the CHURCH IS BIGGER THAN YOU THINK

Structures and Strategies for the Church in the 21st Century

PATRICK JOHNSTONE

William Carey Library
Pasadena, California

CHRISTIAN FOCUS
Good Books with the Real Message of Hope

WEC INTERNATIONAL

© Patrick Johnstone

ISBN 1 85792 269 7

This Special Edition published for:
William Carey Library Publishers
P.O. Box 40129
Pasadena, CA 91104

Phone (in the U.S.): 1-800-MISSION (1-800-647-7466)
Fax: 1-626-794-0477
Email: orders@wclbooks.com

Published in 1998
Reprinted 1998
by
Christian Focus Publications,
Geanies House, Fearn, Ross-shire, IV20 1TW, Great Britain.
and
WEC,
Bulstrode, Gerrards Cross, Bucks, Great Britain, SL9 8SZ

Contents

Diagrams, Tables and Maps

All the maps and diagrams in this book are available in colour or in black and white on Overhead Transparencies from:

WEC International Research Office, Bulstrode, Gerrards Cross, Bucks SL9 8SZ, UK.

Or by e-mail: <IRO@IO.wec-int.org>
               <iro@opwld.demon.co.uk>
Web Site   <http://wec-int.org>

Abbreviations

AD2000 Mvt.	The AD2000 and Beyond Movement
AIDS	Auto-Immune Deficiency Syndrome
CIM	China Inland Mission (today Overseas Mission Fellowship
DAWN	Discipling a Whole Nation
GCOWE	The Global Consultation on World Evangelization, 1997
HIV	Human Immuno-deficiency Virus
KJV	King James Authorized Bible
LCWE	The Lausanne Committee for World Evangelization
MARC	Missions Advanced Research and Communications; a division of World Vision
NT	New Testament
NGO	Non-Government Organization
NTM	New Tribes Mission
OM	Operation Mobilization
OT	Old Testament
RC	Roman Catholic
SIM	SIM International, formerly Sudan Interior Mission
WEC	Worldwide Evangelization for Christ
WEF	World Evangelical Fellowship
YWAM	Youth With A Mission

Forewords

The growth of the church today is on a scale that is unique in the history of the world. That is the thesis of THE CHURCH IS BIGGER THAN YOU THINK. Comprehensive in scope and contemporary in accent, this volume is rich in missiological insights.

Anchored in the eternal perspective of Biblical truth, this book guides the reader through the historical development of the Christian Mission before launching into a practical discussion of the structures and strategies needed. Practical suggestions for breaking down the barriers among local churches, training institutions and mission agencies abound. Graphs, charts and diagrams facilitate understanding and a sprinkling of appropriate personal illustrations adds to the vitality of the book.

Although encouraging, Johnstone is also sobering as he identifies the challenges – geographical, urban, cultural, sociological, ideological and spiritual – to be met in order to accomplish the goal of *a church of every people and the gospel for every person.* An incredibly rich source of recent statistics, this book is also a devotional masterpiece. Johnstone carefully unpacks the global vision inherent in Isaiah 52:13-53:12 and Ephesians 1:3-10, underscores the centrality of the cross and resurrection and concludes with an explanation of God's six fold blessings for harvesters.

This book is one of a kind. It is an indispensable companion to Operation World. It provides the framework to understand what God is doing in our world, why He is doing it and how you can be part of the action.

Dr. Kenneth B. Mulholland
AD2000 & Beyond Presidents and Academic Deans (PAD) Track, North American Coordinator.
Academic Dean, Columbia Biblical Seminary and Graduate School of Missions, a division of Columbia International University, P.O. Box 3122, Columbia, SC 29230.

I don't like books on mission. They usually tell me what I already know and then make me feel guilty for not doing more about it! Patrick Johnstone has managed to give me quite a few facts I didn't know, some insights I hadn't really grasped ... and I don't feel guilty. Inspired? Yes! Envisioned? Yes! Challenged? Yes! Guilty? No!

I thoroughly recommend this book to everyone in Christian leadership. It places mission at the heart of the church – local, national, and global. With this book in one hand, and *Operation World* in the other, we have two strategic resources. Now all we need to do is to go into all the world and preach the gospel!

Stephen Gaukroger
President of the Baptist Union of England and Wales, 1994.
Senior Pastor, Gold Hill Baptist Church

Introduction

Why the title? There is really a triple meaning in that title, and these three meanings give the reason for writing the book.

First, I want to show that the Church is bigger than you may think in TIME. The Church was planned by God in Eternity before time began, and its destiny is to be with God for all Eternity when time is no more. We are part of that eternal body. Even now we are already inhabiters in that Eternity. Intercession is an activity that impinges upon eternity and belongs to eternity.

Second, I want to show that the Church is bigger than you may think in SIZE. Few today realize the tremendous growth and expansion of the Church in all its variety and ministries in the twentieth century. We are part of this growth. My aim is to encourage and build faith in God's sovereignty in the world with information on what has and is happening. This is contrary to the negative portrayals of the media which tend to over-emphasise the bad. I am very conscious I live in Europe which is a continent where there is a scepticism about the present and a cynical pessimism about the future that has penetrated into European world-view which seems to expect the worst. I may therefore appear optimistic to such readers – I believe I have grounds for this! Then my aim is to give a challenge concerning the task of world evangelization to be completed in the twenty-first century by demonstrating that though unfinished, it is finishable and finishable soon – if we mobilize. My desire is to see a far greater and wider involvement of churches in joyfully heeding the Great Commission.

Third, I want to show that the Church is bigger than you may think in STRUCTURE. We live in a time when our perception of what constitutes the structures of the Church has been moulded by inadequate theology and distorted patterns inherited over the centuries. The effects of these have been the marginalization or elimination of vision and mechanisms for world evangelization. Few realize the impact of these distortions on congregational life, training systems and the mission enterprise. My aim is that we repent of past failures, and rectify what is deficient at every level of the life of the Church so that we become more effective in mission.

This book has emerged from some years of ministry to Christian workers and leaders in conferences and seminars. Many have asked me if the content of what I share has been put into writing. This book is my attempt to do that.

I am so grateful for the many who have shared in the birthing of this book. I can only name a few.
- Edson Qeiroz, a Baptist pastor in Brazil, who first opened my eyes to the three basic structures of the Church.
- My dear wife, Robyn, who encouraged and supported me in undertaking this task in the midst of our busy lives. She has also worked hard with me in the writing and editing of this book.
- My WEC colleagues in the International Office who were patient when I committed much time to its writing and even gave many hours to check the manuscript.
- The many who have helped with ideas, corrections and sources of information. Of special mention, Leslie and Jill Brierley, David Phillips, Evan Davies, Dieter Kuhl, Alastair Kennedy of WEC, also Steve Gaukroger of Gold Hill Baptist Church, England and Ken Mulholland and Phil Steyne of Columbia International University, USA.
- My valued colleagues of Christian Focus Publications, especially William Mackenzie and Ian Thompson who have patiently advised and encouraged through the painful process of publishing such a book.

Part 1

Eternity

The Vision Given

Isaiah 52:13-53:12

* * * * *

Blessed be the God and Father of our Lord Jesus Christ,
Who has blessed us in Christ with every spiritual blessing in the
heavenly places,
Even as he chose us in him *before the foundation of the world,*
that we should be holy and blameless before him.
He destined us in love to be his sons through Jesus Christ,
according to the purpose of his will,
to the praise of his glorious grace
which he freely bestowed on us in the Beloved.
In him we have redemption through his blood,
the forgiveness of our trespasses,
according to the riches of his grace which he lavished on us.
For he has made known to us
in all wisdom and insight the mystery of his will,
according to his purpose which he set forth in Christ
as a plan for *the fulness of time*, to unite all things in him,
things in heaven and on earth.

Ephesians 1:3-10

The majestic words of Ephesians are a statement of God's eternal plan for his people. This is the eternal perspective with which we begin this book. These words resemble the passage in Isaiah (52:10-54) which is the Scripture on which this book is based. God wants us, his Church, to share in that eternal perspective. Mission is its heart. Mission is God's heart. Mission is ours too. May it be so.

Several Definitions

I need to define several fundamental terms used in this book.

Church – Church capitalized in this book has specific meanings. There are three levels depending on context:

1. All believers of all time from creation to the consummation whether the Church Militant on earth or the Church Triumphant in heaven.[1]
2. The whole company of the redeemed on earth at the present time. It includes all those who are the Church of the Firstborn, whose names are written in the Lamb's Book of Life. The number is immense, but unknown. None of the statistics in this book can measure this.[2]
3. The whole visible Church on earth including all who call themselves Christian. The latter also includes those whose faith is suspect or whose doctrine may not be in accordance with an evangelical understanding of Scripture. It is possible to count or estimate their numbers, and for statistical purposes, this is what is quantified in this book.[3]

church – in lower case means a local church or congregation of believers.

mission[4] – The loving work of God to bring humankind to himself as the Church. As a secondary outworking of this, mission is the overall ministry of the Church for world evangelization.

missions – Any activity in which Christians are involved for world evangelization.

---

[1] Matthew 16:18-20; Ephesians 2:11-22; Revelation 21:1-26; 22:17.
[2] Hebrews 12:22-24; Revelation 20:12.
[3] Matthew 13:1-23; 13:24-30; 13:47-50.
[4] Bosch 1991:391. Bosch gives an expanded definition of the terms **mission** and **missions**.

Chapter 1

God's Vision – Eternity to Eternity

The Vision for Eternity

God is before time was. He is completely sufficient in himself. The perfect fellowship and love between the Father, the Son and the Holy Spirit lacks nothing for perfection. Yet God inexplicably desired to lavish his love on the creation he planned and include us in that perfect relationship.[5]

He created time and a universe. He then created one special place unique in that universe – the earth. That earth was a small planet of a middling star among the 200 billion stars in an ordinary galaxy among the 200 billion galaxies. But these had not the capacity to respond to his love. He went further, he created life in its myriad forms. Out of those millions of species, he created one species, humankind, in his own image that had the capacity for fellowship with himself. That meant choice; a choice that could mean rejecting the love of the Creator. His plan was that those who believed in him should become an Eternal Companion to his Son as his Bride and to share his throne and authority. This is the whole purpose of creation, the existence of the universe and of history itself[6]. Otherwise how could Paul say in Romans:

> … for creation was subjected to futility, not of its own will but by the will of him who subjected it **in hope**;
> because the creation itself will be set free from its bondage to decay and obtain the glorious liberty of **the children of God**. We know that the whole creation has been groaning in travail until now … *Romans 8:20-22*

The coming of evil is a mystery, but before time began God had a plan to overcome that evil. The remedy was too terrible for any but himself to comprehend. It had to be through God himself, the Son, to die for sinful man and rise as conqueror of sin and the separation and death it brought. This redeeming act became the

---

[5] Sauer 1912 & 1978. Erich Sauer in his book *From Eternity to Eternity* gives a glorious panorama of the whole of eternity with time just a little part of the whole.
[6] Billheimer 1975:19-27. *Destined for the Throne* is a masterpiece describing God's ultimate goal of the universe – the Church.

focal point of earth, history, time and eternity itself. It becomes the focal point of the worship of the Redeemed not only on earth, but throughout the universe and heaven itself for all ages to come.[7]

The victory of the Lord Jesus Christ on the cross was final, complete and sufficient for completely reversing all the pernicious effects of the fall of both Satan and man. That evil and Satan still exist is God's grace and forbearance that more may become part of his Church, and then part of the final application of that victory. The Church thereby becomes strong through praise, intercession and spiritual warfare and prepared for the role of Bride with her heavenly Bridegroom through all the ages to come. That Bride is to come from every part of the human race to be with him for all eternity. The redeemed of the Lord will bow before and reign with God in that glorious consummation.[8]

Paul Billheimer wrote a powerful book *Destined for the Throne*. In the introduction are these magnificent words:

> The author's primary thesis is that the ONE purpose of the Universe from all Eternity is the production and preparation of an eternal companion for the Son, called the Bride, the Lamb's Wife. Since she is to share the Throne of the Universe with her Divine Lover and Lord as a judicial equal, she must be trained, educated and prepared in the midst of all this evil for her queenly role. Because the crown is only for the conqueror the Church must learn the art of spiritual warfare... to enable her to learn the technique of overcoming... It is his way of giving the Church 'on-the-job' training in overcoming the forces hostile to God...[9]

The Vision for Time

The Bible reveals that eternal plan. This book is based on just over two sublime chapters of the Bible. I believe that Isaiah 52:10-54:17 shows us more of the plan of God's loving redemption and its cost than almost any other part of Scripture.

He has also made it equally plain that his plan is to be carried out through those he has redeemed. This is a major emphasis of Isaiah 54. He makes his redeemed people one with himself in

---

[7] John 1:1-18, Ephesians 1:3-10, Revelation 5.

[8] Isaiah 66:22-23, Revelation 21:1-2, 5-7.

[9] Billheimer 1975:15.

intimate fellowship to proclaim the good news so that more may share with him in eternity.

From beginning to end, the Bible is the story of how God steadily revealed more of that plan to his people. It came to full disclosure[10] when he sent his beloved Son, the Lord Jesus Christ, to live, die, rise again, ascend to heaven and pour out his Holy Spirit. Mission is God's mission, or to use the Latin term, *Missio Dei*. Mission is a divine activity.[11] God's mission has purpose for him and for us. His purpose has the wider aspect of rectifying all that Satan's pride distorted and the more focused aspect of ushering in the Kingdom of God by bringing back the King with world evangelization complete. We only find meaning in our faith when gripped by this purpose. We then eagerly await the return of Jesus while giving our all to make way for his return.

The Lord Jesus Christ was the first missionary of the gospel; He is THE missionary on which all missionary work is to be modelled, for He said, "As the Father sent Me so send I you."[12] This, as we will see later, was not an exclusive command to the eleven apostles to whom he spoke, but to all believers of all time.

What an awesome privilege, a thrilling prospect, a vital ministry, a future to live for, and an expectant hope for us! We are a people of destiny in Jesus. Right through the Old and New Testaments is the truth that God calls us to share with him in his mission. We are never closer to God than when our lives are involved in his mission. His promise in Matthew 28:20 that he would be with us always was given to those who go making disciples.

I expand on this in the pages that follow. I want to show the heart of our Father for a lost world, the burden of the Lord Jesus Christ that sinners might be saved and the earnestness of the Holy Spirit in motivating us to proclaim Christ to every race, tribe, people and tongue.

---

[10] Galatians 4:4.

[11] Burnett 1986. Burnett's book, *God's Mission: Healing the Nations* is one of the most balanced and lucid books I know for giving an understanding of God's heart for the whole lost world from the Bible, yet expressed in contemporary language and understanding of the missiological scene today.

[12] John 20:21.

The heart of the Father

Isaiah 52:10-53-12 is one of the most magnificent and powerful passages in Scripture. It reveals the heart of our loving heavenly Father for us, his creation. It speaks of God's Suffering Servant who came that we might be recreated and bring satisfaction to him. No part of the Bible more clearly reveals the Messiah as the Suffering Servant. The plan of God is revealed that his Servant should bear away our sin by a substitutionary death as a sacrificial lamb:

> All we like sheep have gone astray;
> We have turned every one to his own way
> and the Lord has laid on him the iniquity of us all.
> *Isaiah 53:6*

Then his overcoming sin and death by rising again is described in powerful words that were surely quoted to the disciples on the way to Emmaus[13] about 700 years later. Note the highlighted words, which, though poetic, clearly speak of his resurrection:

> ...when He makes himself an offering for sin,
> He **shall see** his offspring,
> He **shall prolong** His days,
> the will of the Lord **shall prosper** in His hand;
> He **shall see** the fruit of the travail of His soul,
> and **shall be satisfied**. *Isaiah 53:10-11*

and then to bring salvation to us sinners:

> ...by his knowledge shall the Righteous One,
> my Servant, make many to be accounted righteous;
> and he shall bear their iniquities. *Isaiah 53:11*

It was fitting that the Moravians, the first great Protestant mission movement launched in 1732, took their motto from these words "To win for the Lamb the reward of his sufferings." It is also fitting that William Carey preached from Isaiah 54 and thus was one of the catalytic instruments in God's hands to launch the modern missionary movement. This passage has had a dramatic impact on the history of the world.

Who can understand the depth of the words which describe the Father's part in the sufferings of his Son? I understand in part what

---

[13] Luke 24:27.

it meant for Jesus to die for my sin. I am guilty for the death of Jesus. I helped to nail Him to the cross. Can I absorb the fact that there is a deeper cause? It was the Father himself who put him there and, indeed, had planned this from all eternity – for me? We will never understand the awesome words in this chapter; we can only marvel and worship:

> …yet we esteemed him stricken,
> smitten **by God**, and afflicted…
> …**the Lord** has laid on Him the iniquity of us all…
> …Yet it was the **will of the Lord** to bruise Him;
> **He** has put Him to grief; … *Isaiah 53:5,6,10*

That God deliberately sent his only Son to us, knowing he would have to turn his back on him because of our sin is a mystery, a miracle, an act of amazing grace about which we will need all eternity to marvel. It is a message that should be shouted from the rooftops and passed on to every person on earth. I was touched when I read about the eighteenth century Moravian missionary to the Inuit (Eskimos), John Beck. He and his colleagues had struggled for five years with no response. He was translating Matthew's Gospel and had just completed the story of the crucifixion when some Inuit visited him to see what he was doing. He had an inspiration and read out the words he had just translated. The Inuit listened amazed and a young man said, "Tell me that again; tell me that again." Kajarnak became the first convert of the work.[14] It was a vision of Jesus dying for him that captured his heart, and cut through all the miasma of spiritist shamanism.

The Burden of the Lord Jesus Christ

No wonder our Risen Jesus was so earnest about telling his disciples to evangelize the world. The whole message of Jesus' ministry before the cross was just this, but he could only say this in parable, delicate hints and example; he could not speak about it openly until after the resurrection, for it would have not been understood by the disciples. Only twice do we have a clear statement of Jesus before his resurrection which is recorded in the Bible about world evangelization – I quote the clearest reference here; the other is in Mark 14:9. It was his confident assertion that in

---

[14] Hutton 1935:55-58.

spite of all future terrible events, world evangelization was an assured certainty:

> And this gospel of the kingdom will be preached throughout
> the whole world, as a testimony to all nations;
> and then the end will come. *Matt 24:14*

The dominant theme in Jesus' ministry during those 40 resurrection days with his disciples was world evangelization. At the end of every Gospel, and then again just before he ascended to the Father[15] he clearly gave command that they should evangelize every person and make disciples of every people. This we often call the Great Commission. Each Gospel and also Acts chapter 1 has another rendering stated at a different time and giving a different aspect of that final command. It is reasonable to conclude that these five post-resurrection statements were representative examples of what may have been much fuller coverage that Jesus gave during those vital forty days.

This Great Commission is far more comprehensive than many had realized. Note the emphases in each of these key passages below – though the particular emphasis indicated here is not exclusive, there is overlap.

1. The Evangelistic Commission of Mark 16

Mark emphasized the need to communicate the gospel to every individual on earth, and with the theological thrust of faith for salvation:

> Go into all the world and preach the gospel to the whole
> creation. He who believes and is baptized shall be saved;
> but he who does not believe will be condemned.
> *Mark 16:15-18*

The concern is that all men might have the opportunity for faith and new life through the salvation Jesus came to offer. The promise to those who believe is also of demonstrations or following signs of the power of the Holy Spirit. The whole colour of the ministry here is that of a pioneer evangelist.

---

[15] Matthew 28:18-20, Mark 16:15-20, Luke 24:44-49, John 20:19-23, Acts 1:1-11.

2. The Church Planting Commission of Matthew 28

The last three verses of Matthew are often considered THE Great Commission. It is certainly one of the most comprehensive statements on the matter that we have from the Lord Jesus.

> And Jesus came and said to them, "All authority in heaven and on earth has been given unto me. Go therefore and make disciples of all nations, baptizing them in the name of the Father and of the Son and of the Holy Spirit, teaching them to observe all that I have commanded you and lo, I am with you always, to the close of the age." *Matthew 28:18-20*

Jesus stressed the making of disciples in this command. This is more than evangelism, though that is implied as part of the whole. An on-going ministry is indicated with baptism and teaching as part of a process of discipling. Baptism is usually an act of obedience of commitment to Christ before others. Teaching can be one to one, but the normal is for more than one to gather regularly for the systematic teaching of God's Word. These imply a range of activities involving other believers being gathered together and having a relationship of accountability in a congregation. Today we would use the term 'church planting' for the ministries in this passage.

3. The Teaching Commission of Luke 24

Luke ends the gospel he wrote with incidents that emphasize the teaching of the whole of the Scripture. Of all the resurrection appearances of the Lord Jesus Christ, Luke alone relates the one to the two disciples walking to Emmaus. It was in this conversation that Jesus said:

> O foolish men and slow of heart to believe **all that the prophets have spoken**! Was it not necessary that the Christ should suffer these things and enter into his glory? And **beginning with Moses and all the prophets,** he interpreted to them **in all the scriptures** the things concerning himself. *Luke 24:25-27*

Specific references to the scriptures are highlighted. How instructive that Bible study must have been. One wonders what passages of the Old Testament the Lord used.[16]

Later in the same chapter Luke again selects words that emphasize the Bible and teaching in his rendering of the Great Commission:

> Then he said to them, "These are my words which I spoke to you, while I was still with you, that **everything written about me in the law of Moses, and the prophets and the psalms** must be fulfilled". Then he opened their minds **to understand the scriptures**, and said to them, **"Thus it is written** that the Christ should suffer and on the third day rise from the dead, and that repentance and forgiveness of sins should be preached in his name to all nations..."
> *Luke 24:44-47*

In these two events, there are six references by Jesus to the contents of the Old Testament, and that the Old Testament actually foretold not only the events of Jesus' atoning ministry, but also the very content of the gospel that would be proclaimed world-wide. The very substance of the gospel was what had to be proclaimed. It is with good reason this aspect of the Great Commission can be called the 'Teaching Commission.' Teaching was also indicated in the passage in Matthew, but here is the main thrust of the ministry.

4. **The Sending Commission of John 20**

Jesus appeared to the disciples, Thomas being absent, and gave them their marching orders:

> Jesus said to them again, "Peace be with you. As the Father has sent me so send I you." *John 20:21*

He gave himself as their example, but this also implied with the same enabling. This then followed as he bequeathed to them the power of the Holy Spirit in verse 22. He also gave to them his divine authority in verse 23. At the beginning of his ministry he showed that the Son of Man has the authority to forgive sins,[17]

---

[16] Hengstenberg. Original English translation 1854. This is a masterly 1,400 page exposition in two volumes of the Christology of the Old Testament.
[17] Mark 2:1-12.

so he was offering to his disciples that same authority. We may find the mention of the forgiving of sins difficult to explain because of abuses in this area in the history of the Church.

5. The Global Commission of Acts 1

The very last words Jesus ever spoke to his disciples were on the Mount of Olives just before his ascension. He gave yet another aspect of the Great Commission:

> ...You shall receive power when the Holy Spirit has come upon you; and you shall be my witnesses in Jerusalem and in all Judea and Samaria and to the end of the earth.
> *Acts 1:8*

Jesus gave a breathtaking global sweep to the task before the apostles. He was strategic. He did not emphasize one part of the task over another. His disciples were to have an apostolic ministry locally in Jerusalem, nationally in all Judea, to ethnic minorities in their land like the despised Samaritans as well as to other lands, continents to the end of the earth. We need to keep that balance too. The Great Commission is not just the glamorous 'far far away', but the humdrum local outreach in the streets and fields where the believers live, and also to the difficult sections of the community nearby that we would normally seek to avoid. Jesus was not giving a range of alternatives from which we could choose, but showing that every Christian has a global concern, even if his calling is to a specific location whether local or afar.

The Lord Jesus was comprehensive. The Great Commission covers a wide range of ministries from pioneer work to church development, teaching, training and they also cover every part of the world. I once spoke at a missions week-end in a church in Canada. They had a banner over the exit in the foyer with the words, "**You are now entering your mission field.**" I like that!

God's passion is for the redeeming work of his Son to be proclaimed to all the peoples of the world. We, as the Church, should be the ones to do it.

The Urging of the Holy Spirit

The Holy Spirit has an intense desire for salvation of the peoples of this world. He is the Lord of the Harvest. It is not surprising to find that Luke tells us of the involvement of the Holy Spirit when Jesus gave the Great Commission:

> ...after he had given commandment through the Holy Spirit to the apostles whom he had chosen. *Acts 1:2*

It is noteworthy that immediately after this, Jesus commanded the apostles to wait in Jerusalem to be baptized in the Holy Spirit. After receiving the power of the Holy Spirit they were to be witnesses to the end of the earth.[18] The Church and its expansion in Acts could equally be called Acts of the Apostles or Acts of the Holy Spirit.

His pleadings to believers for action are insistent. He guides us, but especially in those matters pertaining to the cause of mission. He gives gifts relevant to the furtherance of the task and also signs that accompany or follow those who go believing.[19] How can any Christian or congregation claim to "have" the Spirit without having the Spirit of mission?

---

[18] Acts 1:4-5,8.
[19] Mark 16:15-18.

Chapter 2

The Church's Vision for the World

It is not just in this sublime chapter of Isaiah 53 that God reveals his longing for a people for himself. The whole of the Bible shows his heart of love, not wishing that any should perish.[20] That his salvation is not just for the Jews, but for every people is strongly, but implicitly, stated in the OT. In the NT it is explicit. Yet it is God's loving plan that his people share his vision.

The Involvement of God's People in the Vision

Scripture, theology, the Church, and even Christians would not exist without mission. Therefore a theology without mission is not a biblical theology, a Church without mission is no longer truly the Church and a Christian without mission is no true disciple. For Christians, mission is not an optional extra for the fanatical few or for the specially anointed, it is a fundamental definitive of who we are in Christ and why we are in Christ. David Bosch, in his outstanding book on the theology of missions, *Transforming Mission*,[21] quotes Aargaard:[22]

Mission… is seen as a movement from God to the world; the Church is viewed as an instrument for that mission. There is a church because there is mission, not vice versa.

The astonishing fact is that God's people, in the main, have not seen this vision, nor have they made the vision central to their life and existence. In this failure, they miss God's purpose, God's intimacy and God's blessing. Living for the fulfilment of this vision of the Father is the most noble, most enriching, most meaningful purpose one can have in life.

How can any child of God claim to be following Jesus if they have no concern for the lostness and need of the peoples of this world? How can they expect the promise of his abiding presence with them, 'I will be with you always,' if they have not been willing

---

[20] 2 Peter 3:9.
[21] Bosch 1991:390.
[22] Aagaard 1974:423.

to obey the command '...go and make disciples of all peoples...'[23] on which it is conditional?

How can any congregation or denomination claim to be biblical or even Christian that does not place at the heart of its ministry agenda God's heart for a lost world? Its budget apportionment, prayer involvement and deployment of workers should show it. The Church of the Lord Jesus Christ is defined by mission – for it is composed of those who were won to salvation by mission, and now have the awesome responsibility to win others as their mission. If it is not missionary in its theology, daily life and commitment, it no longer has the right to claim to be the Church. The viability and health of the Church and of ourselves, as children of God, cannot be separated from the task of world evangelization.

There has been a cataclysmic decline in commitment and membership in the past 40 years of denominations that became theologically liberal. It is in these denominations that biblical mission has been redefined in humanistic terms and evangelism replaced by dialogue, tolerance and a socio-political agenda far removed from the intent of the Lord Jesus Christ.[24] Sadly many Evangelicals have not done much better in their involvement in mission.

There has been a tragic separation between soteriology (the doctrine of salvation) and missiology (the doctrine of missions) in the thinking and theology of most Christian leaders and expositors. To take this further, a soteriology without missiology is no longer the true message of salvation. Look again at the words of the Lord Jesus in Luke 24:47:

> Then he (Jesus) opened their minds to understand the scriptures, and said to them, "Thus it is written, that the Christ should suffer and on the third day rise from the dead, and that repentance and forgiveness of sins should be preached in his name to all nations (peoples), beginning from Jerusalem..."

---

[23] Matthew 28:18-20.
[24] McGrath 1995:17 *et seq.* This book gives a powerful account of the history of the rise of Evangelicalism in the twentieth century. At the gateway to the twenty-first century he shows it to be the wave of the future of Christianity.

This is a single sentence. The work of Jesus in suffering and rising again, the content of the gospel to be preached, and the mission task are all included in that one sentence. One without the other would be an incomplete message. Note that mission here must include local evangelism in Jerusalem, nation-wide evangelism in Judea, outreach to ethnic minorities within the nation in Samaria and world-wide mission to the end of the earth.

The question is not whether missions is for me, or whether missions should have a part of my ministry, but rather what is my part in missions because I am a believer. Missions are not a matter of a special calling for some, but a matter of asking God for his direction in his mission now. There is a "You" shaped hole in God's kingdom. Find it and fit into it!

The Great Commission is a command for the Church to eagerly obey as a love response to the God who had already poured out so much love for her. Every Christian of all time and of every place and culture has both the privilege and responsibility to be a Great Commission Christian. Later we will see reasons why this has not been the case. I just take the life of William Carey as an example of one for whom this vision became a consuming passion, and through whom countless others have been similarly motivated in the ensuing two centuries.

William Carey as a Visionary

May 31, 1792 was a pivotal day in William Carey's life. It also became pivotal for world history. That an impoverished pastor in rural England should so impact history is improbable, but he did. He was not the first person to challenge the Church to missions, but he was the one under God who broke the log-jam that prevented the Church flowing out to the world for the gospel.

He was preceded and influenced by great preachers and theologians among Puritan divines[25] in the seventeenth century and later by Jonathan Edwards.[26] The accounts of great missionaries such as John Eliot, David Brainerd in North America and also Ziegenbalg and Plütschau in India also moved him. However it was Jonathan Edwards who had the widest impact through his writings

---

[25] Murray 1971.
[26] Davies in the *International Bulletin of Missionary Research* April 1997.

which so influenced Andrew Fuller and Carey.[27] His reading about the Concerts of Prayer (which started in 1744 and were associated with the Scottish Cambuslang Revival in 1742) and his editing of David Brainerd's diary turned him into a passionate advocate for missions. He then published his *A Humble Attempt to Promote an Explicit Agreement and Visible Union of God's People through the World, in Extraordinary Prayer, for the Revival of Religion and the Advancement of Christ's Kingdom on Earth, Pursuant to Scripture Promises and Prophecies, Concerning the Last Time* [what a title, but apparently the original title was 187 words long!]. In his latter years Edwards himself became a missionary to the Native Americans. If Carey was the father of modern missions, then Edwards was the grandfather.[28]

There were even mission bodies active before the Baptist Missionary Society was formed such as the SPCK (Society for Promoting Christian Knowledge founded in 1699)[29] and the Moravians (who began sending out missionaries in 1732 after they experienced revival in 1727).[30] All these were precursors of the modern mission movement, but the *chairos* time of God had not yet struck.

For years Carey had lived, prayed, studied and worked towards the realization of that moment when others would begin to share his vision, but all appeared futile. The day before he had preached a passionate and well-reasoned sermon to fellow ministers meeting in Nottingham, England. His vision was for the evangelization of the whole world. This "deathless sermon", as it came to be called, had had an electric effect. John Ryland, who had baptized Carey nine years before, made this comment:

> Had all the people lifted up their voice and wept, as the children of Israel did at Bochim, I should not have wondered, so clearly did he prove the criminality of our supineness in the cause of God.[31]

---

[27] Van den Berg 1956:93.
[28] Davies 1997:60-67. Davies rightly calls the remarkable Jonathan Edwards the "grandfather" of the modern mission movement.
[29] Latourette 1975.
[30] The Moravian mission story is described in more detail in Chapter 16.
[31] George 1991:32.

Although it had a profound effect on these men, they had neither the faith nor the courage to do anything about it. Their meeting was breaking up with no decision; the immensity of the task overwhelming them. Carey turned to his friend, Andrew Fuller, who was also a pastor, gripped his arm and cried out, "Is there nothing again going to be done, sir?" This emotional outburst from his distraught friend broke through Fuller's doubts and hesitation and he threw his weight into persuading the meeting to reconsider their lack of response. That carried the day. A resolution was passed that 'a plan be prepared against the next Ministers' Meeting for forming a Baptist Society for Propagating the Gospel among the Heathens.'

Four months later that meeting took place in Kettering and 12 men committed themselves as the first members of the new missionary society. They contributed the, then, large sum of just over £13 – collected in a snuff box!

So was born the modern missionary movement. It was a movement that, despite its many weaknesses, was to lead to an astonishing and unprecedented expansion and growth of the Church over the following 200 years. Over this period the largely isolated, introspective Protestant Church in north-west Europe was transformed into a global multi-cultural family of churches in which those of European origin were to be a distinct minority. Just to give one statistic, in 1792 only 7 in every 1,000 Protestants was an African or an Asian, but by 1992 this had risen to 580 in every 1,000. Scurrilous pamphlets were written against Carey's challenges by his contemporaries in the established Church. These only revealed their utter spiritual bankruptcy and supineness in refusing to take up the task which they were maligning.

William Carey was not the first child of the Reformation to preach missions, nor was he the first to go overseas as a missionary but he is rightly called 'the father of modern missions,' justifiably shown by:

1. His study and understanding of the modern world

He lived in a time when Europe was discovering the existence of the wider world. Explorers were returning to Europe with detailed maps of new worlds and descriptions of peoples and cultures. The published accounts of the discoveries of Captain Cook were a significant contribution to Carey's thinking of missions.[32] The trading companies were sending their representatives to every corner of the world for financial gain. The industrial revolution was gathering momentum. Yet how a poor rural pastor in a remote part of England could acquire the reports, books and information is astonishing. His carefully crafted and coloured wall map and personally hand-sewn leather globe reflected the latest discoveries of his time. It was this map Andrew Fuller noticed in Carey's workshop that gave fuel to his stirring message on Haggai 1:2 entitled *The Pernicious Influence of Delay;* a passionate plea for the necessity of taking the gospel to the heathen, which, in turn, had a significant impact on Carey in his personal call to the mission field.

The world survey in his famous little 87-page book, *An Enquiry,* is a masterpiece of factual accuracy, balanced assessments and global comprehensiveness. We have the advantage of extrapolating backwards from our more extensive knowledge to verify the validity of these statistics.

2. His perception of mission as the heart of God and the message of Scripture

He passionately and persuasively preached and wrote portraying the Great Commission as being just as valid for modern Christians as for the apostles to whom Christ addressed it. He had plenty of discouragements. At one ministerial meeting when he raised the issue of the Great Commission, his old pastor, John Ryland retorted: "Young man, sit down. When God pleases to convert the heathen, He will do it without your aid or mine."[33] The prevailing attitude for the previous three centuries had been that the Great Commission was exclusively for the apostles to whom the words were originally addressed.

3. His years of pastoral ministry and church planting in rural England

His years of service in congregational work together with his assiduous gathering of information about the entire known world gave him a wholeness in his understanding of missions hitherto

---

[32] George 1991:20.

[33] George 1991:53. It is also reported that Ryland added a further pungent comment about him being "a miserable enthusiast" for even raising the issue!

unknown. He saw missions as involving the whole Body of Christ to evangelize the whole world.

4. His ability to communicate that vision by both word and print

His ministry, both in his *Enquiry* and in his sermon in Nottingham, to which reference is made above, had a ripple effect across the Christian world. Note these comments:

> "Believed by some to be the most convincing missionary appeal ever written, Carey's Enquiry was certainly a landmark in Christian history and deserves a place alongside Martin Luther's Ninety-five Theses in its influence on subsequent church history."[34]

> "Carey's Enquiry marks a distinct point of departure in the history of Christianity. It laid the foundation of missions in accurate information, careful consideration, wise use of means as well as in the obligation of Christian duty."[35]

> "I call the sermon of Carey wonderful, because there has, perhaps, been no sermon preached in modern days, which has had so distinct and traceable effect on Protestant Christianity throughout the world."[36]

5. His proposal of a mechanism for mission work to be initiated and sustained

His models were more from his times than from the apostolic models of Scripture, but in doing so he stumbled across a thoroughly biblical structural model for the successful evangelization of the world. The very title of his *Enquiry* indicates this. The full title is as follows; *An Enquiry into the obligation of Christians to Use means for the conversion of the Heathens.*[37] (emphasis mine). The means advocated were the practical structures required to get the task accomplished. His outlining of the strategy for mission work on the field was far ahead of his time. Many later mission agencies failed to heed his wise advice. The structure proposed by Carey was that of a society, a structure born

---

[34] Kane 1971.
[35] Carey, S. Pierce, 1923.
[36] ibid.
[37] Carey 1792.

out of the culture of the time – many such religious societies had
been springing up in Britain over the seventeenth and eighteenth
centuries and had been formative in social reform and the
conservation and growth of the great Methodist Revival over the
eighteenth century.[38] The dynamism and daring of the structure was
more modelled on the big international trading companies which
had carved out powerful trading empires across the oceans. The
form of the structure was culturally moulded, but the **principle** of a
separate structure is supra-cultural and eminently biblical.

6. His faith in God

He allowed no discouragement of those around him to deflect
him and no obstacle to hinder him. He became the embodiment of
the words he preached in his epochal sermon: "Expect great things
[from God]; attempt great things [for God]."[39]

7. His example in going as a missionary himself

Despite many obstacles with finance, opposition of his own
countrymen in India, disease, disastrous setbacks in ministry, and
even the unwillingness of his first wife (would Carey have ever
been accepted by a modern mission board?), he plodded on with
unswerving dedication to become one of the greatest missionary
Bible translators and church planters of all time.

Carey was a visionary, researcher, theologian, linguist, writer,
preacher and an effective communicator all rolled into one – a rare
combination indeed. He claimed to be no genius and just a plodder
– but what a plodder! No wonder he became a catalyst in the hand
of God that generated a growing involvement of Christians in the
mission enterprise – first from Europe, then from North America,
and, in the last twenty years, from nearly every nation of the world
where the Church has taken root. We are privileged to be alive
today. What appeared to Carey's contemporaries an impossible
dream is becoming an attainable reality. We are poised on the brink
of the realization of Carey's dream – the completion of world
evangelization. It could be in our lifetime.

William Carey has been an example to me ever since I became a
Christian at university. I never realized that in my calling to be a

---

[38] Skevington Wood 1960:32,166-241.
[39] George 1991:32.

missionary I would also become a world researcher and mission strategist and, hopefully, motivate many for the same task. My book, Operation World, is successor to his Enquiry. Later in this volume I will compare the statistics in these publications and show what has been achieved over these 200 years.

It was a great privilege for me to be invited in 1991 by my friend, Harry Godden, then the Superintendent of the East Midlands Baptist Association, to speak at their annual gathering in Nottingham. It was only after I had accepted this invitation that I realized that these leaders were the direct successors of the Northampton Baptist Association for which Carey preached his famous message from Isaiah 54 those 199 years before. I therefore used Carey's own text at that time. It was a good meeting, but I could not claim that it contained the drama and the amazing results that followed from Carey's sermon! This passage of Scripture, with its strong missiological message, has become part of my life.

Conclusion to Part 1

The basis of this book is for the Church to have a vision for world evangelization. The fundamental reason for this is that God has a vision from all eternity for a Bride for his Son. This Bride is to be the completed and perfected Church at the consummation of all things. The Church here on earth needs to have that vision too, but has, to a great measure, lost it.

William Carey was then put forward as one of the key figures of church history for the restoration of that vision to the Church. That work of restoration is not complete, and to further that is the reason for this book.

Part 2

The Past

The Marginalization of Mission

Isaiah 53:12-The Gap-Isaiah 54:1

Therefore I will divide him a portion with the great,
and he shall divide the spoil with the strong;
because he poured out his soul to death,
and was numbered with the transgressors;
yet he bore the sin of many,
and made intercession for the transgressors.
Isaiah 53:12

...THE GAP...

Isaiah 54:1
Sing O barren one, who did not bear;
break forth into singing and cry aloud,
you who have not been in travail!
For the children of the desolate one will be more
than the children of her that is married, says the Lord.

Introduction

Here in Part Two I share from my heart a deep concern that has developed over the years. Why has the interest in world evangelization been so little? Those of us involved in spreading the gospel to the ends of the earth can see this lack, but how has this deficiency arisen? The problem is more than a problem of priorities or coldness of heart. There is a blindness that seems almost impenetrable.

We soon find out that bashing congregations with the challenge, or attempting to prick consciences in public meetings bears meagre fruit. Even books that eloquently show the biblical basis for mission, and the failure of churches to be involved is not the real answer, for those who most need to hear the message would not even be attracted by the subject matter. The roots of the problem lie far deeper, and these must be addressed.

In the chapters that follow I have sought to give an explanation, from my perspective, of where we went wrong – often way back in history. There may be some surprises and you may disagree with some of my conclusions, but I aim to challenge what may be long-held views which govern our response to mission. My prayer is that both our theology and practice of mission in many congregations and theological schools may be significantly changed.

Chapter 3

Mission Belittled in the Church

We find in the Church today an inherited mind-set or world-view which has excluded mission altogether. If the term "mission" is used, its meaning is so redefined or watered down that the evangelization of the world appears of little importance for the average Christian.[1] To many today, mission means little more than the general work of the Church in the world to alleviate social ills but with the evangelistic and missionary sending component ignored or despised.[2] We always must keep a balance between the evangelistic and the social aspects of mission (see Chapter 23), but prevailing attitudes are shown in financial giving. Raising money for famine or landmine victims or for adopting an orphan is easier than for building a Bible school, or sending support to a missionary or for broadcasting the gospel by radio.

The general culture of many Christians would probably have a mish-mash of half formed ideas and impressions such as:

- Mission work – isn't it rather arrogant to think that our religion is better than other people's? Surely it's OK if people follow their religion sincerely. Why change them?

- Surely mission work ended ages ago! Isn't that something to do with colonialism, pith-helmets, jungles, old ladies and slide shows? Isn't that job done? Look at the use of mass media, all the Bible translations that there are, and what about all those people who went out in the past as missionaries?

- Missionaries – the need is so great here at home, we need them to come over to be missionaries here!

---

[1] **Mission and missions.** We need to define the two before we go further. Sadly the term "mission" has been so broadened and distorted in some Christian circles that it has lost its punch by including anything that ought to be done and lost its meaning by downplaying the spiritual and emphasizing the political and physical. **Mission** is God's overall plan for the redemption of humankind and for the world itself at every level (Rom 8:18-25). **Missions** are the varied human initiatives to further God's mission.

[2] Stott 1975:15-20; Burnett 1986:12.

Where have these ideas come from? One source is our complex, pluralistic world that has no rhyme nor reason for the origin of the universe, or its purpose in which our generation-X young people are moulded, but the other is the prevailing theology, structures, activities and attitudes that make up much of Christian culture today. Let us look more closely at some of the roots of the prevailing attitudes.

I start by way of an illustration from our passage in Isaiah. This is symbolic of the marginalization in the Church of the Lord Jesus Christ between what is considered its normal life and missions.

I believe the Bible to be totally true and without mistakes – as originally given. Precious parchment space in Bible times was not wasted with such frills as paragraph and word spaces, nor were there any identifying numbers to find places in a long book like Isaiah. Imagine how hard it must have been for the Lord Jesus in the synagogue at Nazareth when he was handed the scroll of the book of Isaiah. Luke adds the comment '...*and when he had found the place....*' He must have taken some while to find the place he wanted in what is now our chapter 61. The numbering of the chapters and verses was a helpful later addition but not part of the original inspiration. We can be grateful for the numbering we now have, but at times it obscures the continuity God intended us to see.

The artificial break which separates Isaiah chapter 53 from chapter 54 is a good example. The section on the cross and resurrection has been separated from the glorious triumph of the gospel in world evangelization that follows by a new chapter heading. The connection between the two is obscured.

Falling where it does the chapter division is symbolic of a tragic separation between church and mission that has permeated every aspect of Christianity. We see it in the handling of Scripture, preaching, curriculum in theological institutions, organizational structures, congregational life and the very thinking of the ordinary Christian. It is a divorce that must grieve the heart of God. It is a divorce that has crippled the Church of the Lord Jesus and robbed it of joy, purpose and blessing. The result is that most Christians down the ages have sidelined the vision for mission that was central to the heart of God and do not seem to have even noticed that this has occurred. The dire consequences are that millions have never been evangelized.

Once we held an Operation World conference in an English city and I used Isaiah 54:1-3 as my text. I applied the barren woman to the Church and the promise of "possessing the nations (peoples)" to us in New Testament terms of making disciples. I was publicly challenged by a lady in the big crowd that I was not justified in doing this; she claimed that the promises were for God's Old Testament people, the Jews, and not for Christians at all. I cannot remember how I replied, but I do remember that I was embarrassed by the emotional vigour as well as the inadequacy of my response! What would have been the better response only came to me after the meeting – as it usually does! I then remembered that Paul had applied this very passage specifically to the New Testament Church:

> "Now Hagar is Mount Sinai in Arabia; she corresponds to the present Jerusalem, for she is in slavery with her children *(The Jerusalem of Paul's day and he spoke of the Jews living there at that time),* But the Jerusalem that is above is free, and she is our mother. For it is written, Rejoice, O barren one who did not bear; break forth and shout, you who are not in travail; for the children of the desolate one are many more than the children of her that is married." *Gal 4:25-27 quoting Isaiah 54:1.*

This passage written by Isaiah had meaning and gave encouragement to the Jewish people exiled in Babylon, but this was only a shadow of the fullness that would come. Just as the full meaning of the Suffering Servant of Isaiah 53 could only be seen after the resurrection of Jesus, so the joyous harvest of Isaiah 54 could be soon after the birth of the Church at Pentecost. The rejoicing is therefore over a spiritual harvest – a gospel promise in which the world-wide Church is gathered through the preaching of the gospel. Yet very few Christians realize this, and few preachers preach on this marvellous passage. The Church is the poorer and Christians more downcast. Unbelief is stimulated that God has somehow abdicated and let Satan control things because few expect the prophesied harvest or actually know about the harvest being gathered in our time! Later, in Part 3, I will give you facts, figures and illustrations to show the unprecedented harvest in the very times in which we live.

The point is that without the Gap we would see the connection between the Suffering Servant crucified in Isaiah 53 and the follow-though in world evangelization of Isaiah 54. We would see the latter with a resurrection outworking and apply the passage and its symbolism to mission to our own times. We have fallen into the unfortunate Gap which separates the cross from mission and this has affected many realms of Christian belief and practice. My burden in this book is that some of these may be exposed and rectified, and that the Church may have the vision that God intended and structures to implement that vision.

Chapter 4

Mission Overlooked in Interpreting Scripture

Here are three illustrations of the many that could be used to show that our understanding of Scripture is often viewed through the spectacles that filter out mission. So deep have these philosophical presuppositions gone that we often miss plain statements about mission in the Bible.

1. God's promises to Abraham

What were the three promises God gave to Abraham before he left his home in Ur? Most would easily mention two – first that God would make of him a great nation and give them a land (Canaan/Israel) and that Abraham himself would be blessed and be a blessing. Many might have difficulty in remembering the third and most important one of all – and it is the one specifically that applies to us today:

"…in you all the families of earth shall be blessed…"
Gen 12:3

These words are so important that they need some explanation. In the previous chapter of Genesis is the tragic account of the Tower of Babel and the confusion of languages. This was the time when ethnicity and cultural diversity became the dominant characteristic of the human race. The very next incident recorded in Scripture is the call of Abraham. Embedded in that calling was the promise that it was for the blessing of every variety of those human cultures. This promise was so important that it was repeated or alluded to many times in Genesis,[3] the Old Testament[4] and also in the New.[5] The climax of the whole Scripture is the heavenly scene where this promise is fulfilled – when redeemed people of **every** race, tribe, people and tongue are gathered round the throne of the Lamb.[6]

---

[3] Genesis 18:18, 22:18, 26:4, 28:14. Also proved in the blessing of Laban through Jacob and Pharaoh through Joseph.

[4] Psalm 2:8, 22:27, 72:8-11, 86:9, Isaiah 45:22-23 are just a few examples.

[5] Galatians 3:8, 14, 29.

[6] Revelation 5:9, 7:9-10.

Paul, writing to the Galatians, explained this promise in a remarkable way:

> "And the Scripture, foreseeing that God would justify the Gentiles by faith, preached the gospel beforehand to Abraham, saying, 'In you shall all the nations be blessed'."
> *Gal 3:8*

Paul stated that the original promise was actually the preaching of the gospel to Abraham. The promise only has its meaning and fulfilment in the peoples of this world when they repent and believe in the Lord Jesus Christ, Abraham's Seed. What a promise it is. This gospel promise is a thread running through the Bible on which the treasures of God's Word and the pearls of theology are strung. Any theology that is not threaded on mission is not a biblical theology. Would that this be understood in all our seminaries and theological schools, for many of them have the pearls, but nothing on which to string them so they roll around unattached!

God's promise to Abraham for the peoples of the world is relevant today. Our post-Cold War world is a demonstration of the importance of ethnicity.[7] Ideology held centre stage for a brief 200 years between the French Revolution in 1789 and the tearing down of the Berlin Wall in 1989. Ethnicity has again returned to become a dominant factor in the affairs of the world with multiplied ethnic conflicts,[8] tribalism, ethnic "cleansing" and outright wars such as we see in Africa, Russia, what was once Yugoslavia, Indonesia, and elsewhere. Ideology, whether colonialism, capitalism, democracy or Communism, only proved to be a lid on the pot of deep ethnic divisions that have boiled out during the '90s with the demise of ideology as a motivating force.[9] One only has to look at the world-wide changes in the attitudes of students over the last thirty years – few protest on the basis of ideology any more. Mission is God's answer to ethnic hatreds, for only in the preaching of the gospel are the dividing walls of hostility broken

---

[7] I elaborate on this theme in chapter 22 of this book.

[8] This is a reflection of the words of Jesus in Matt 24:6 about the world since his ascension.

[9] Please see Chapter 25 for the future challenge presented by ideologies to our proclamation of the gospel in the twenty-first century.

down.[10] The blessing of the nations through mission is fundamental to the ministry of the Church and the life of the world.

2. Psalm 22

Psalm 22 is the companion chapter in the Old Testament to Isaiah 53 and 54. In Isaiah we see the Father's heart revealed in sending his Son to suffer on the cross for a sinful world. In Psalm 22 we see the heart of the suffering Son himself. The Psalm opens with the very words of the Lord on the cross, '*My God, My God, why have you forsaken me?*' The Psalm goes on to give a most graphic account of the events around the time of the crucifixion, though, of course, in poetic language. I was amazed when I carefully studied this Psalm, for in it I found 16 prophecies that were fulfilled in specific events at the time of the crucifixion. All took place over a period of a few hours, but that was a millennium after David was inspired by the Holy Spirit to pen those words. To further add to the wonder of it all, these words were written at a time when the very mode of execution by crucifixion was unknown. I am a scientist by training, and the likelihood of all the quotes of Jesus on the cross, and of his enemies at its foot, and the references to his hands and feet being pierced, his thirst, his bones unbroken, the blood and water that flowed, the soldier's spear-thrust and his death – all happening over those few traumatic hours is not a miracle, it is God-ordained; supernatural; divine! It fills me with wonder that it is only in this Old Testament passage that Scripture reveals a fact we know by tradition that not only were Jesus' hands nailed to the cross, but his feet too. None of the Gospel accounts tell us this.

The pathos and power of the first 21 verses of the Psalm can distract from its victorious ending. The following three verses speak of the resurrection of Jesus. In verse 22 come these triumphant words:

> I will declare your name to my brothers;
> in the congregation I will praise you. *Ps 22:22 NIV*

In fulfilment of this word Jesus appeared only to those who had believed – another indication of the divine origin of Scripture. Verses 25-26 speak of Jesus' triumphal entry into heaven whereby

---

[10] Ephesians 2:11-22.

he completed eternal salvation for us – a foreshadowing of the teaching of Hebrews 9 & 10 and Revelation 5.

> From you comes my praise in the great assembly;
> before those who fear you, I will fulfil my vows
> The poor will eat and be satisfied;
> they who seek the Lord will praise him –
> may your hearts live for ever. *Psalm 22:25-26*

This is Old Testament poetry, but contains New Testament truth! I paraphrase this and include some of the concepts mentioned in Hebrews chapters 9 and 10. Jesus entered into that greatest assembly of all, heaven, where there is a sanctuary not made with hands. It was there he fulfilled his vows by appearing as the final sacrifice for sin, and through his blood opened up the way for a satisfying salvation for poor sinners who then gain a new song of praise and hearts that live for ever.

Then comes the dramatic conclusion in the final verses which speak of world evangelization:

> All the ends of the earth shall remember and turn to the Lord;
> and all the families of the nations shall worship before him.
> *Ps 22:27 RSV*

Here is that promise to Abraham yet again – at the conclusion of the Psalm that best describes the saving work of the Lord Jesus Christ. Here again we see that the cross and world evangelization are bound together into a divine wholeness. Salvation and mission cannot and must not be divorced from one another. How often have you heard the full message of Psalm 22 preached? This lack is indicative of the reality of the divorce.

3. The slowness of the disciples to catch the vision

God's revelation of his love and concern for the salvation of the Gentiles is constantly restated in the Old Testament. Yet the people of Israel failed to see their role as a blessing to the world. Reluctant Jonah was commanded to go to Ninevah, but he did not want the people of Ninevah to repent and escape God's judgement! Through their later history they were more concerned that they be separate from the Gentiles, whether from the spiritual pollution of their idolatrous and immoral religions or from their conquering armies. The devastating effects of spiritual failure in the time of the Kings of Israel and resulting pain of defeats and exiles that followed were so burned into their thinking that these attitudes are understandable. By the time of Jesus this world-view had so permeated the thinking of the post-exile Jews that social and spiritual contacts with the Gentiles and Samaritans were reduced to the absolute minimum and the coming Messiah was conceived in terms of his military conquest of the Gentile nations, and, by implication, the Jews to become the world superpower. After all, the Jews were at that time possibly 13% of the population of the Roman Empire and 3.5% of the world population. The furthest the Jews were prepared to go was to welcome individual Gentiles as proselytes, but only after rigorous initiation.[11]

All this helps us understand how hard it was for the disciples to grasp the revolutionary nature of Jesus' vision. The writers of the Gospels are at pains to show by illustration and teaching the way in which Jesus sought to challenge that world-view. David Bosch[12] masterfully shows how the whole of both Matthew and Luke's writings reveal this. Look at the way Jesus spoke of and ministered to the despised Samaritans, Greeks, traitorous tax-collectors and the hated Romans with whom he came in contact. His teaching also struck at the core of the erroneous world-view of the Jews and the disciples. Luke even shows the opening of the public ministry of Jesus to be a dramatic enunciation of his global vision which then provoked a violent reaction from the Jews.[13]

This incident in the synagogue at Capernaum is only explicable in the light of this challenge. Luke records that Jesus stood to read from Isaiah 61 with startling results. In our English translation we find rapt attention in verse 20, then open admiration in verse 22, but by verse 28, a short while later, they are so violently opposed to him that they are trying to murder him by throwing him over a cliff. What went so badly wrong? Maybe our English translations

---

[11] It is extraordinary how much searching after righteousness there was among the pagans of the time of Jesus. Some reckon that there were 500,000 Gentile proselytes to Judaism at the time of Christ. This was a significant number, for according to a recent investigation by the Hebrew University in Jerusalem, there were 45 million inhabitants of the Roman Empire at the birth of Christ. Of these 6-7 million were Jews. Normal demographic growth would have resulted in 350 million Jews in 1995 instead of the present 14 million remnant.

[12] Bosch 1991:56-122.

[13] Luke 4:16-30.

have missed the point – because the missiological nature of Jesus' announcement was not understood by the translators. The RSV rendering of Luke 4:22:

> And <u>all spoke well of him</u> and wondered at the gracious words which proceeded out of his mouth;...

The underlined words could be translated literally from Greek as *"all bore witness to him,"* which is ambiguous and could also have a negative meaning *"and all condemned him."* A novel and illuminating translation and paraphrase goes as follows:[14]

> They protested with one voice and were furious because he only spoke about (God's year of) mercy (and omitted the words about the Messianic vengeance).

The Jews knew the passage well, and expected Jesus to go on to read the words in the second phrase of Isaiah 61:2, but he ended the reading in mid-sentence and omitted these words:

> ...and the day of vengeance of our God.

The astonishment of the Jews quickly turned to anger because the expected vengeance on the Gentiles was not expressed. Jesus made it worse by reminding the protesters of the ministry of Elijah to a leprous Syrian general and a Sidonian widow. He amply demonstrated that he had deliberately omitted that phrase and that his intended ministry was not to wreak vengeance on the Gentiles, but to save them – even passing over the most needy people of Jewish society, the lepers and widows. This the Jews could not accept and provoked the extreme response of an attempted murder.

It is therefore not surprising that it took so long for the disciples to see the point. They were astonished that Jesus sat at the well in Samaria and spoke to the Samaritan woman. He later reprimanded them that they should even think of calling down fire from heaven to burn up the unwelcoming Samaritans.[15] Neither could they really take in the implications of the Lord's final parting words that they were to be witnesses in Samaria. It took years and persecution to get the disciples to actually go to the Samaritans with intent to bring them to Christ. Philip's remarkable ministry caused a great

---

[14] Bosch 1991:108-112 and Lewis 1992:22-25 elaborate on the logic and exegesis of this passage.
[15] Luke 9:51-56.

stir among the believers in Jerusalem. So a powerful delegation of Peter and John was sent there to investigate. Wonderfully they saw the work of God begun in their hearts, and God's approval was demonstrated by an outpouring of the Holy Spirit.[16] At last they understood that the Samaritans were equally candidates for salvation.

The Samaritans were part Jews in customs, beliefs and religion so the psychological leap to accept the Samaritans was not so great. It needed a much bigger leap for the Gentiles to be seen as also worthy of the gospel and equal inheritors of eternal life with the believing Jews.[17] The vengeance and conquest concept was still strong among the disciples. The Jews expected the Messiah to lead them to military victory, and even though Jesus entered Jerusalem triumphantly, it was not on a war-horse, but a peaceful donkey. The disappointment was vividly expressed by the two disciples walking to Emmaus after the death of Jesus in saying '*we had hoped that he was the one to redeem Israel.*' They were still looking for physical rather than spiritual deliverance from oppression. The hope was again stated just before Jesus ascended to the Father when the eleven raised that issue again: '*Lord, will you at this time restore the kingdom to Israel?*'[18] All the kingdom teaching of Jesus had fallen on deaf ears. I am sure he was disappointed.

His major challenge for world evangelization became more explicit and urgent after he had risen from the dead. All the expressions of the Great Commission are a climax to three years of the same message. This was the dominant theme of the Lord's ministry during those 40 days before his ascension. Even after Pentecost there were years of hesitancy on the part of those disciples who had heard these challenges. It is the failure to grasp the importance of that final command of Jesus as an integral part of their identity as his followers which has been repeated down the succeeding centuries to our own day.

I realize that in arguing this point, I am arguing from a silence in Scripture. There are specific references before Acts 11 to the importance the apostles attached to the evangelization of non-

---

[16] John 4, Luke 9:52-56, Acts 1:8, 8:4-24.
[17] Acts 11:18.
[18] Luke 24:21; Act 1:6

Jews.[19] It was probably a combination of a number of practical factors that hindered a wider implementation of the Great Commission – the apostles were caught up in an amazing revival and enormous church growth. They took too long to delegate authority, as the later appointment of deacons showed. There were simply not the structures and mechanisms at the beginning for a deliberate widening of the ministry to the Gentiles even if they had had the time to think much about it. It was the martyrdom of one deacon, Stephen, and the preaching of another, Philip, which actually provoked the spread of the gospel to the Samaritans and Gentiles.[20] It was the deacons who became the apostles; they did not do much 'deaconing'!

How similar to today! Many pastors of busy churches are so overwhelmed by the pressures and needs of their own congregation and local challenges that there seems no time for what is only going to create more work – promoting missions. It may take the same combination of sufferings and delegation of authority in modern congregations to provoke obedience to the Great Commission!

The divorce has continued to be perpetuated through the centuries. Our present-day marginalizing of missions is only a reflection of the failures throughout the history of the Church.

---

[19] Acts 2:29; 3:25; 4:29.
[20] Winter & Hawthorne 1981:A110. Don Richardson covers this ground in his article, *The Hidden Message of Acts*.

Chapter 5

Mission Bypassed In Terminology and Theology[21]

The lack of a clear vocabulary in common theological use, or the distortion of biblical terms that relate to mission in the course of history has done much to blunt the clear challenge to missions in God's plan. It is perturbing that this has not been pointed out more clearly in doctrinal formulations of the Church and its theologians from the early Church onwards.

Barrett and Johnson[22] have made a study of the terminology of the New Testament. It is astonishing to see the extent and richness of this vocabulary. This is a comprehensive summation of God's burden for the ministry of Christians and the Church with regard to mission. The diversity of vocabulary and number of references is convincing proof that the Great Commission verses are central to a right understanding of the whole New Testament. God's passion for the redeeming work of his Son to be proclaimed to all the peoples of the world is shown in the Bible. How can we Christians miss this centrality?

Look at several key words and phrases pertaining to world evangelization and how they have been handled in the Bible translations we use:

Evangelize

Barrett and Johnson[23] marshall an extraordinary collection of terms. In all the references to mission in the New Testament there are seven key mandates or actions commanded. These have an impact on how mission is to be implemented. These are listed in the table that follows.

---

[21] Olson 1993. Olson's book *What in the World is God Doing* is an excellent brief coverage of the history of missions and the causes for the vision to be almost eliminated.

[22] Barrett & Johnson 1990:13.

[23] Barrett & Johnson 1990:12-17.

English	NT Greek	Occurrences in NT[24]	Describing Mandate	Dominant Characteristics	Human Role
Overall Mandate **Evangelize** *euangelizo*		133	Type of **Evangelization**	Authoritative	**Method of Evangelism**
Receive	*labete*	263	Pneumatic	Spirit-dominated	Prayer
Go	*poreuthentes*	154	Preparatory	Person-implemented	Pre-evangelism
Witness	*martyes*	173	Presence	Unorganized, private	Personal
Proclaim	*keruxate*	72	Proclamation	Ordered, public	Preaching
Disciple	*matheteusate*	266	Pressure	Convert-oriented	Persuasion
Baptize	*baptizontes*	111	Plantation	Church-oriented	Planting
Train	*didaskontes*	212	Pedagogical	Ministry-oriented	Pastoral

The Great Commission can be summed up in the one key Greek verb *evangelize! [euangelizo]*. This word is used 56 times in the New Testament in addition there are 10 close variants based on the root verb *angello*. There are a further four close synonyms and a further 19 near-synonyms all expressing aspects of the same concept, as well as a further 500 close cognate words (nouns, etc.). The task of evangelizing is elaborated by the Lord Jesus Christ in seven mandates, which are imperatives, and these comprise the Great Commission. They are *Receive!, Go!, Witness!, Proclaim!, Disciple!, Baptize!, Train!* All these Greek words are translated into 596 English terms which are listed in the above-mentioned book as amplifications of the sevenfold Mandate. The New Testament is therefore saturated with a whole range of words which refer to world evangelization and local evangelism.

Now we come to the sad part. The word "evangelize," though in common use in its Greek form in the New Testament, is never ONCE translated in this form in the KJV or in most of our English Bible translations. Many substitutes are used such as *preach the gospel, tell the good news*. They are good and helpful, but they obscure the wider challenge for mission because there is no obvious single root which links them together, but which is there in the Greek text.

---

[24] These occurrences include all variations of the verb and immediate cognates (adjectives and nouns derived from the verb) in the New Testament.

Apostle/Missionary

The Greek verb *apostello* is its root. It means "I send out, send away, put forth." Luke says that Jesus prayed before the selection of his disciples, and then chose the twelve whom he named apostles.[25] They were disciples, but the intent was that they be sent out into the world. There is a uniqueness about the Twelve as witnesses of the life, ministry and passion of the Lord Jesus Christ. They were the Apostles of the Lamb[26] and, under God, the human founders of the Church. In Acts and in the writings of Paul we find many others were termed 'apostles' – James the brother of the Lord, Paul himself, Barnabas, and, by implication, Silas and others.[27] It is also interesting to see that in his dispute with false apostles, Paul's arguments were not on the basis that they had been present as witnesses of the ministry of Jesus or had a personal revelation of the Risen Lord, but rather on the evidence of falsehood in their life, words and ministry.[28]

There was no indication that the apostles were to remain permanently based in Jerusalem to run the Church, nor was there any concept of the common idea today in certain sections of the Christian Church that sees the 'apostle' as the top leadership in a family of churches. Where Paul speaks of "God has appointed in the church *first apostles...* " in I Corinthians 12:28, he could have been speaking of either first in time or first in place. I believe that the root meaning would indicate the former – the usual pattern was for an apostle to be the one who first planted a church; other ministries then followed. Paul never maintained a dominating 'apostolic' control of the churches he planted.

We use the words *mission, missions* and *missionaries* today but these are absent in the English Bible – unless as a heading above the biblical text such as: "Paul's second missionary journey." The use of the word mission has only been widely used among Christians comparatively recently. The biblical words *apostleship* and *apostle* have fallen into disuse among most Evangelicals. So the two words we most use to express mission do not appear in our

---

[25] Luke 6:13.
[26] Revelation 21:14.
[27] Galatians 1:19, Acts 14:4+14, 1 Thessalonians 2:6, Romans 16:7.
[28] Douglas 1962:48-50 gives a fuller argument about the meaning and function of apostles.

English Bibles at all. Mission is sidelined because it is not biblical terminology even though the meaning and concepts are biblical.

Today we use the word *missionary* and that should be equivalent to *apostle*. The word is derived from the Latin equivalent to *apostello* which is *mitto*. Both words have almost the same meaning, but in the history of the Western Church (which was basically Latin in language) we have tended to use this latter form. I have been a missionary for over 30 years and do much public speaking, but if I were to stand up in a pulpit and say, 'I am an apostle,' most people would think that I have no right to make such a claim for there are no longer apostles, or that I was head of some deviant sect! In the process of the word-switch the biblical meaning and context of the word *apostle* are replaced with *missionary* which gradually assumed a cloud of meaning no longer anchored to Bible terminology. Today we can argue extensively about the definition of missionary and never once refer to the biblical definition because we do not realize that there is one, because the two words should be synonymous.

The ministry of apostleship was to be the growing edge of the Church, so a missionary should be one on that growing edge – planting or strengthening churches. But we have divorced the term missionary from church planting. So anyone who goes overseas with church support is therefore called a missionary. It is tragic that the link between the two is lost. Every missionary should see him or herself as part of a team which has the objective of planting or strengthening churches.

Kingdom of God

When we pray the prayer the Lord Jesus taught us, do we ever think that we are praying a powerful prayer for world evangelization? As you pray these words *"Thy Kingdom come, on earth as it is in heaven,"* do you think of this in terms of mission? The very term "Kingdom of God" has been applied to so many different situations and even misused that we have lost a clear concept of that kingdom. It becomes a vague ephemeral entity; we know we are part of it and involved in it, but the richness of all that the kingdom of God means is lost to most of us. In the teaching of Jesus constant reference is made to *the reign of God, kingdom of God, kingdom of heaven*. The concept was fundamental in his thinking. It is not always easy to discern all that he meant, for much was taught in parables. However it is plain that the Kingdom and mission cannot be separated. A new world opens up when we understand this, and Jesus' teaching takes on a new mission perspective. Some equate the kingdom of God with the Church, but the Kingdom is much wider, for it is wherever Jesus reigns or is working by his Spirit to extend that reign in the hearts of men and women. One could say that **Church + Mission = The Kingdom**.[29]

It is noteworthy that Luke records in Acts 1 that Jesus gave a commandment (the Great Commission) to the apostles (v2) and told them to be witnesses to the ends of the earth (v8), but between these is the statement that he spoke of the kingdom of God (v3).[30] The response of the apostles to such a statement was to ask about the restoration of the kingdom to Israel (v6). The vigorous reaction of Jesus (v7) showed them that he was not speaking of a limited ethnic Jewish kingdom.[31] Immediately he gave them their marching orders to go to the kingdoms as far as the ends of the earth. The Kingdom of God is wherever the reign of God is being applied by the Holy Spirit in the affairs of this world and its kingdoms as well as in individual hearts. Mission is the work of extending and establishing the kingdom.

The Great Commission

The Great Commission is a term also used by William Carey,[32] but he was not the first to use it. It was fundamental in the theology and vision of the main streams of the much-maligned and persecuted Anabaptists in the early years of the Reformation. This

---

[29] Perhaps the formula could be more correct theologically by being even more mathematical by writing it as:

    The King*(Church+Mission)[Holy Spirit]

or in words, The King multiplies his kingdom through the Church in world evangelization by the power of the Holy Spirit!

[30] Acts 1:2-3,8.

[31] The question of the disciples and the ambiguous response of Jesus implies a future restoration of the kingdom to Israel. Many commentators such as David Pawson, Lance Lambert and others would strongly maintain this. I am not desirous of discussing the context and form of that restoration eschatologically here. The important point here is that this was not the priority for the impending ministry of the apostles, nor of the Church, but that their focus should be world evangelization.

[32] Carey 1792:4-8.

is effectively shown in the writing of Franklin Littel in his article on *The Anabaptist Theology of Mission.*[33]

> In right faith the Great Commission is fundamental to individual confession and to a true ordering of the community of believers. The Master meant it to apply to all believers. The proof-text [*Matthew 28:18-20*] appears repeatedly in Anabaptist sermons and apologetic writings.

Then on baptism and the Great Commission:

> The Great Commission was the stock argument for the use of the sign [of baptism]. The Article on Baptism in the Five Articles (ca. 1547), a Confession of Faith and second most important document of the Hutterians, found its cornerstone in Matthew 28 and Mark 16. Hans Hut, foremost missioner of the South German Brethren, used a standard formula as he baptized hundreds: He told them to obey the commandments, preach the gospel and baptize others in the Great Commission."

Many died for proclaiming this faith in the ensuing century – a history that few Protestants know.

In the following centuries its use was limited in the English-speaking world. As Sydney Rooy says,[34]

> The Great Commission does not occupy a large place in Puritan thought. In itself this is not strange, since the command to evangelize had played but a small part in mission motivation in the primitive and medieval Church. Nor did Luther and Calvin see its significance. The Puritans did point to the continuing validity of its call to mission duty. Sibbes cited it,[35] Baxter expounded it [*as applicable to every age*],[36]

---

[33] Shenk 1984:13-22.

[34] Rooy 1965:319-321.

[35] Rooy 1962:15-64, especially p42. Sibbes: "Every Christian has a divine appointment to spread the gospel." Richard Sibbes (1577- 1635) was one of the great Puritan preachers.

[36] Rooy 1962:66-155 gives a detailed account of Richard Baxter's theology and teaching. Baxter explicitly said (Rooy 98), "This [Great] commission was not restricted to the apostles for the following reasons..." He then listed six cogent reasons.

and Eliot fulfilled it [*as missionary to the native Americans 1640s-1690*]. (*Author's explanation*)[37]

Rooy's point is well made, but he apparently did not actually read what Luther said on missions. J. Montgomery convincingly showed that Luther's commentaries, sermons and even his hymns contained references to the value and rightness of taking the gospel to the nations.[38] It was the next generation of Lutheran theologians who adopted such a negative stance, which was then reflected back on Luther himself. This then influenced later Pietistic and Evangelical writers in their criticisms.

The mainline Reformers and those that followed them assumed that the key Great Commission text, Matthew 28:18-20, had been obeyed and achieved by the apostolic Church, and that all which remained was to evangelize locally.[39] This key challenge of the Lord Jesus was largely ignored or glossed over from the Reformation through to Carey's day. Carey wrote a devastating critique and demolished these arguments by showing that if the command to make disciples of all peoples was no longer valid, then nor was baptism any longer incumbent on Christians. In fact, any who presumed to disciple peoples in subsequent ages were doing so without biblical or divine warrant because it was not preceded by going to make disciples of all nations. Also he showed that the wonderful promise of Christ's presence with us would no longer be true without the obedience upon which it was conditional.

During the subsequent 200-year modern missionary advance, the Great Commission has become the key phrase for that movement – almost to the exclusion of all else. So the wider context of Matthew, and the overall message of the Bible on mission was not adequately developed. The theology of mission by the proponents of the Great Commission has therefore been often too simplistic and lacking in comprehensiveness. The phrase has therefore been over-exploited by those committed to its

---

[37] It is interesting to realize that Isaac Watts in penning the famous hymn, "*Jesus shall reign where'er the sun*" was motivated by the preaching of Baxter.

[38] Montgomery 1967:193-202. Also see the *Evangelical Missions Quarterly* Summer 1967 Vols. 3-4:193-202.

[39] An Anglican priest, Hadrian Saravia, advocated that Matt 28:19 was binding on the apostles and all future times in a tract he wrote in 1690. Barrett 1987 (2), 35.

implementation, and ignored by the rest of the Church. Truly the divorce appears to have been finalized in the main stream of the theological world.

A Deficient Theology

Lack of adequate terminology concerning mission has led to a more serious distortion of theology itself. This has characterized nearly every expression of Christian theology from earliest times. The lack is demonstrated by failure to even mention mission in credal statements so painstakingly compiled to formulate the theology of the Church. This astonishing lack of any reference in these to the resurrection ministry of Jesus or the task of the Church for world evangelization is an error of enormous proportions, and has distorted theological education to the present day.

The most famous and widely used is the Apostles' Creed. Its origins are not clear, but it is probable that it developed out of the Great Commission text as a baptismal confession. It was only finalized in the sixth century, but many of its statements probably go back to the first century and apostolic times.[40] The main motivation for the formulation of the theological expressions in the Apostles' Creed was not world evangelization, but combating the error of Marcionism. The only mission concept that remains is in its title, but "Apostle" here has no relationship to messengers of the gospel being sent out to the non-Christians. It is tragic that the major formulation of Christian theology which is most often read and studied in churches around the world has no single word about the Church and its responsibility to a lost world!

The Nicene Creed of 325 was also formulated to deal with error. In this case it was Arianism. Once more there was no mention of mission, but an elaboration and re-statement of the Apostles' Creed with more carefully defined statements about the person and work of the Lord Jesus Christ. Although mission activity still continued at the time, it was mainly directed at the completion of the Christianization of the degenerating Roman Empire and the conversion of the barbarian hordes that assailed it. Wider activity was hindered by the lack of theological expression of the need and also the lack of effective structures (of which, more later) within the main stream of church life to promote world evangelization.

The words of the reformers, Luther and Calvin, in writing and preaching are positive about the Scriptures that spoke of mission, but this was not their major emphasis. They laid a good foundation on which a missiology could emerge. Calvin overreacted to the erroneous teaching on apostolic succession of the Roman Catholics, and therefore did not apply the apostolic commission to later generations of the Church.[41]

Many of their successor theologians were actively hostile to any thought that mission was the responsibility of the Church.[42] The great statements of the Reformed Faith, whether mainland European Belgic or Heidelberg Confession, English Westminster Confession or the Anglican Thirty-Nine Articles, are all silent on the issue. A few Lutheran and Reformed theologians in the Netherlands, Britain and Germany did seek to stem the theological tide, but little of any practical outworking was manifested in the actual sending of missionaries. Mission work was carried out by the Anabaptists, Pietists[43] and Moravians in the two centuries that followed, but this was ignored by the theologians of the day.

One of the surprises of history is that the Reformation recovery of the Bible did not result in a surge of vision for world evangelization. There are practical political reasons which mitigate the enormity of the failure, but do not fully excuse our forebears in the faith.

1. The tender plant of the Reformation was threatened by an aroused Catholicism and the most powerful rulers of the age. They were determined to eradicate the Reformation *heresy* by force. They had at their disposal vast armies enriched by the plunder of the New World. Survival rather than expansion was the issue; an issue only settled over a century later at the Peace of Westphalia in 1648. This Treaty ended the Thirty Years War that had devastated much of Germany and Central Europe and almost led to the military conquest of all the lands that had embraced the Protestant faith.

2. Christianity was hemmed in by an implacable Muslim foe. Islam had wrested from Christians the areas won by them over

---

[40] Latourette 1975:134-6.
[41] Rooy 1962:98.
[42] Bosch 1991:243-246.
[43] Many of these Pietists were actually Lutheran.

the previous thousand years in the Middle East, North Africa, Asia and even much of south-east Europe was under its heel. Just a few decades before, in 1453, Constantinople, one of the Christian capitals of the world, had fallen to the Turks and Vienna itself was under threat of capture by them in 1529 and 1683. Europe was hemmed in and isolated from the rest of the world as never before.

3. Added to the barrier of Islam shielding Africa and Asia were also the Catholic Empires of Spain and Portugal dominating the oceans, effectively isolating north-western Europe from meaningful contacts with non-Christians. This meant there were not practical openings for Reformation missionaries to consider missions. It was only at the end of the sixteenth century that the British, Dutch and French[44] gained sufficient naval power and financial resources to project their influence beyond Europe. These fleets frequently took with them chaplains with the hope that they might evangelize native populations. This rarely happened – trade was more important. Stirring up the natives with a new religion was too threatening to the former.

4. One of the tragic spiritual reasons was failure of the Reformers to face up to the need for structural reform. They left unchanged the parochial system, which the main stream of the Reformation inherited from the Roman Catholic Church.

The Radical Reformers or Anabaptists wanted to reform the structures too, and were persecuted for it. The very term 'Anabaptist' or re-baptizers was a derogatory epithet. They rejected the rigid parish structure. The Great Commission became their prime motivation and their explanation for their widespread evangelization and mission among those who were nominally Christian as well as the heathen. They became a threat to the status quo. Broadbent describes this dilemma in Luther's life:[45]

> Luther had seen the Divine pattern for the churches, and it was not without an inward struggle that he abandoned the New Testament teaching of independent assemblies of real believers, in favour of the National or State Church system which outward circumstances pressed upon him. The

---

[44] At that time the Huguenots were still politically significant in France.
[45] Broadbent 1931:144-149.

irreconcilable difference between the two ideals was the essential ground of conflict...

The glorious and tragic history of the Anabaptists has not been adequately described outside Mennonite writings on church history. Wilbert Shenk edited an excellent book *Anabaptism and Mission*. In this Franklin Littel wrote an article on "The Anabaptist Theology of Mission." Here is a quote which indicates the centrality of the Great Commission among the original leaders of the Movement.

No words of the Master were given more serious attention by his Anabaptist followers than his final command. ...In right faith the Great Commission is fundamental to individual confession and to a true ordering of the community of believers. The Master meant it to apply to all believers at all times. The proof text appears repeatedly in Anabaptist sermons and apologetic writings...

Tragically, there were some Anabaptist leaders who advocated violence to set up the kingdom of God on earth. It was an aberration from mainstream Anabaptism and a disaster. The short-lived Anabaptist kingdom in Münster of Jan van Leyden fell in 1535. This further deepened the hostility of the Reformers to all Anabaptists, most of the latter were apolitical and pacifist in inclination. They were fiercely persecuted throughout the sixteenth century by the Roman Catholic Inquisition and also, sadly, by the majority of the leaders of the Reformation. Many were exiled, stripped of all their possessions, tortured, executed and burnt at the stake for their ardent proclamation of the gospel. Theirs is an amazing and little-told account of courage and determination for mission.[46] One wonders how much the Reformers' rejection of the Anabaptists underlay their rejection of their emphasis on the Great Commission. So brutal was the persecution that following generations of Anabaptists did not show the same commitment to outreach, becoming more known for their introspective, secluded communities, a pattern still common among their modern descendants, the Mennonites and the Hutterites.

From the Reformation on the tide began to turn – in spite of, rather than because of, the Reformation. However that tide was

---

[46] Shenk 1984.

turned by the Roman Catholics, who spent the three hundred post-Reformation years in an extensive expansion through missionary enterprises. For 200 of those years, Protestants did virtually nothing to the scorn of Roman Catholic writers. I believe at the heart of the problem lie two serious internal deficiencies – one was theological and the other structural.

1. There was no theological framework that could provide the basis for mission.

The Reformers Luther and Calvin were sympathetic to the concept of world evangelization. Some of their commentaries and writings are positive to the taking of the gospel to the heathen. Calvin prefaced his *Institutes* to the King of France, giving his reason for writing as he did – the salvation of his native people,[47]

> …I toiled at the task chiefly for the sake of my countrymen the French, multitudes of whom I perceived to be hungering and thirsting after Christ, while very few seemed to have been duly imbued with even a slender knowledge of him…

The devastating Thirty Years War (1618-1648) led to the decision that Roman Catholic, Lutheran, Reformed and Anglican political rulers should determine the religion of their subjects, which was a further damper on any mission activity. The rigidities of the parochial system and the passivity encouraged in the reformation creeds, all hindered the development of a biblical understanding of mission. These developments influence our Christian world-view to this day.

A good example is the massive work of A.H. Strong. A century ago he wrote a three-volume Systematic Theology.[48] It is a masterpiece of Baptist evangelical theology and from a Christian tradition that had contributed as much as any family of denominations to world evangelization, yet his entire work only once refers to mission, apostleship, evangelization or the Great Commission.[49] His quotes of Matt. 28:19 are not to support the idea of making disciples or for world evangelization, but as a proof text

---

[47] Calvin 1536:3 in Vol. 1 of *Institutes of the Christian Religion*.
[48] Strong 1907.
[49] Strong does mention the preaching of the gospel to the whole world and quotes Matthew 24:14 on page 1008, but this is only as a sub-set of his presentation of the second coming of Christ.

for baptism only. How can any theology claim to be biblical or even Christian that ignores this?

Few other great theologians do better. It would be an interesting study to assess the coverage of the Great Commission and missiology in all similar works by major theologians. I believe the results would reveal exceptions, but in the main, the lack would be glaringly plain, and my point confirmed.

Our seminaries and theological colleges often display the same attitude, and missiology is just an optional extra subject for those interested in that branch of learning. I will return to this issue when I deal with structures in chapter 26.

In his book, David Bosch refers to a 1986 report[50]

"…one may appreciate the frustration and distress of Cracknell and Lamb who, surveying the British scene, find that the theology of religions (indeed the entire area of missiology) is either virtually unknown in theological institutions or relegated to the position of an unimportant subsection of pastoral theology." What a condemnation.

James Scherer, a long-time Lutheran missionary in China and Japan and then a professor of missions in a Lutheran seminary in the USA had this to say:

"It has always struck me that the teaching of missions had no clearly defined or adequate place in the theological curriculum of mainline seminaries. Whatever place it once had seems to have further diminished in recent years. This lack of status contrasts sharply with the central place of mission in the New Testament and in the early church… It seems to me that the dominant Western model of theological education is one devised in the late period of Christendom. It presupposes a static condition of Christian community and is geared toward the maintenance of existing congregations and received traditions. Issues such as evangelism, conversion, church growth, witness to people of other faiths, and mission in unity seem largely foreign to it." [51]

---

[50] Bosch 1991:477. Quoting Cracknell and Lamb in a British Council of Churches survey.
[51] Scherer 1996:72.

I would agree heartily with the sentiment, but question the time of origin of this theological deficiency. I would put it back to Roman Catholic Medieval times when theological education became the main function of universities. The Reformation perpetuated the system.

Theological education has made a Cinderella of missiology when mission was actually the source of all theological study. Bosch quotes Martin Kähler's suggestion and added comments,[52]

> ...in the first century, theology was not a luxury of the world-conquering church but was generated by the emergency situation in which the missionizing church found itself. In this situation, **mission became the mother of theology**. However as Europe became Christianized and Christianity became the established religion in the Roman Empire and beyond, theology lost its missionary dimension." (*author's emphasis*).

How this needs to be changed. Unless our theological institutions recover a biblical centrality of mission and insist on it as the core and inspiration of their instruction, we will perpetuate the error of nearly two millennia.

2. There were no structures to sustain mission.

It is hard for us in our pluralistic age to conceive the degree of control of the Pope and the Roman Catholic Church in the Middle Ages. Rulers, governments, universities, daily life and the home were in fear of the all-embracing system which controlled life on earth and beyond the grave too. When the Reformers began to unravel the intricate web of control, not every strand was untied. The post-Reformation Roman Catholic Church, with all its failings, still retained an integrated system that was able to sustain mission with their monastic orders. The Reformation dispensed with the largely corrupt monastic system, but took centuries to find an equivalent alternative because they rejected the one to hand.

The close relationship between church and state of pre-Reformation times remained largely intact for centuries afterwards. The rigid parochial system and, in many cases, a territorial episcopacy were effective means of control for the secular rulers but not for inspiring mission. The pervading attitude was that

---

[52] Bosch 1991:489.

making Christians of the heathen was somehow the government's job. So most of the few Protestant mission efforts before 1790 were through the initiative of godly secular rulers – King Gustav in Sweden encouraged work among the pagan Lapps in the north of Sweden in 1559. Oliver Cromwell, when ruling England in the Commonwealth period (1649-1660), sought to promote mission in North American colonies. Then, in the seventeenth and eighteenth centuries colonial chaplains had some impact as the Netherlands, Denmark and Britain expanded their trading empires in Asia. Though with the latter, the trading companies were usually hostile to any mission work in their territories as being detrimental to trade. Through the concern of King Frederick the small Danish territories of Tranquebar and Serampore in India became the bases for Ziegenbalg, the great Pietist missionary (1706-19), and later for William Carey in 1792 and not the extensive British domains that surrounded them. During the whole eighteenth century only one Indian from British controlled areas was baptized.

Whenever state control of religion was weaker, and dissent[53] permitted, there was a blossoming of new ideas with outworkings for world evangelization. This was true when the Dissenters under Cromwell won the British Civil War (but in the resulting Commonwealth (1649-1660) lost the peace), and in New England where the Puritan settlers had a measure of freedom of action.

In the next section I take four examples of missionary movements before 1790 which had a measure of success. I draw a few conclusions about their achievements. These I will expand when I deal with the structures for mission for the future in Part 4.

The effects of these negatives are shown in the next diagram which shows the percentage of the human race that was Christian over two millennia. After 650 years of Christian growth, the decline set in with the rise of Islam. In 650 AD one quarter of the world's population professed Christianity; a figure not to be attained again until the middle of the nineteenth century.

---

[53] Dissenters were those who did not agree with state control in the affairs of the Church. From them came the Baptists, Independents, Quakers and others.

The Growth and Decline of Christianity
Comparing Caucasians and non-Caucasians
AD100-2100

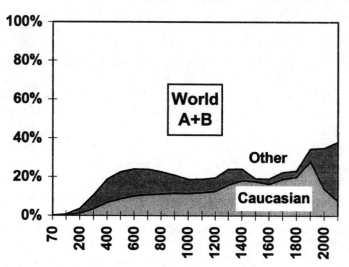

The losses are even more dramatically shown when comparing Caucasian (European-origin cultures) and non-Caucasian Christians. For the first 800 years of the Church, non-Caucasians were in the majority; by 1500 this was reduced to less than 8%. Christianity had largely become a localized religion limited to parts of Europe. A later diagram on page 67 shows how World B had shrunk to almost vanishing point; for 1,000 years the number of non-Christians being brought into meaningful contact with Christianity gradually shrank to just 2% of the world's population. Missions had, in effect, ceased to exist as an activity of the main body of the Church. This is not to say that missionary activity ceased, but it was mainly confined to the despised or ignored fringes of the Church. God has carefully preserved a visionary and pure remnant in all ages of the Church – this is a fascinating story beyond the scope of this book.[54]

---

[54] Broadbent 1931, Kennedy 1965. These two books give a history down the ages of the Pilgrim or Remnant Church which remained more true to the Bible than the main body of nominal Christianity. Described are such as the Montanists, Donatists, Albigensians, Waldensians, Hussites, Lollards, Anabaptists, Moravians, Christian Brethren, etc. Most historians follow the virulent criticisms of the threatened

Chapter 6

Mission Sidelined in the History of the Church

How is it that Christians down the ages have failed to see the centrality of mission? For most of the Church and the majority of individual Christians it is as if those last words of Jesus were never spoken. The Great Commission has become *The Great Omission*, the appropriate title of J. Robertson McQuilkin's challenging book.[55] I give several historical examples of this failure to incorporate mission in the life, teaching and ministry of the Church and from these to deduce lessons that are applicable to us today.

The New Testament Church

This neglect was just as apparent in the Church in Acts. The early Church is often held up as a model to be followed by all subsequent generations of Christians. That is certainly true of some aspects of the life of primitive Christianity, but there are also aspects that we should note and avoid. That passionate concern of the Father which was communicated by the Son for a needy world was not in evidence in the first 5-6 years of the Church.

Luke called the Eleven "apostles." Luke was sure of their main ministry – they were, as the Greek word means, "those sent away with a message." They didn't; they remained based in Jerusalem for about 6 years and in their ministry were involved with Judea and the Jews.[56] There was little world vision manifested[57] and the Church was very much identified with Jerusalem, continued use of the Temple and house meetings for teaching, fellowship and breaking of bread. Organization and structure squeezed out the visionary and mobile aspects of church life. The Church became centripetal and inward looking. There must always be a finely

---

establishment in painting these bodies in dark colours. They were usually closer theologically to the Evangelicals of today.

[55] McQuilkin 1984.

[56] I am assuming a chronology based on Jesus' ministry being over the period AD29-33 and Peter baptizing the household of the Roman centurion, Cornelius, in AD38 (Barrett 1987, 21). If, as is eminently possible and better fits the 30-year pre-ministry life-span for Jesus (Luke 3:23), his ministry were from AD26-30, this could have been 8-9 years.

[57] Except those points to which I referred in the last chapter on p 42-43.

balanced tension between the institutional and the mobile, between maintenance and vision, between the pastoral and the apostolic. I will return to the need for multiple structures in the Body of Christ in Part 4 of this book. The results were almost inevitable. Dissension arose over a seemingly trivial issue – the distribution of food to widows, and the accusation that the Hebrew speaking believers were favoured over the Greek speaking believers. The Church faced division over the ethnic issue but the practical reason was the issue of food for the members! Any Christian body that becomes inward looking and selfish is doomed to spiritual decline or acrimonious division for it is no longer living for the will of God. A divorce because of a breakdown of relationships leads to many other divorces. The Church at the time addressed the issue wisely, and God was able to use this.

The Holy Spirit used this breakdown to thrust the Church into mission. Deacons were appointed to handle the practical matters of food distribution, but several of those men of God were of true apostolic calling! Stephen preached so effectively that he became the first known martyr to shed his blood after Jesus himself. The persecution that then broke out scattered the believers, including another deacon, Philip, who became the evangelist to the Samaritans. The apostles still did not move from Jerusalem; the ones who were commissioned to be sent away stayed and the ordinary believers went out.[58]

The Holy Spirit had to use a triple vision in Joppa to shake Peter out of his blindness. After this he was willing to take the plunge and preach the gospel to the Romans in Cornelius' house. His graphic account of the visions and resulting conversion and outpouring of the Holy Spirit on the Gentiles at last largely convinced the Church in Jerusalem in these remarkable words:

> When they heard this they glorified God, saying,
> "Then to the Gentiles also God has granted repentance unto life." *Acts 11:18*

Until then most of the disciples had not seen this as an option – even after all Jesus' Great Commission challenges. The following verse shows that some still remained unconvinced. Only after that affirmation was it possible for the scattered disciples to actively

---

[58] Acts 8:1-8.

win Gentiles to the Faith; the church in Antioch was the result. It was this church rather than the Jerusalem church that became the launch pad for world evangelization. The issue of how to handle the Gentile believers was only finalized about 16 years after Pentecost at the Council in Jerusalem[59]. It was only then that the apostles began to go out to far-distant lands and peoples with the Gospel. We are not told of their ministry in the Bible, but there are strong traditions that are hard to confirm that all, with the possible exception of John, died a martyr's death – Peter and Paul in Rome, Philip in Asia Minor (Turkey), Matthias in Crimea, Judas Thaddeus in Armenia, Bartholomew in Albania, Andrew in Achaia, Matthew in Persia or Ethiopia and Thomas in India.

The Sinful Delay of the Church down the ages

The New Testament Church eventually obeyed the Lord Jesus, but lost nearly half a generation. Every generation has the challenge and theoretical possibility to obey the Great Commission in their own generation. Is this what Jesus implied in some of his simple, but puzzling statements?

> So also, when you see these things taking place, You know that the kingdom of God is near. Truly, I say unto you, this generation will not pass away till all has taken place. *Luke 21:31,32*

Was he referring to the destruction of Jerusalem or to the end of the age? Both are part of his discourse. Then in the discussion at the end of John's Gospel about the future for Peter and John, Jesus could have implied that his return would come before John's death:

> When Peter saw him *(John)*, he said to Jesus, "Lord, what about this man?" Jesus said to him, "If it is my will that he remain until I come, what is that to you? Follow me!" The saying spread abroad among the brethren that this disciple was not to die… *John 21:21-4*

I do not want to build a theology on these statements alone. There is an ambiguity in the prophecies of Jesus, which the Holy Spirit uses to stimulate every generation. Nevertheless this could be an indication that the completion of the basic elements of the Great

---

[59] Acts 15, ca. AD 48/50 (Conybeare & Howson 1957, 832; Douglas 1962, 227).

Commission of preaching the gospel to every person and making disciples of every ethnic group would open the way for his return and could have been achieved in their lifetime. Through the whole New Testament is the pervading thought of the imminence of the return of the Lord Jesus. Did delayed obedience mean the non-fulfilment of the words of Jesus to those disciples? Is that why so many generations have passed without that awaited return? Can our obedience hasten his return or our disobedience delay it?

The sermon of Andrew Fuller in 1791 mentioned above was entitled 'The Pernicious Influence of Delay', and later this was phrased by the founder of my own mission agency, C.T. Studd, as 'The Sinful Delay'. This was the major theme of Alexander McLeish's writings half a century ago.[60] McLeish propounded the principle that every generation has had the responsibility and potential to evangelize their own generation fully. I personally would not want to build a theology or stake my reputation on this. But if so, then truly the unfinished task before us is to be blamed on the sinful delay of the Church. Will our generation be likewise guilty? There is an urgency that is very biblical, but there is an immediacy of achievement for each generation that is more disputable. We should take this latter possibility seriously, while not making a theology of it!

I have a responsibility for the evangelization of the generation now living and I ought to throw my whole being into the achievement of this. I do not want to lose our present window of opportunity for world evangelization through my own or our collective disobedience.

The diagram opposite shows how much progress those early apostles made. We see three worlds of humankind and their proportions for each century over the last 2,000 years.[61] These worlds are not defined geographically, but rather on the basis of response to the Christian faith.

---

[60] McLeish 1952.
[61] For these definitions and statistics I am indebted to David Barrett (Barrett 1990:25 et seq.).

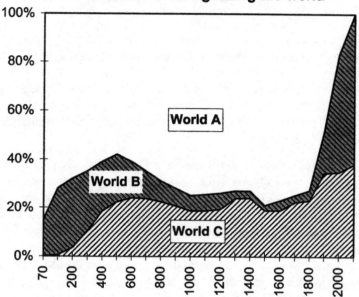

The Spread of Christianity
Two millennia of evangelizing the world

1. **World C** – all persons who individually are Christians anywhere in the world. This is Christianity in its broadest expression and includes Roman Catholic, Orthodox, Protestant, Anglican, Evangelical and all derived or deviant forms of Christianity. The growth and declines of Christianity over these two millennia as a percentage of the world's population is clearly shown.

2. **World B** – all non-Christians who have heard the gospel, or who live within societies and areas where they were or are likely to hear it during their lifetime. These are evangelized non-Christians.[62] It is a measure of the growing edge of the Kingdom of God which should be much bigger than the

---

[62] Barrett 1987 (2) for clear definitions which demonstrate that evangelism and conversion are not the same in biblical teaching, though in many modern books the two are equated.

visible Church. Only in the early church and in our day has this been true.[63]

3. **World A** – all non-Christians who are unevangelized and likely to remain so without a new effort by Christians to bring the gospel to them.

It is possible that in the space of those first 45-50 years nearly 30% of the world's population at that time had been exposed to the Good News. Those early apostles certainly made up for initial lost time. They truly were turning the world upside down. By the end of the fifth century this had risen to about 40%. Despite the slow start we can certainly admire the extraordinary achievements of Apostolic Christianity.

Then followed a millennium of conflict and decline as Christianity increasingly became a European phenomenon. Notice how from 500 to 1800 the non-Christian proportion of the world was increasing, the Christian population was either static or in decline and the proportion of the world's population even being exposed to the gospel in serious decline. Only in our times has the percentage of the world's evangelized population rapidly increased. This graph shows that the Mark 16:15 command of Jesus that the gospel be preached to every person is at last attainable in our own times. Of course this is not the whole Great Commission. Exposure to the gospel is an inadequate first step, but a necessary precursor to the discipling and church planting ministries which we find in Matthew 28:18-19.

Church Historians and Mission

Church historians have been just as guilty of bias, for here again world evangelization has not been a chief focus. Some of the greatest mission movements of history have been little publicized. Church history books often speak more about the leading personalities, internal structures and theological disputes of the centre and say little about the growing edge of the Church. Some of the missionaries involved were so busy and so isolated that they

---

[63] I do not want to imply that mission work is only valid in World A. This is not true. There are many millions in World B and C who have need to hear and understand the whole gospel, and have not had that opportunity. However the individuals in Worlds B and C have the probability of hearing the gospel with existing outreach.

could record little of, or report rarely on, their accomplishments. So the really exciting part of church history has had a poor and limited write-up.

Those that had a vision for world evangelization were few and usually not part of the mainstream of the Church. Had they been, centralized leadership, rigidities of structure and tradition would have stifled that initiative and little would have been done. Vision and flexibility of action are the hallmarks of the mission enterprise. Institutionalization and hierarchical leadership kill vision. Leaders within these are far more concerned at maintaining the status quo. It is the latter that prevails in the end – both in visibility and in the history books.

Yet there is a remarkable and less well-known *continuity* of the mission vision all through the ages. Through this ignored remnant came a quiet maturing of the vision which began to come into full flower just two hundred years ago. Note the comments of Barnes in his book *Two Thousand Years of Missions before Carey*:

> The missions of the two thousand years before the time of Carey were scattered over the world ... They were conducted by the most widely divergent sects of the children of God. But nothing in either the physical or the spiritual realm is entirely isolated. There are always lines of continuity which give coherence to the whole and show the process of development. To discover the Plan of Development is to think God's thoughts after him ... We may be sure that if the records had been made and if sufficient attention could be given them, not one of the 2000 years would be found devoid of true missionary effort, and not one of the efforts could be fully appreciated except as connected with every other one.[64]

The dynamic ministry of the Holy Spirit has kept up the momentum towards world evangelization in spite of the failures and disobedience of the Church as a whole. This is a wonderful, but little known story. The Holy Spirit takes hold of a person and imparts a vision which launches a movement; however it is sadly true that this later becomes a machine and often finally ends up a monument.

---

[64] Barnes 1902: Chapter 25.

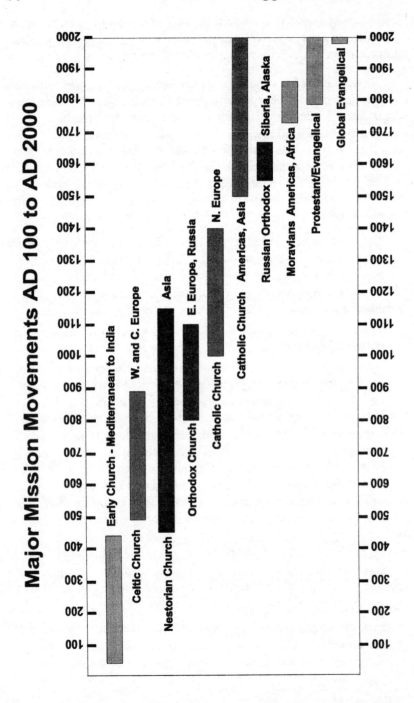

Major Mission Movements AD 100 to AD 2000

The Church needs both stability and continuity together with dynamism and flexibility, but the latter is harder to describe. Our church history books are more filled with describing dying monuments than with dynamic movements. I briefly describe below just four of the most dynamic mission movements which preceded the present modern missionary era. These are to show their importance and also how small a part they have played in most church history writings.

The diagram opposite gives an overview of the most significant missionary movements after the collapse of the Roman Empire in the West. This shows something of that variety and continuity. The Eastern Empire continued for another millennium as a Greek-speaking Christian Empire until the combined assault of Western Christian Crusaders and Muslim Ottoman Turks led to its destruction in 1453. Some of these missionary movements would have had aspects of theology of which we may not approve while others used dubious methodologies and were even barbaric in their "Christianization" of subjugated peoples. I select these few to illustrate the point, and also draw some lessons from their successes and failures.

1. The Celtic Mission thrust to Europe, 500 - 800 AD

The story of how Celtic itinerant monks evangelized much of Britain and West and Central Europe is one of the great missionary feats of all time.[65] The Irish were never conquered by the Romans but ultimately became the means by which many of the pagan invaders of the Empire and their homelands were evangelized. A vital indigenous Celtic Christianity arose which was not dependent on imperial favour for survival and which was autonomous of the Pope in Rome in both doctrine and structure. It preserved much of the Latin and Greek classical learning from destruction during the dark ages which had so debased Western Europe over the period of the sixth to the eighth centuries. It also retained something of apostolic Christianity in its vision for mission which was lost by the centres of power in the Christian world.

Its origins give some explanation for its spiritual strengths and organizational weaknesses. As Roman power waned in Britain, an Irish band of marauders seized some Roman British and enslaved

---

[65] Addison 1936.

them.[66] One was a nominal Christian, Patrick. During his servitude as a swineherd in largely heathen Ireland he came to a living faith in God. After six years he managed to escape to France. There he entered a monastery. Twenty years of spiritual growth were preparation for what was to become his life-work – the conversion of Ireland. His thirty years of evangelism with dramatic power encounters that confounded his opponents were so successful that by his death in 461, the heathen druidic religion had been routed and replaced with Christianity.

His pioneer mission work, methods, earnest prayer life and his godly character made a deep impression on the Irish. They became one of the great Christian missionary peoples of history extending even to the present day – whether Celtic, Catholic or Protestant. Organizationally the strength of the Celtic Church lay in its monasteries and their abbots which became more influential than the territorial episcopacy initiated by Patrick. The sodality (brotherhoods) became the focus rather than the modality (organizational structures)[67] – a phenomenon that became prominent in twentieth century Protestantism.

The most famous monastery was that of Iona, an island off the west coast of Scotland. The abbot of Iona, as with many other monasteries, was a presbyter, not a bishop; but there were always bishops connected with the society and subject, by their monastic vow, to the abbot. The bishops were honoured as such, and their exclusive power to ordain was respected. But over all the monks, bishops included, the abbot was the supreme autocrat.[68]

Spiritually the strength of the Celtic Church was found in the emphasis on the study of Scripture and the godliness and dogged faith of those who followed in Patrick's footsteps.

Celtic missionaries such as Ninian, Columba (Scotland), Aidan (England), Columbanus (France, Switzerland and N. Italy), and their British Catholic successors such as Wilfrid (Frisia), Boniface (Germany) were the leading missionary thrust of Western Christianity. This early effort was autonomous from Rome, and it was only two centuries later at the Synod of Whitby in 664 that

---

[66] Bruce 1958:371-383.
[67] See p178 for a fuller explanation of this terminology. Also Winter 1971, 193.
[68] Addison 1936:77.

Papal authority began to gain the upper hand. Ultimately Celtic Christianity and its hero saints were claimed by Rome as her own. Nevertheless the spirit of Celtic Christianity had a deep impact on the life and development of the English Church for centuries to come and from the British isles a series of missionaries journeyed to the Netherlands, Germany, Switzerland and even as far as Kiev in today's Ukraine and Iceland (then still uninhabited). This great missionary advance was gradually halted by institutionalization internally and the fearsome destruction of the coastal regions of Western Europe by the Vikings. The institutional Latin Church won the control, but the missionary Celtic Christians won the heathen.

2. The Nestorian evangelization of Asia, 480 - 1250 AD

The story of world evangelization would be incomplete without an account of the Nestorians, but few Christians know anything of the outstanding missionary outreach generated and sustained by these Christians. By the year 1000 the Nestorians had spread from Syria to Iran and Yemen and then across central Asia, Mongolia, Tibet, China, parts of India, Thailand and Burma. It was the dominant faith between the Caspian Sea and the borders of China. There were then 12 million associated with this Church in 250 dioceses. By the thirteenth century there were 72 metropolitan patriarchs and 200 bishops in China and surrounding areas.[69] This represented 24% of all Christians in the world of that time, and over 6% of the population of Asia.[70] Yet we know so little about them. Why is this?

Nestorius was Bishop of Constantinople, but in 430 a synod in Rome excommunicated him for various heresies. However the excommunication was as much attributable to cultural differences, breakdowns in inter-personal relationships and personal ambition as to doctrines.[71] This was the time of intense dispute about the relationship between the divine and human in the person of the Lord Jesus Christ. The Nicene Creed had defined Jesus as equally God and man. The dispute was also strongly coloured by power politics in the church and intense personality clashes. The Monophysites (now found in the Coptic Orthodox Churches of

---

[69] Tucker 1983:45
[70] Barrett 1987a:29 & 96.
[71] Latourette 1975:322-5.

Egypt and Ethiopia) emphasised the divine aspect of the nature of Christ and the Nestorians the human – Nestorius taught that in Christ his divine and the human natures were effectually two persons – meaning that Christ's divine and human natures were never really united.

Those who held this theological position were pronounced heretics and banished from the Empire taking refuge in what is today Iraq and Iran. Nestorianism became, in effect, a Persian form of Christianity and was inaccurately called the "Nestorian" Church. Sadly so, because ever since then the main body of Christianity has virtually ignored them as heretics. This isolation was further enhanced by the Muslim conquest of Persia in 640. At that time there were a million Christians in the land in what then became known as the Catholic Apostolic Church of the East or Assyrian Orthodox Church. By 1300 a large minority of Persia was still Christian. They and the Muslims were then under Mongol rule.

For 600 years very little news of Asia beyond the Muslim barrier was heard in the West. We must admire the vision and courage of the early pioneers who pressed through tremendous difficulties on immense journeys through some of the most demanding terrain on earth to spread their message. They took with them much knowledge of the Scriptures and theology, a strong missionary monasticism similar to the Celtic Church, and a willingness to learn languages and translate sacred writings into them. The Nestorians were the missionary church *par excellence* of a millennium ago. The supreme leader of the Nestorian Church elected in 1281 was a Mongolian monk.

By 1500 Nestorians had been virtually wiped out over much of Asia leaving little behind them but archaeological evidence. What went wrong? The early dynamism and vision was replaced by dependence on tradition and ecclesiastical structures; formalism, syncretism and compromise were the result. The Nestorians were nearly always in a minority except for a time in Syria and Iraq, so political patronage was rarely their lot. They had not the spiritual stamina and commitment to withstand the opposition and persecutions of highly organized and dominant religions. The Taoist Emperor of China banned Nestorianism and their monasticism in 845, but there was some recovery. The Muslim rulers in Mesopotamia (Iraq) assumed the right to appoint the

Nestorian Catholicos, the supreme head of the Church in 987. The Mongol empire, by now largely Muslim, systematically destroyed Christianity from the Mediterranean to China from 1358 onwards. Today the Church is a pale shadow of its past with less than 200,000 adherents. Mission vision was crushed by persecution and squeezed out by ecclesiastical organization and the Church died. It is a solemn warning to us today that enormous effort and seeming fruit can ultimately disappear in subsequent generations without trace within the cultures it once leavened. Is this happening in Western Europe today?

3. Roman Catholic missionary orders, 1209 AD onwards

The Western Church under papal leadership was more inclined to spreading Christianity by political pressure or military action than by evangelizing through the preaching of the gospel. This pattern emerged during the Dark Ages after the fall of the Western Roman Empire. The military challenge of Islam reinforced this attitude, for they had taken all the Christian lands of the Middle East and North Africa and were a constant threat to Europe. The sad result of this thinking surfaced in the cruelties of the Crusades against Islam in Palestine, the Inquisition against Muslims and Jews and, later, Protestants. The Inquisition was especially powerful in Spain and Portugal and behind the forcible "Christianization" of the indigenous Americans.

The founding of the mendicant orders began to change this thinking. The Franciscans were founded by Francis of Assisi in 1209 and the Dominicans by Dominic in 1215. Their commitment to poverty, mobility and to preaching provided both an army of missionaries and a mission structure with sufficient autonomy to initiate bold advances to non-Christian peoples. A further order, the Jesuits, was founded by Ignatius Loyola in 1534.

Columbus' discovery of the Americas in 1492 and the Portuguese discovery of the ocean route to Asia round Africa in 1498 ended the isolation of Europe from the rest of the world and the mighty barrier of Islam was breached. World evangelization again became a possibility. The double impetus of both the opening up of the oceans to Spanish and Portuguese traders and the shock of the Reformation on the Roman Catholic Church provided the transportation and motivation to spread to the Americas and to

Asia, and, to a lesser extent, Africa between 1500 and 1700. The growth of these three orders was dramatic:

Order	Year Founded	Totals	
		1400	1770
Franciscans	1209	60,000	77,000
Dominicans	1215	12,000	est. 10,000
Jesuits	1534	n.a.	22,500

The commitment of the population of Spain and Portugal to spreading the Catholic faith was extraordinary, for the great majority of these numbers came from these lands. This represented nearly 1% of the total population of the two countries that were involved in these orders – many of them overseas. One can only be amazed at the fortitude and dedication of the missionaries sent out. The ruthless commitment of the Jesuits to spreading the Catholic faith was awesome, though we have to question some of their methods, motives and teachings. The cruelties and evil perpetrated on conquered peoples were terrible. The naked use of the secular power and military might for the propagation of Spanish Catholicism, prohibition of Protestants from labouring in their sphere of influence and the crushing of indigenous cultures will for ever remain a scandalous blot on this period of mission endeavour. However when one sees what was accomplished by some and how much of the work remains to this day, it has to be acknowledged that there was often lasting fruit. Baptisms were performed on a level never before seen. The great Jesuit missionary, Francis Xavier, baptized 750,000 Asians in ten years. There is not the space, nor is this the object of this book to give a full account of this work.[72] Some of these results are given in a tabular form on the opposite page.

The numbers involved were staggering. In some countries such as China and Japan there were waves of fierce persecution which virtually wiped out the Catholic population, in others such as Mexico, Philippines and parts of the East Indies (Indonesia) almost the entire population is nominally Catholic or, in the case of the Moluccans, Protestant today.

---

[72] Latourette 1975, Barrett 1987a:33-40.

People & Area/Country	Mission Order	Year begun	Year of stats.	Numbers baptized	%[73] of country
Amerindians, Mexico	Span. RC	1519	1536	6,000,000	?80.0
Indians, Kerala India	Jesuit	1536	1559	300,000	0.3
Indians, Tamil S.India	Jesuit	1544	1703	200,000	0.2
Filipinos, Philippines	Franciscan	1577	1589	100,000	16.0
Moluccans, Indonesia	Jesuit	1534	1569	80,000	1.0
Japanese, Japan	Jesuit	1549	1614	750,000	3.5
Chinese, China	Jesuit	1582	1700	300,000	0.2
Vietnamese, Vietnam	Jesuit	1627	1700	200,000	6.7

The Roman Catholic missionary surge slowed during the seventeenth and eighteenth centuries, but picked up again in the nineteenth and twentieth in parallel with the Protestant mission mobilization.

What conclusions can we draw from this? Once more we find that it was the monastic structures that initiated and sustained the mission thrust, and, more specifically, monastic orders which were deliberately mobile and trained for preaching and converting non-Christians (and "heretics"). These orders had accountability to Rome, but also a degree of autonomy of the ecclesiastical structures to initiate new advances and develop appropriate local strategies. So great was the latter with the Jesuits that the Pope dissolved the order in 1773. The Roman Catholics had a dual structure of modalities and sodalities which the Protestants lacked. As a result, all this activity took place in a time when Protestants did virtually nothing for world evangelization.

A major problem was the rivalry between the three major missionary orders, and comity arrangements had to be instituted. It is possible that it was this rivalry that provoked the Japanese rejection of Christianity and the massive persecutions that followed. The reverberations of that rejection cripple mission work in Japan to this day.

4. The Moravians from 1727 onwards

As already stated, Protestantism was not noted for mission concern during its first 275 years, yet there was an "apostolic succession" of vision passed on from German Pietism to Denmark

---

[73] The populations of the nations at that time as given in McEvedy, & Jones, 1978 are used to calculate the percentages.

and Norway (Egede was a Norwegian missionary to Greenland), and then to Count Nicolaus Ludwig von Zinzendorf.[74] He was the leader of the Unitas Fratrum or Moravian Brethren. This small community became one of the greatest missionary churches of history. Not only did they commit themselves in a unique way to mission work, but also became the means for blessing of John Wesley and the beginning of the Great Awakening in the English-speaking world which, in turn, became the platform for Carey and the modern missionary movement.

How did this small rural group of poor artisan refugees become such a blessing to the world?

1. **The godly leadership of Zinzendorf**. He was one of the great missionary statesmen of history. He had welcomed a community of Christians fleeing persecution in Moravia[75] and had given them a home on his estate in Saxony, Germany. They became the launch-pad for this mission movement.

2. **Revival.** The Holy Spirit was poured out upon them in 1727 and gave them a new zeal for God. This gained focus after Zinzendorf had a vision for mission in Denmark where he met a West Indian slave and two Eskimos from Greenland who pled for missionaries to come to their people. He returned home and passed on that vision. Within a short period missionaries were called to St Thomas in the West Indies in 1732 and to Greenland in 1733 – both Danish colonies. Other fields soon followed – Arctic 1737, Algiers and China 1742, Persia 1747, Ethiopia 1752. Fields were opened in Surinam, West and South Africa and North America.

3. **Prayer**. Soon after the revival a prayer chain began that continued for over one hundred years without a break. Prayer was fundamental to the spread of the gospel and the subsequent revivals.

4. **Commitment**. Between 1732 and 1760 227 workers were sent out. Then over the years between 1732 and 1930 over 3,000

---

[74] Neill 1964:227-240; Tucker 1983:67-82.

[75] Over a century before Luther's conversion, the Moravians had their roots in the ministry of the remarkable Reformer John Hus (1375-1415) of Moravia (today's Czech Republic) where there were already 200 Protestant churches by 1500. See Langton 1956.

missionaries were sent out to serve the Lord, representing an average of one out of every 12 communicant members. This was almost a tithe of their membership. How many congregations today would dare to make such a tithe?[76] All went out as tentmaking missionary evangelists with little other support than prayer. Many gave their lives for the Master, but their places were soon filled by others who followed.

What were their successes? Their ministry was bathed in prayer by a whole denomination committed to world evangelization. Ordinary Christians without much education or theological training gained a vision which was very simple – to win the heathen even if they had to give time to secular pursuits for survival. The Moravians started more missions in ten years than the whole of Protestantism over the previous 200. What were their failings?

1. The initial thrust lost momentum for some years because the leadership in Germany, and Zinzendorf in particular, lost some of the vision with a mystic preoccupation with the physical death of Christ. It is an indication that if the leadership of the sending churches retains the control of the overseas mission enterprise, the vision will surely suffer if there are any problems at the home base.

2. There was also no clear plan for converts won to the Lord. A long-term church-planting strategy was lacking, as a result there are few enduring evidences of the work today in many of the early Moravian fields. All communicants of the Moravian Brethren today number no more than 500,000 – mainly in the West Indies, Surinam, North America and Tanzania.

3. Over recent years liberal theology and institutionalization have sapped the spiritual life and mission vision of the Church.

Conclusion to Part 2

I have sought to bring together four strands of developments to explain the patent failure of the Church to embrace the vision of mission. It was a failure which began with the slowness of the first disciples' understanding of the message of Scripture, which led to

---

[76] I know several congregations in which 10% of their membership are in full-time service in home and foreign missions. One such is Gold Hill Baptist Church in Buckinghamshire, England; another is the Tulsa Christian Fellowship of Tulsa, OK, USA.

the early Church failing to understand its role. Christian terminology developed over the centuries which resulted in theology itself ignoring missiology and church history down-playing the importance of mission advances. The marginalization of mission has become a part of our Christian thinking, teaching, acting. Later we will see the damage this did to the structures of the Church. It will take a mighty act of the Holy Spirit to reveal the truth and dispel the blindness because this strikes at the heart of so much in the modern Christian world-view. The vision must be restored to the Church and, praise God, this is happening on a scale unprecedented in the history of the Church.

Part 3

The Present

The Harvest Gathered

Isaiah 54:1

Introduction

After reading in chapter 53 of the indescribable sufferings of the Servant, the Lord Jesus Christ, we find a dramatic change in chapter 54. Here is the fruit of the Cross. Tears become joy because of a spiritual harvest. The Cross leads to world evangelization and a world-wide ingathering of people into the kingdom of God.

The future people of God are the subject of this chapter, those who would live after the Day of Pentecost. This is the final outworking of the ministry of Jesus for the world's salvation. Now, 2,500 years after this prophecy was given, we can look back to see the spectacular outworkings of the sufferings of Jesus through his Body, the Church.

Chapter 7

The Vision Regained

William Carey was the main character in chapter one. He was one of the chief instruments in God's hand for the restoration of mission into the mainstream of Protestant Christianity through his writing, emphasis on prayer for world evangelization and promotion of practical structures for mission.

By 1792 the initial push by missionaries of the Danish-Halle Mission in India and the Moravians in the New World and elsewhere was slowing down. The harvest of converts and churches established on the fields was still meagre. They were certainly not evangelizing more than a small fraction of the surrounding indigenous populations. Nor were they impacting the wider Church in traditionally Protestant countries with new vision and recruiting a stream of new workers for world evangelization. They did not yet have an adequate mechanism for information, recruitment and channelling[1] for missions.

William Carey not only challenged the Church to action but also promoted a simple, but effective theological and structural framework to channel that effort into church planting ministry. The two diagrams on pages 62 and 67 show the effects of what happened. The earlier diagram shows that World B, the evangelized non-Christian population, started to climb rapidly from 1800 – many more were being exposed to the Good News. Then in the second diagram it is plain that from 1850 onwards the proportion of non-Caucasian Christians in the world population grew rapidly, showing that many of those being evangelized were now becoming Christians while in traditionally Christian lands the actual percentage of Christians as a whole were either stagnating or even in decline. After many centuries of relative barrenness and retreat, the Church was becoming the Church militantly triumphant – at least, in parts! This was foretold by Isaiah two and a half millennia ago. No generation before ours, with the possible exception of the first century Church, could lay such claim to be the fulfilment of this prophecy.

---

[1] The Pietist A.H. Franke published the first known mission magazine in Germany around 1707.

The Biblical Basis for a great harvest

Isaiah 53 describes the plan of God for the redemption of sinners to be achieved through the Suffering Servant. This had meaning to the Jewish people as a portrayal of the Messiah, but its full meaning could only be seen after the atoning death of the Lord Jesus Christ. It is a spiritual redemption, therefore it follows on that the words in Isaiah 54 also have a spiritual application – more meaningful to the Church of Gentiles and Jews of the new covenant than to the Jews of the old. The language is of physical restoration from Babylon after exile but this was a faint foreshadowing of the greater spiritual truth of a return to God that had global implications and related to the preaching of the gospel. Earlier I showed how Paul himself applied Isaiah 54:1 to the Church. Many great commentators have also applied this prophecy primarily to the Church. James Denney said:

> "By coming to the Church, Isaiah causes us to understand more deeply the value and efficacy of the servant's atoning work. The sufferings of the servant were for the Church, his body, not for himself." [2]

I therefore unashamedly make the same application here. The verse itself is extraordinary:

> Sing O barren one, who did not bear;
> Break forth into singing and cry aloud,
> you who have not been in travail!
> For the children of the desolate one will be more
> than the children of her that is married, says the Lord.

The barren woman is no longer grieving over the shame of her childlessness, but suddenly rejoicing over a mighty increase of spiritual progeny rather than over the few physical children expected of a married woman.

There is the note of restoration, new life and resulting joy. It is the language of life, revival and of abundant spiritual growth. God does give times of awakening, times of refreshing and times of restoration. Some have a pessimistic view of the world and of ourselves as the Church in it, "Things will only get worse!" Often this comes from a gloomy perspective of Scripture and

---

[2] Denney 1972:360.

understanding of how things will be when Jesus returns, "...when the Son of Man returns, will he find faith on earth?"[3] Many use this verse as a justification for an unbelieving heart. Jesus was challenging us not to be gloomy and give up, but to believe in him when we intercede. In Isaiah 54:1 is a promise for us to expect the present and coming world-wide harvest into the Kingdom.

The Historical Basis for expecting a harvest

There are many periods in the history of the Church where there have been times of barrenness and spiritual life was at a low ebb. God then stepped in with outpourings of his Holy Spirit in local, national and even regional revivals.

The first and most remarkable was at the first post-resurrection Pentecost. It was there that the barren Old Testament Church among the Jews was empowered by the Holy Spirit to spread across the known world of that time. This prophecy in Isaiah 54:1 had special meaning for that time and, no doubt, Jesus expounded on this in his resurrection ministry. It was likely to have been in his thinking when he promised that the gates of Hades would not prevail against the Church.[4] However this was certainly not the last, and all through the history of the Church there have been such revivals. These have been meticulously researched and described in Edwin Orr's volumes on the history of revivals.[5] The frequency and impact of these awakenings and revivals has markedly increased in the past two hundred years. Those living in the West long for such again and wonder whether this could ever happen, but maybe do not fully realize what amazing awakenings and revivals have burst out on other continents in recent years.

Many examples of national revivals could be given. Britain has had such century after century – through Wycliffe in the fifteenth century, the Reformation in the sixteenth, the Puritans in the seventeenth, the Wesley-Whitefield revival in the eighteenth and the Evangelical Revival of the mid-nineteenth. Lutheran Finland, Norway and Sweden have had series of revivals over the past 200

---

[3] Luke 18:8.
[4] Matthew 16:18-19.
[5] Orr 1973. This book recounts the way God used William Carey and others to start the Union of Prayer which began the Second Great Awakening in Britain and then in the USA and provided the impetus for the new mission movement.

years. The effects of the Welsh and Pentecostal Revivals at the beginning of this century continue to reverberate around the world to this day. Millions in the last 50 years have been revived and sinners added to the Kingdom through such outpourings. A few of the more significant ones were in East Africa in the 1940s and '50s,[6] Korea in the midst of the terrible Korean War[7] in the 1950s and '60s, China (1945-48) and Cambodia (1975)[8] in the lull before the storm of Communism decimated the Church in those lands, Indonesia – especially West Timor[9] – and also many other parts of that largely Muslim nation. Nagaland and Mizoram, remote states in north-east India, became the most evangelical states in the world in recent years in which the majority of the population was radically changed by the reviving work of the Holy Spirit. In the 1970s and '80s came the massive turnings to God in China and in Latin America which decisively shifted the centre of gravity of Evangelical Christianity away from the lands that were for centuries its birthplace, haven and prison.

There is much cause for rejoicing. The growth of the Church today is on a scale that is unique in the history of the world. The outpouring of the Spirit at the birth of the Church was world-wide in its scope and outworkings, but the numbers involved were not on the scale we have seen in increasing numbers over the past 200 years. We can expect this to happen, for what else would give the convincing proof of the victory of Jesus other than a world-wide demonstration of that victory? I would go further, I believe we are now in the time of the final ingathering before the end. During the last 10 years, more were added to the Evangelical community, through new-birth conversions and birth into evangelical families, than the population on earth in that Pentecost year.

We are far closer to achieving the basic goals set out for us by the Lord Jesus in his resurrection ministry than many have given credit. We still have an enormous task, but it is a task that can be

---

[6] Roy Hession in his book, *The Calvary Road*, spread the message of that revival round the world. The revival began in the land of Rwanda in the1930s and spread to much of East and Central Africa. It is tragic how the land of revival of two generations ago became that of ethnic hatreds and genocide in the 1990s.

[7] Campbell 1957.*The Christ of the Korean Heart*. London, England: Christian Literature Crusade.

[8] Burke *Anointed for Burial*.

[9] Koch, Kurt. 1970.

accomplished. Jesus gave us an achievable goal, and I want to demonstrate that this is so in this section. Jesus told us plainly that the world will become a most unpleasant place and evil will multiply and even apparently triumph,[10] but at the same time his people will multiply and spread across the face of the earth. Everything is heading towards a climax – both evil and good. It will be high tide at midnight. The darkness will increase at that midnight hour, but that will also be the high tide of the Church as she is readied for the Bridegroom.

We have much about which we can rejoice. I delight in sharing with believers the factual basis for such a statement. Speaking about the kingdom does not always have to be a gloomy affair; it is often one of rejoicing. There are many causes of concern and rightly so, but many preachers dwell too much on the negatives, and this is communicated in their public ministry. I believe that one of the hindrances to vision for mission in past centuries has been a profound pessimism about the world and the future. People respond better to encouragement. They are better able to face the negatives from the strong positive ground of the promised hope of the growth and success of the Kingdom of God. Isaiah does just this, he offers hope of a mighty harvest to the discouraged people of God. This is now my aim. I believe that every preacher and every teacher should be armed with facts of the world-wide kingdom with its challenges and growth and communicate these to their people. This will stimulate vision, intercession and action.

The Statistical Evidence for expecting a harvest

People are wary of statistics. Pages of figures and graphs repel as often as attract. The English language has many hackneyed jokes about statistics and statisticians. The common perception is that one can prove anything with statistics. There is substance to these cautions. Few of us have come through life unscathed from being manipulated by a clever juggling of figures for promotion of life insurances, the sales pitch for an unorthodox sale of goods or even the hype of Christian organizations.

Christian statisticians need great openness, humility and integrity in every aspect of presenting a scenario with figures and graphs. Sources must be traceable, estimates and extrapolations

---

[10] Matthew 24.

made plain and a balanced objectivity made obvious. The heart motivation for using figures must be pure, or the presentation will be warped or biased. A partial presentation of facts can become a lie. Truth can degenerate to propaganda. King David numbered Israel in his pride[11] and brought terrible retribution from the Lord.

This latter event has often been used by Christians to show that even the *counting* of the people of God is a sin, whereas it was the motivation that was wrong rather than the act. Many denominations and churches therefore do not keep adequate records, using this reason as the justification. Dr Frederick Tatford was the great historian of the widespread mission work of the "Open" Brethren. He described this history in 10 well-researched volumes.[12] He tactfully stated, "The Brethren have always manifested a supreme lack of interest in their numerical strength. Their numbers are difficult to assess, partly because no precise statistics are available..." However in a private letter, he told me of his extreme frustration that these figures had not been available. My suspicion is that the sin of David in numbering Israel played a significant part in this. The result can be a false humility that conceals an independent spirit and lack of accountability to the wider Body of Christ. I believe that this lack of accountability is one of the reasons that in many countries Brethren growth has been so poor.

The Bible is full of numbers and totals; indeed, one whole book is called "Numbers." The weight of evidence is that our God commends counting and statistics when the motive is right. There are many occasions when it was God who was the initiator of the counting – in Moses numbering the people of Israel and in the spies sent to research Canaan. God told Elijah of the 7,000 who had not bowed the knee to Baal. Revelation is filled with numbers with special meaning.[13] The Church in Acts gave statistics of numbers baptized on two occasions.[14] These latter were probably given to encourage the Church to praise and action. It is for this reason we need to use statistics today. So now follows a brief account of global surveys of the Church and its growth.

---

[11] 2 Samuel 24.
[12] Tatford 1982.
[13] Numbers 1:1-3; 3:40; 13:1, 17-24; 1 Kings 19:18, Revelation 7:4-8, etc.
[14] Acts 2:41; 4:4.

For centuries it was not possible to take a census of the Church, but there have been those who have sought to do so. David Barrett described some of these in his article *The Five Statistical Eras of the Christian Church.*[15] The most remarkable was the amazing Nestorian theologian, explorer and geographer, Cosmas Indicopleustes[16] who produced a 12-volume survey entitled *Topographia Christiana* from AD 535 to 547.

William Carey's *Enquiry* in 1792 was the first real statistical global survey ever undertaken, and that was only just over 200 years ago. It became a stimulus for opening up many countries for Christian missions. The statistics in Carey's work, and comparison to today is given in the next chapter.

The nineteenth century produced much more survey and research information with the momentum picking up towards 1900. The great drive towards the completion of world evangelization by the end of that century was the motivation to give as accurate a picture as possible.[17] In the 1880s surveys of every province of China were done and the results published in an atlas with meticulous detail. In 1887 appeared a little book that had a big impact entitled *The Evangelization of the World* written by B. Broomhall. In it was a powerful diagram – an adaptation of which is shown on the next page.

Between 1906 and 1925 a series of Mission Atlases was produced in which the position of every Protestant mission station in the world was shown, and large tables of Christian statistics recorded for every country. Yet still no comprehensive picture of all religions of the world's population was given. Nothing compared to these were produced by Protestants for another nearly 50 years.

---

[15] Barrett 1983:160-169
[16] Barrett 1982:ix. In the introduction to the Encyclopedia Barrett gives a brief description of the 40 or so known global Christian surveys up to 1980.
[17] Johnson 1988.

Population of World 1887

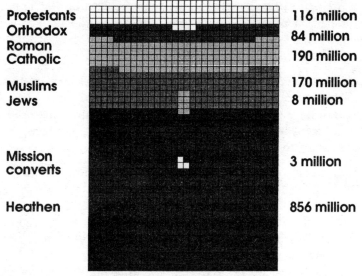

Protestants	116 million
Orthodox	84 million
Roman Catholic	190 million
Muslims	170 million
Jews	8 million
Mission converts	3 million
Heathen	856 million

Each square = 1 million souls

World Dominion Press in the United Kingdom carried the mission research flag between 1930 and 1962 culminating in the production of the World Christian Handbooks of 1948, 1952, 1957 and 1962 and Lutterworth Press the last Handbook in 1968. Sir Kenneth Grubb was the author of these volumes.[18] His coverage was good, but incomplete due to Grubb's unwillingness to even mention Orthodox and Roman Catholic statistics except in later editions as an appendix. He was also suspicious of Pentecostalism, so I suspect that his coverage of the Pentecostal denominations was only partial.[19]

---

[18] Kenneth Grubb was, for a time, a WEC missionary in Amazonia. He was the brother of Norman Grubb, who later became WEC's International Director.

[19] Johnstone 1993:25. This graph shows the growth rate of Pentecostals between 1960 and 1990. There is an irregular spike in the curve. The data in the *Operation World* database prior to 1970 was heavily dependent on data in the *World Christian Handbook*, but the 1970 data in the *World Christian Encyclopedia* gave a more complete picture, hence this anomaly.

In 1963 Leslie Lyall of Overseas Missionary Fellowship wrote a little world survey with some statistics[20] entitled *Missionary Opportunity Today*. I was so grateful for this survey and the statistics in the 1968 World Christian Handbook for these were my best global resources for statistical information as I compiled the first full *Operation World* in Zimbabwe (then Rhodesia) in 1972.

The pace of firm statistical research picked up with the advent of a remarkable phenomenon, Donald MacGavran. His books on church growth,[21] and the need to carefully quantify the growth of churches and test the methodologies used brought a whole new dimension to missions. From this catalytic work emerged a whole range of well-researched country surveys by numerous authors over the following 20 years.[22] The work of Ralph Winter at the US Center for World Mission in founding the William Carey Library was a major factor in making it possible for otherwise obscure missionary researchers to publish their results in this form. The Church Growth Movement has been much criticized in recent years, and the publication of such books has virtually ceased. A sad loss; the baby was thrown out with the bath water.

However from out of this came the ministry of Jim Montgomery and the DAWN movement (Disciple A Whole Nation). Starting with the vision in 1973 in the Philippines for mobilizing denominations to set goals to plant churches in every community. The remarkable survey of Ghana by the Ghana Evangelism Commission between 1986 and 1993 set new standards for meticulously researching a whole nation and planting churches in every community. The successes in these lands have stimulated like initiatives in many other countries around the world. Here we see research leading to mobilization, goal-setting and, in many cases, staggering growth in numbers and vigour in the churches involved. The DAWN concepts have now been taken up by the

---

[20] Lyall 1963.
[21] McGavran 1955, 1966, 1970, 1987.
[22] Countries such as Mexico (1963), Korea (1966), Latin America (1967), Liberia (1968), Sierra Leone (1969), Finland and Italy (1970), Philippines (1971), Taiwan & Thailand (1980), etc. were covered by a series of missionary researchers.

Church in many countries and we are gaining a better picture year by year of the growth (and decline) of the denominations.[23]

In 1968 the truly global surveys began. Two books became pivotal for numerous other global surveys linked with the Lausanne Movement, World Evangelical Fellowship, and numerous unreached peoples surveys by MARC/World Vision and others. These were the *World Christian Encyclopedia* and *Operation World*. Both were originally researched and written in Africa, not in the West! The authors of these two books have worked closely together for over 20 years with a significant exchange of data and interaction of ideas.

The work on the *World Christian Encyclopedia* (WCE) was begun in 1968 by David Barrett in Nairobi, Kenya as a successor to the *World Christian Handbook series*, but only published in 1982. The Encyclopedia was an immense task and unique in the history of Christian research. Barrett's aim was "...a critical, scholarly, and scientific approach to data describing the Christian world." He succeeded and produced a work of high academic excellence and so comprehensive that most ordinary Christian workers find it hard to comprehend or apply more than a fraction of its contents! Nearly 20,000 of the WCE were printed.

There was also *Operation World* authored by myself in Zimbabwe in 1970 and first published in 1972. That 1972 edition was the first effort to give complete denominational and religious population breakdowns for each country and the whole world, as did the later *World Christian Encyclopedia*. The purpose of *Operation World* was very different and was written to stimulate prayer for the nations of the world, and to give needed information to mobilize Christians around the world for mission outreach. Cumulatively the total number of copies of *Operation World* printed in over 10 languages between 1972 and 1993 is about 1,500,000.

---

[23] There is not the time to mention the many research initiatives to quantify the growth of the Church over the past 20 years, but the outstanding research work of Peter Brierley of MARC-Europe and then the Christian Research Association in the UK is worthy of mention. Through Brierley's work and stimulus a whole family of Christian Handbooks for many countries of Europe and beyond have been published since 1973.

I have had the privilege of being part of this thrilling work of the Holy Spirit over the centuries of informing, activating and mobilizing the Church for mission. It is in this effort that I have spent much of the last 25 years gathering all the factual information I could find about the world and its spiritual need and the Church and its growth. This body of information gives the basis for the dramatic figures in the chapters that follow. It is the combination of statistics and factual accounts that assure me of the climax of Kingdom harvesting that still lies ahead of us.

Chapter 8

The 200-year harvest since 1792

William Carey concludes his Enquiry with a brief survey of the world's continents and countries giving names, sizes, populations and their religious affiliations. With our present knowledge we can project back to 1792 and cross-check the results. The overall picture was generally close to what we know today, but there were a few large errors in estimation of populations.[24] It is amazing how this rural pastor was able to glean all the information that he did and give results that were so reasonable.

Comparing his statistics in 1792 with those in *Operation World* in 1992 gives interesting conclusions, as shown on the next graph .

1. The population of India today at 920 million is far more than the population of the whole world, at an estimated 731 million, in Carey's day. The width of the bar is proportional to the population of the world.

2. Carey listed the major religions: Christian (RC, Orthodox and Protestant), Jews, Muslims and "Pagans" (subsuming all other religions such as Hinduism, Buddhism, Animism, etc.). The term "Pagan" is not politically correct language today, but in our sophisticated and tolerant age we need to be reminded that whatever appellation we use, their eternal destiny is just as tragic if they remain without the grace of God extended to them in the preaching of the gospel.

3. The vertical axis shows the percentages of the various religions. The Pagan and Jewish components have declined but, interestingly, the Muslim percentage is about the same today as it was 200 years ago. Present Muslim growth is more through a higher birth rate than through conversions.

---

[24] Carey's estimates and those of *The Atlas of World Population* of 1978 can be compared for the year 1790. The first figure is Carey's, the second the AWP: World 171m/170m, China 60m/330m, Anatolian Turkey 20m/9m, Arabia 16m/5m, Brazil 14m/2.5m. Carey underestimated East Asia and over-estimated the Middle East and South America.

Religious changes in World

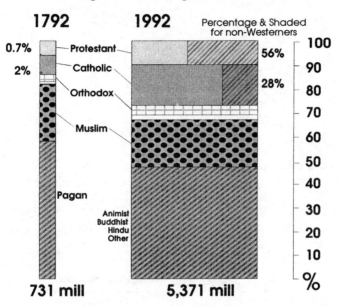

4. Christians of all types have grown as a percentage of the world's population – especially during the nineteenth century. These figures are not remarkable in themselves, for Protestants have only doubled as a percentage of the world's population over 200 years. This hides the steep decline in Europe and spectacular gains in Africa, Latin America and Asia. The following diagram illustrates this. The overall growth in Protestant numbers is shown in the relative sizes of the pie charts, however it is the proportion of Protestants that are non-Western which is impressive. Protestants in these two continents outnumber all other Protestants in North America, Europe and the Pacific. It is only because the overall population is so much bigger that the percentage of the population that is Protestant is lower.

The Four Waves of Protestant Mission Expansion

The neglect of mission during the first 270 years of Protestant history is clearly illustrated by the maps[25] on succeeding pages.

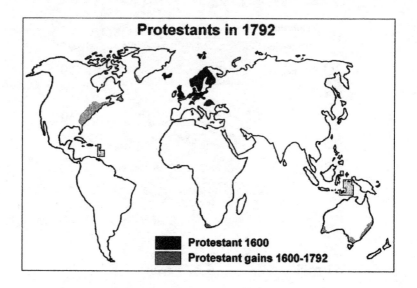

Protestants in 1792

Protestant 1600
Protestant gains 1600-1792

In 1790 the daughter churches of the Reformation were almost entirely confined to the north western edge of Europe, the eastern seaboard of North America, a few islands in the Caribbean and the Cape of South Africa. The only mission advances were the outposts in the Dutch East Indies (the Spice islands of today's Indonesia) and the work of a few Danish-Halle missionaries in India and of the Moravian missionaries in the Americas and Africa. It was only in the latter two that the motivation was primarily winning souls. In all the other instances conversion of native or subjugated populations followed European colonial settlements, trade and promotion of slavery.

It is sobering to observe the expansion of Catholicism over the same period. The motivation for these advances was usually colonization by Europeans, greed for gold and wealth and a despising of indigenous cultures. Nevertheless despite all the

---

[25] These maps cannot give much detail, but at least will convey the extent of mission outreach in each period.

cruelty, use of the Inquisition and insensitivity to cultures, the number of non-Caucasian Catholics increased – even if that Catholicism was steeped in pagan concepts and ceremonies. This map shows the geographical spread of Catholicism; in the previous chapter were given some statistics of the numerical increase of Catholics in these areas.

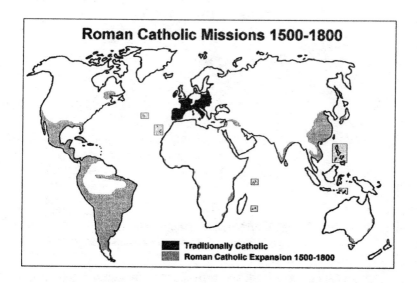

Roman Catholic Missions 1500-1800

Traditionally Catholic
Roman Catholic Expansion 1500-1800

Protestant missions have advanced and slowed in four distinctive waves. Each wave has lasted for around sixty years or two generations before a new wave has arisen, sweeping on to new fields hitherto little touched by the gospel and, in the process, rejuvenating aspects of the previous waves. Various writers have used slightly different dates, but I have used significant events that I believe represent a paradigm shift in mission strategy.

The First Wave: Denominational missions to the continental coastlands (1792-1865)

This period was bracketed by Carey and the formation of the Baptist Missionary Society (as it later came to be named) and by Hudson Taylor and the founding of the China Inland Mission. This was the period of predominantly denominational missions with long sea voyages or massive land journeys to distant mission fields. It is hard for us in today's world to conceive how difficult were communications and provision of supplies. Missionaries in China had to wait a year for a reply to a letter sent to Europe, and London Missionary Society missionaries to the Buryat Mongols in Siberia in the 1830s had to wait even longer. It is not surprising that it was predominantly the islands of the seas and the coastal fringes of continents that were evangelized at this time.

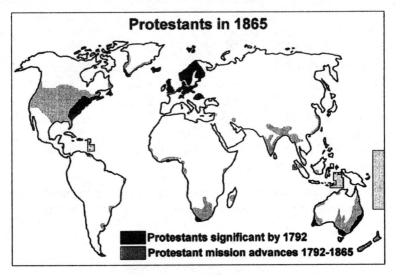

During this period Protestant missions were established and, in many cases, churches also planted. The dynamism and drive of the early missionaries were gradually restricted as the home denominations often began to exercise more control of the field ministries. The map opposite shows the extent of that advance.

The Second Wave – Interdenominational missions to the continental heartlands (1865-1910)

A new vision, a new paradigm, a new way of working was essential if the gospel were to be taken beyond the bounds of areas reached hitherto. One of the major characteristics of this new wave was geographical penetration and preaching the gospel to every person, and less on discipling and church planting. Another was the recruitment of ordinary people without the years of systematic theological studies expected of those ordained to pastoral ministry. Some would call this a "lay" movement – a term I dislike, for it is a non-biblical term that both artificially divides the Church into "clergy" and "laity" and defers to post-biblical structures and hierarchies which were part of the reason for the stifling of mission in the first place!

The agonising struggles of Hudson Taylor during his first term in China led to the birthing of a new type of mission – the China Inland Mission (now Overseas Missionary Fellowship) in 1865. The recruiting appeal was to the less highly educated that other existing missions would not have accepted, the emphases were on faith in God alone for the provision of finances, direction of field ministries from the field and not from the sending country, willingness to "go native" and live as the indigenous population and vision for unevangelized inland regions. Many hundreds of new missions modelled on the CIM came into being over the following years. It is interesting to see how many missions in this wave included in their name words such as "Inland" or "Heart" the Africa Inland Mission (AIM), Sudan Interior Mission (SIM), Heart of Africa Mission (WEC) being examples.

This new dimension for missions led to an expansion to many hitherto unevangelized parts of the world. The map below shows this.

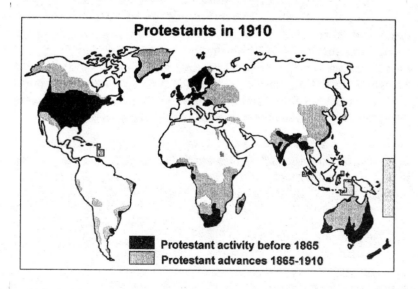

Protestants in 1910

Protestant activity before 1865
Protestant advances 1865-1910

Great gaps still remained. Huge areas of the world were only just being explored and mapped and vast territories then were without a single witness for the Lord Jesus such as the Middle East, Central, West and North Africa, Central Asia, many areas in the Indian sub-continent, most of the East Indies and the mountains and tropical forests of Latin America.

Such was the success of this wave of advance that there was rising expectation towards the close of the nineteenth century that world evangelization was a real possibility. The rousing challenges of Royal Wilder[26] promoted what became known as "The Watchword" which was **The Evangelization of the World in This Generation**, and A.T. Pierson's vision:

> "...that before the year 1900, the gospel shall be preached to every living soul."[27]

These inspiring words galvanized a larger number of Christians than ever before to greater action for world evangelization. However the mobilization was only partial and the dream unfulfilled.

The privilege of hindsight grants us a perspective which shows how enormous was the task that they had to complete. No one then knew that there were as many as 6,500 or more languages in the world, and that only 537 had anything of the Scriptures in their own language at that time. The total community of Protestant Christians in Latin America, Africa and Asia in 1900 was about 4 million; or 0.4% of the total population in those lands. There were also then only about 8-9,000 missionaries seeking to reach them.

It was the pivotal Edinburgh World Missionary Conference in 1910 that marked the end of this wave. The momentum was slowed by the discouragements of non-achievement of the 1900 goal and virtually stopped by the advent of a World War of unprecedented savagery between "Christian" nations in 1914. These events shook the confidence of many Christians and aided the rise of a cynical pessimism in the West,[28] an ecumenism with eventually a greater

---

[26] Johnson 1988:6 & 7.
[27] *Missionary Review* Nov 1881:437.
[28] This is especially true of Europe, and has been cruelly but accurately described as "Euro-pessimism". This has sadly dampened the faith and hope of millions of Christians in that continent.

concern for structural unity at the expense of biblical truth and passion for mission. These events also hastened the transfer of mission initiative from Europe to North America for the next wave.

The Third Wave – Evangelical Missions to the countries of the world (1910-1966)

The two World Wars and the marginalization of Evangelicals over this period and the dramatic decline of the Student Volunteer Movement after 1920 dealt severe blows to any development of global initiatives and extensive surveys of global need that characterized the second wave. The number of evangelical missionaries and missions steadily increased after each World War in spite of the hostile theological, social, economic and political climate. These agencies just got on with the job. Over this period, nearly every country in the world was either entered or targeted for entry. It was a slow slog of laying foundations for growth, of seeing churches planted and of training indigenous leadership. Over much of this period the blanketing influence of European colonial domination and control of much of the non-Western world often stifled spontaneous developments of indigenous Christianity. Church growth in the non-Western world was only moderate.

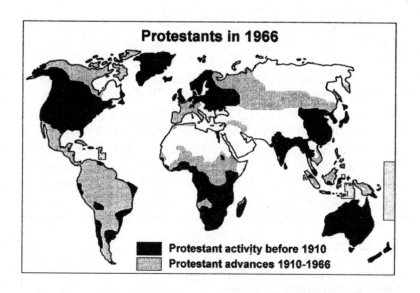

Protestants in 1966

Protestant activity before 1910
Protestant advances 1910-1966

The change came after World War II. One of the chief human agents for this change was the evangelist Billy Graham. His Christian integrity backed up a forthright and earnest presentation of the good news to many countries around the world. He restored respect to the ministry of evangelism and gained credibility for Evangelicals. Evangelicalism steadily gained the initiative in the Church world-wide over the following decades when all other mainline Christian streams were stagnant or in decline. Graham also poured much effort, prayer and finances into a succession of global conferences, the first of which was the Berlin Conference on World Evangelization in 1966 which then brought mission and the Great Commission to centre stage in the Christian world. The time of great breakthroughs for the gospel was dawning. If any Christian deserves the accolade as the Man of the century with regard to world evangelization it is Billy Graham. In the light of eternity, we may find that Graham's contribution to global mission far exceeded his high-profile evangelistic crusades.

The Fourth Wave (1966-Present) – Global missions to the peoples of the world

The fourth wave is still in full flood. Its characteristics are an emphasis on peoples rather than countries and a globalization of the missionary force with a growing component of Asian, Latin American and African missionaries. Over this period the centre of gravity of Protestantism and, even more, of Evangelicals has moved decisively away from the Western world. This will be shown in the next chapter. The geographical areas without active church planting ministry in the year 2000 can no longer be adequately represented on a map, for there are virtually no countries and very few major peoples without some effort being made to plant churches. Most of the white areas of the 1966 map are being covered by ministries that often have to be kept confidential. Please study the 10/40 Window map on page 219.

The people emphasis started to gain momentum long before 1966. The sterling work of the Bible Societies must be acknowledged, for they have long championed the need of peoples for the Bible in their own language. William Carey himself had seen this as the fundamental ministry on which he and his team should concentrate for the sake of those missionaries who would follow and would need these vital tools. However in the main this people emphasis did not receive a high profile in mission strategy for many years.

C.T. Studd was one of the famous Cambridge Seven who went out to China with the CIM in 1885. He was one of the strong promoters of the Student Volunteer Movement and later pioneered an unevangelized area of the Congo in Central Africa and, in the process, started a new mission, Worldwide Evangelization Crusade in 1913. Studd formulated the basic vision and wording that became the primary objective of the new agency:

> To reach the remaining unevangelized peoples on earth in the shortest possible time.

William Cameron Townsend,[29] the founder of Wycliffe Bible Translators, was another pioneer for peoples. His experiences in Central America and involvement in Bible translation spurred him to launch a specialist mission in 1934 dedicated to the translation of God's Word into the thousands of languages with nothing of the Scriptures. This was a revolutionary emphasis at that time, but something we almost take for granted today as a part of our mission task for discipling the peoples of the world.

Then arose a whole range of new specialist ministries emphasising languages and peoples – Clarence Jones and Radio HCJB in Ecuador (1931), Joy Ridderhof and Gospel Recordings (1941), New Tribes Mission (1942), Far East Broadcasting Company in Philippines (1946) and many others.

It was the Lausanne Congress on World Evangelization in 1974 that brought the people emphasis to the forefront of mission thinking and strategy through the impassioned pleas of Ralph Winter. He challenged Christians to concentrate their efforts on the 16,000+ Hidden (or, in today's terminology, Unreached) Peoples of the world.[30]

After much subsequent discussion various generations of definitions for peoples and unreached peoples have been agreed

---

[29] Hefley 1974.

[30] The term "unreached" was promoted by MARC-World Vision in the first lists of peoples without a known witness in the early '70s. Winter's term was expressive, but easily misunderstood. Winter later graciously agreed to use the other term, despite its manifest inadequacies, so that all were able to use the same language.

upon and refined. This is the definition used by John Gilbert of the International Mission Board of the Southern Baptists:

> An ethnolinguistic people within which there is no viable indigenous church movement with sufficient strength, resources and commitment to sustain and ensure the continuous multiplication of churches.[31]

There were inadequate lists of peoples, too little research done, and too little information to have much more than a generalized picture. Investigation had to follow the vision. Over the following two decades a clearer picture has emerged through the meticulous efforts of Barbara Grimes with successive publications of the Wycliffe Ethnologue,[32] MARC/World Vision with much dedicated efforts to produce the Unreached Peoples Annuals between the years 1972 and 1984,[33] David Barrett and his Peoples Database associated with the World Christian Encyclopedia,[34] The Gospel Recordings Language Lists, and more recently the work done for the AD2000 and Beyond Movement's Joshua Project listing of least reached peoples.[35]

Now we can begin to see how we have progressed in discipling the peoples of the world. This is so fundamental to the whole vision for fulfilling the Great Commission that this will be given in some detail. First, the following diagram gives a picture of the progress over the 2,000-year history of the preaching of the gospel.

The two lines in the diagram show first the estimated number of peoples over these two millennia. We have listed in Genesis 11 the 70 peoples that were recorded after the Babel fiasco. No one knows how many ethno-linguistic peoples there were at the time of Christ – this is a reasonable estimate. The number of peoples has considerably increased over the last two centuries for two main reasons, the numerical increase of nation-states dividing peoples into multiple components and the migration of ethnic communities from continent to continent. We reckon that there are now nearly

---

[31] Gilbert 1995.
[32] Grimes 1996.
[33] Dayton 1972-1980.
[34] Barrett 1998.
[35] The Joshua Project was launched in 1990 as a means of focusing the vision of the Church for the remaining decade of the millennium on the least reached peoples on earth. This is more fully described and defined on pp 107-8.

13,000 distinct ethno-linguistic peoples in the countries of the world.[36]

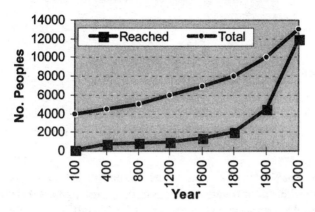

Two Millennia of evangelizing peoples

We can be more sure about the number of peoples that were evangelized at different periods in subsequent history. It is interesting to see how few of the world's peoples had been reached by 1800. The number of peoples reached had considerably increased by 1900, but even then more than half the peoples of the world were still completely unreached. The dramatic change has been in the latter part of this century.

Although many peoples are still unreached, the number is only a fraction of that of 100 years ago. The goal is attainable in our generation – if we mobilize prayer and effort and work together to disciple the remaining least reached peoples.

The next diagram gives a breakdown of the 13,000 peoples in the world by the penetration of the gospel. These are approximated to the nearest 500 for simplicity.

This simplified representation of the state of discipling of the world's peoples gives a measure of the progress. Briefly, here is the meaning of these four columns:

---

[36] The probability is that in the next century the number of spoken languages is likely to go down rapidly as smaller languages die out. Some have said that we may lose 3,000 languages and their associated cultures. The rapid urbanization of the world and the use of mass media are two major contributory factors.

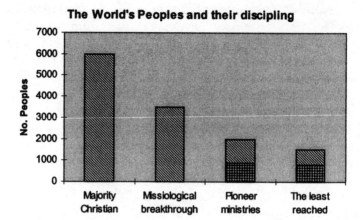

1. **Column 1:** Nearly half the world's peoples today have a majority of their population that would claim to be Christian. This would include all Protestant, Catholic, Orthodox, indigenous and fringe sectarian groups. This is what an individual would perceive his or her religious identity to be, whatever our value judgements as to the validity of that claim. This is the basis of all the statistics used in the *World Christian Encyclopedia,* Barrett's annual Statistics Table on World Mission and in *Operation World.*[37] These are cultures that have been permeated with the gospel and Christian values – even if later generations only retain a notional concept of being a Christian.[38]

2. **Column 2:** Missiological breakthrough is the term coined by Ralph Winter[39] to define that point in the evangelization of a people when the impact of the gospel becomes so significant that there is both a "critical mass" of indigenous believers and where Christianity has become a viable component of the indigenous culture. The 3,000 or so peoples in this category would also include peoples such as the Koreans among whom

---

[37] Barrett 1998, Johnstone 1993, The January Issue of the *International Bulletin of Missionary Research* over the years 1985 onwards.

[38] Brierley 1996. Peter Brierley of the Christian Research Association has developed this term ***notional Christian*** in the various Christian Handbooks to categorize the large numbers of individuals in long-Christianized countries who retain no meaningful link with organized Christianity, nor have any clear understanding of the content of the gospel, but who would still think of themselves as "Christian".

[39] Winter, in many issues of *Mission Frontiers* Magazine, USCWM.

enormous church growth has taken place this century, yet Korean Christians are still under one third of the total population. The same is true for such peoples as the Singaporean Chinese, the Indian Tamil and the Kenyan Turkana.

3. **Columns 3 and 4** represent the 3,500 or so peoples in the countries of the world that are still pioneer fields for mission endeavour. The indigenous Church is either non-existent or still too small or culturally marginalized to impact their entire people in this generation without outside help. Of these, probably about 1,200-1,500 peoples have either no indigenous church at all or no residential cross-cultural team of missionaries seeking to reach them.

4. **The shaded sections of Columns 3 & 4** represent those peoples listed in the AD2000 Mvt. Joshua Project List. The criteria for inclusion are: Population over 10,000 and less than 5% Christian or 2% Evangelical.[40]

Never before have we had so clear a picture of the boundaries of the unfinished task in discipling peoples. We dare not underestimate the tough challenges we face in order to accomplish this task, but at last we can see that the achievement of the task is within our grasp.

The Joshua Project of the AD2000 and Beyond Movement is the largest strategic mobilization of Christians in history to disciple the peoples of the world. Support and enthusiasm has come from across a wide spectrum of denominations, agencies and countries. In the latter, the involvement has been predominantly non-Western, but, sadly, with Christians in European countries showing the lowest level of interest. The vision is for a church for every people by the year 2000. That vision may not actually be fully attained by that year, but we are already seeing a significantly increased level of commitment for church planting ministries to the specific peoples without churches. My desire is that by the end of the year

---

[40] The Joshua Project list was compiled by researchers using various listings of the world's peoples from 1994 onwards. The 1,700 ethno-linguistic peoples listed are for use in mobilizing prayer and outreach to them from the global Church. The smaller peoples and those with marginally more Christians and ministry to them are not forgotten; these are more the concern of national, regional and more specialized agency/church partnerships for groups of similar peoples.

2000 we should have committed teams of cross-cultural workers to every significant ethno-linguistic people in the world. The actual conversion of individuals and the timing of the breakthrough for the gospel is the work of the Holy Spirit in whom we must trust, and not in our grandiose planning or clever techniques. Strategies needed to reach these peoples will be developed later in this book.

Chapter 9

The 40-year Expansion of Evangelicals since 1960

One of the great untold stories of Christianity in this century has been the astonishing growth of vital, indigenous Christianity in nearly every country of the world. How have we missed this? There are a number of reasons:

1. **The massive decline of Christianity in Europe and also in the Pacific** has made it appear that Christianity is only just holding its own and that Secularism, Islam, and in the Pacific island states, sects are growing far faster. In terms of global percentages this is true. However the real decline has been the loss of nominal and notional Christians in the West and not those with a vigorous faith. During this decline, Evangelicals, and even more of Evangelicals that are of a charismatic or Pentecostal persuasion have grown significantly – both in numbers, conversions and as a proportion of Christianity.

2. **The difficulty of counting Evangelicals.** Evangelicalism is basically a theological position on the supreme authority of Scripture in faith and practice and an experiential profession of personal salvation and a personal faith in God. This often results, or should result, in a disciplined lifestyle, holy living and a commitment to share one's faith with others. This cuts across all denominational boundaries, even within denominations that do not have a specifically evangelical doctrinal basis. Evangelical Christians are found in every Protestant denomination – also in significant numbers in other streams of Christianity. Measuring the number of evangelical Christians is therefore a complex and imprecise science! This was attempted in the denominational databases used as the basis for the statistics in *Operation World*.[41] Of course not every Evangelical is necessarily "born again" – the statistics in the Lamb's Book of Life are still not accessible! The figures used

---

[41] Johnstone 1993:16-17, 652-653. This is where the definitions, terminology and methodology are explained. The entire database for *Operation World* has been published by Global Mapping International both on disk and on CD ROM, and every figure used to derive figures for Evangelicals in every denomination of the world may be accessed and checked.

for Evangelicals are for the wider evangelical community, which may then be directly compared to Roman Catholic, Hindu and Muslim statistics.

The above-mentioned ministry of Evangelist Billy Graham was one of the factors that gave Western Christians a new confidence. It indirectly led to a greater emphasis on mission which was centred on evangelism and church planting. Many of the converts of post-war evangelistic crusades went out as missionaries. The surge in pioneer efforts, conversions and churches planted was astonishingly successful. The following diagrams demonstrate this massive increase of Evangelicals in the world.

These two curves in the first diagram tell a dramatic story.

1. Western Evangelicals have slowly but steadily grown in numbers in a time of significant decline in Christianity as a whole in the West.

2. The real growth has been in Latin America, Africa and Asia. This is shown in the "non-West" curve. In 1960, non-Western Evangelicals were half as numerous as Western Evangelicals. But by 2000 they will be four times more numerous, and if such growth rates continue, in the year 2010 they will be seven times more numerous.

Evangelicals 1960-2010

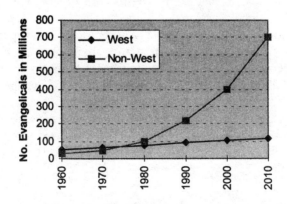

Many make the comment that Islam is the fastest growing religion in the world. This is not wholly incorrect, but it must be added that this needs to be qualified. Firstly, in many Muslim countries, little effort has been made to control population growth, so possibly 90-95% of Muslim population growth is due to higher birth rates. Further, some of the growth is due to the deliberate Muslim strategy for Muslim men to marry Christian wives, some of whom become Muslim, and bear Muslim children. Actual conversions to Islam are not as numerous as many would suppose – these are predominantly among Blacks in the USA, parts of West and Southern Africa, and some areas of Indonesia. The higher visibility of Muslims in Western countries is largely through increased immigration and retention of the open symbols of their religion together with vocal and well-organized publicity, which is often in opposition to other religious communities.

The diagram below shows the growth rates for Muslims, Roman Catholics, Protestants and, in a separate line, Evangelicals (as a section of Protestantism).

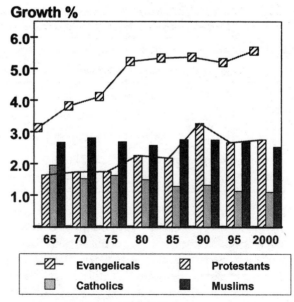

Average Annual Growth Rate
Muslims and Christians

There are several interesting facts revealed here.

1. Although **Christianity as a whole** is growing more slowly than Islam, Protestants are growing slightly faster at 2.9% and about double world population growth at 1.7%.

2. **Roman Catholics** are growing more slowly than the world population, so their actual percentage of the world's population is decreasing. This is largely due to losses in Europe to secularism and Latin America to Evangelicals.

3. **Protestant** Christians are growing at about twice the rate of the world's population, but this is almost entirely due to Evangelical growth. Non-evangelical Protestantism is in serious decline. Liberal theologies are preached to dwindling congregations in emptying churches.

4. **Evangelicals** are growing at over three times population growth rate and are the world's only body of religious adherents growing rapidly by means of conversion. This is shown by the table below which also gives the percentages of Muslims over the same period.

	Evangelicals		Muslims	
Year	Population Millions	Annual Growth	Population Millions	Annual Growth
1960	81 mill	n.a.	464 mill	n.a.
1970	114 mill	3.5%	608 mill	2.7%
1980	180 mill	4.7%	788 mill	2.6%
1990	303 mill	5.3%	1034 mill	2.8%
2000	480 mill	4.7%	1340 mill	2.6%

The growth of Pentecostal and Charismatic denominations since 1960 has been even more striking. This would be even more remarkable if we were to add to these the growth of the Charismatics within denominations that do not have a specifically Pentecostal doctrinal position. However we do not have enough data for the whole period to show this.

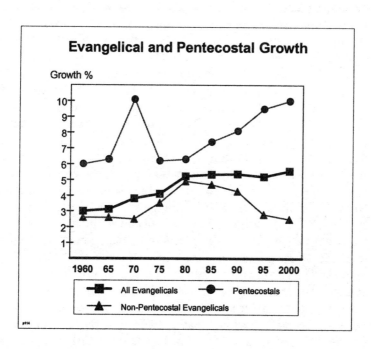

The consistently high growth rates are exceptional, and even though we have extrapolated these growth rates into the next decade, one wonders if this level will continue to be maintained. However, daring goals for growth and dramatic increases in membership as with the Assemblies of God Decade of Harvest or the Deeper Life Christian Church of Nigeria and many others could indicate this. Here is the statistical evidence for Evangelicals taking the Christian centre-stage in the Western World in the twenty-first century.[42]

The unusual global growth spurt in the 1960s I have not been able to explain – it may be the under-reporting of Pentecostal figures in the 1962 World Christian Handbook![43]

The growth of Evangelicals over these 40 years has shown a distinct continental prominence for each decade.

---

[42] McGrath 1995.
[43] See footnote on Sir Kenneth Grubb on p89.

1. **In the 1960s** the growth in **Africa** was the most marked. This growth has continued, but it would be reasonable to say that the 1960s were Africa's decade. The massive increase followed the ending of colonial rule when most African countries became independent states. Christianity became indigenized in a remarkable way – some groups being more syncretic, others more evangelical and charismatic in flavour. Never before in history has a whole continent seen such a radical change with Christianity gaining over 50% of the population in a single century. The spiritual turning to God has, sadly, not impacted the politics of the continent. Numerous dictators such as Idi Amin in Uganda or Mengistu in Ethiopia, gross corruption and mismanagement as in Zaire, terrible wars as in Ethiopia, Nigeria, Southern Africa and Liberia and the ghastly genocide of Rwanda and Burundi have all occurred in countries with many active Christians. Yet in many of the countries of Africa with the worst conditions, the Christian Church is one of the only stable structures that remain. It is a disappointing truth that evangelical churches have, by and large, failed to have an impact on political structures and attitudes. There seems to have been an implied teaching that politics is dirty, so committed Christians need to keep out of it. It is an indictment of our past discipling patterns.

2. **The 1970s** were marked by the rise to prominence of Evangelicals in **Latin America**. The continent had been nominally Catholic for much of the previous 500 years. Over this century the number of Evangelicals has multiplied from under 250,000 in 1900 to around 40 million[44] in 1990 and possibly over 60 million by the end of the century. There are now more Evangelicals in church on an average Sunday than in Roman Catholic churches – and this in a purportedly "Catholic" continent. Even with the recent more modest estimates for the larger Brazilian denominations, there are still more Evangelicals in Brazil than in the whole of Europe. By the 1990s the social

---

[44] This figure is lower than that given in the 1993 *Operation World*. We have since found that the exuberant reporting of the growth of some churches was based on flimsy statistical evidence and a large element of guesstimation. This was especially true of the Brazilian Assembles of God where the estimated numbers were claimed to be 16 million for 1991, but later investigation will probably reveal that this was nearer 8 million.

and political influence for good on society was becoming significant. Evangelicals have become a force that cannot be ignored.

3. **In the 1980s** it was **East Asia's** turn. The growth of the Church among South Koreans, the 50 million Overseas Chinese and the Javanese in Indonesia was followed by the extraordinary growth of the Church in the post-Mao era in China. The result of this has been that Evangelicals in Asia have become more numerous than in North America. The Singaporean Church has now become the most missionary-minded Church in the world in terms of the number of missionaries sent out for every 1,000 Christians. Of the ten largest evangelical congregations in the world, seven of these are in one Korean city, Seoul – a city where only 110 years ago there was not one single congregation. Today it's night skyline is dominated by thousands of red neon crosses on church buildings. There still remain vast areas and many large peoples of Asia where there has been no breakthrough yet, so this positive picture is still only partial.

4. **In the 1990s** the spotlight moved to **Eurasia** – that vast area of the world that comprised the Communist Bloc and where for decades Christians have been marginalized and often brutally persecuted. The spectacular disappearance of the Iron Curtain led to extraordinary changes, with the resurrection of the older indigenous Churches (mainly Orthodox) and also a massive growth in evangelical activity, both indigenous and foreign. Sadly much of the latter was stronger on zeal and finances and weaker on cultural sensitivity and co-operation with often devastating effects unforeseen by the perpetrators. The reaction of Orthodox Churches has been to limit or even outlaw foreign and evangelical activities.

Stepping back we see a remarkable pattern emerging of the 200 year growth as it gathered momentum –1700s the North Atlantic, 1800s the Pacific, 1960s Africa, 1970s Latin America, 1980s East Asia, 1990s Eurasia. This one and a half times encirclement of the globe now leaves us with the challenge of the 10/40 Window area. Central and South Asia and the Middle East are the remaining major areas of challenge. Where will the breakthroughs of the coming first decade of the next millennium come? Will it be among Muslims, Hindus or Buddhists? These are the final unpenetrated bastions of the enemy's hold on the souls of men. The rising tide of the gospel is lapping ever higher round this area, and we are even having foretastes of what that breakthrough might mean. Would that I had the space and the freedom to tell of amazing things going on in these seemingly impenetrable ideological fortresses. In Part 5 this will be covered in more depth.

Yet we must be careful not to overlook those sections of the world's population of this generation that are now unreached even though in "Christianized" areas. What about the need of a Europe that has departed so far from the gospel it once cradled? Then what about the Jews who are prophesied to come back to their Messiah when the full number of the Gentiles is come in to the Kingdom?[45] Our task is not yet complete, but the finishing line is in sight!

---

[45] Romans 11:28.

Chapter 10

Growth through God's interventions

The twentieth century has been notable for terrible wars, famines, tyrannies and immense natural catastrophes. These tragedies have occurred throughout history, but the number and intensity that has visibly increased. The media have helped spread this feeling of apocalyptic doom, for an event on one part of the world is broadcast in every country of the world within a few hours. This gives us a cumulative concentration of woes bombarding our consciousness hitherto unknown. News is depressing.

Yet it is these traumatic events that have contributed to the harvest into God's Kingdom. Some question whether a good God could exist if he "allows" such terrible things. What about Hitler's murder of 6 million Jews in the Holocaust or the warped ideology of Pol Pot which led to the murder of 2 million in the Killing Fields of Cambodia in the 1970s, or the callous genocide perpetrated by Hutu extremists on 1 million or more Tutsi in Central Africa in the 1990s? We will never see the whole picture this side of eternity, nor be able to give a logical reason for all of these events.

We can only say with Abraham,[46] 'Shall not the Judge of all the earth do right?' However our confidence is in our heavenly Father's absolute goodness and *agape* love for us and all men. It is in the light of his love that we will one day see the solutions to the presently insoluble woes that befall us and all humankind. The Lord Jesus Christ taught us that human failures and natural disasters have a redemptive core.

> ...And Jesus answered them, "Take heed that no one leads you astray. For many will come in my name, saying, 'I am the Christ,' and they will lead many astray. And you will hear of wars and rumours of wars; see that you are not alarmed; **for this must take place**, but the end is not yet. For nation will arise against nation, and kingdom against kingdom, and there will be famines and earthquakes in various places: all this is but the beginning of birth-pangs." *Matthew 24:4-8*

---

[46] Genesis 18:25.

In the midst of speaking of spiritual deception, wars and natural disasters, he utters those words "**this MUST take place.**" It is part of a bigger plan of which the negatives are an essential component. Somehow his redemptive purposes are worked out in love, but in the context of tragedies that open hard hearts and break down barriers to the gospel.

One fact has become clear to me in my gathering of information from around the world; the sound bites and the news flashes on our television screens do not tell the full story. God is doing an unprecedented work in our day. These mighty works are not in spite of the disasters, but even *because of* them. Jesus spoke to his disciples in Luke 17 of the terrible events that would precede his return and he ended that discourse with the enigmatic statement, "Where the body is, there the vultures will be gathered together." Could he perhaps have prophesied about television cameramen? They certainly flock together wherever there are dead bodies! The wars, disasters, blood, pain, sorrow, suffering and sin of our world are vividly portrayed on our TVs. Sadly the cameramen do not wait around long enough to record the testimonies or show how God's grace changes lives of those who suffered.

In 1995 I had the privilege of preaching in the Cape Town cathedral of the Church of England in South Africa. A terrible incident had occurred several years before. Guerrillas had burst into a Sunday morning service and sprayed the large congregation with machine gun bullets. Many were killed, and many more were injured. Within minutes the television cameraman of the world were there to record the horrors. In the subsequent agony and heart-searching, God met with those believers in a deep way. Not only did they forgive those who had injured them or caused their bereavement, but also others were added to the Body of Christ as a result. Some time later the leaders of the congregation wanted to tell the world of the great things that God had done, but the media were not interested in broadcasting this. No wonder we get depressed with the news.

This is why it has been so exciting for me to link the outpourings of God's love and power in today's world to the negative secular events which provided the backdrop. I am more than ever convinced that history is just a backcloth for His-story. Historians have usually missed the ONE important theme that gives meaning and excitement to history – it is God's redemptive plan for humankind. Here are a few examples of national awakenings through different human disasters.

I must add a word of caution here. There has been a tendency for Evangelicals to exaggerate exciting stories for publicity or fund-raising. Mass evangelism has turned up many lurid claims of thousands, or even hundreds of thousands of conversions through some medium or evangelistic campaign when a little careful verification would have shown that thousands of people may have shown some interest and this was easily equated as conversion. After the collapse of Communism in Europe, there were many truimphalistic reports of whole gatherings responding to an invitation. All that these unfortunate people were saying was that they hated the old system and were interested in anything that could provide answers that were lacking in Communism. Evangelicals in Russia and the Ukraine would be many more if all the responders had actually been converted and become disciples. We evangelicals can rightly be accused of speaking evangelastically.

Wars

El Salvador is better known to the world as the small Central American republic torn by a bitter civil war that raged for 12 years and only ended in 1992. The brutality, the destruction and the floods of refugees unsettled much of the continent. Yet few realize how fast Evangelicals multiplied during the desperate years of war. In 1965 Evangelicals were only about 2.5% of the population, but by 1990 they had become almost 20%. This figure does not include the many Salvadoran Evangelicals who became refugees in other lands.

Argentina began this century as one of the most prosperous countries in the world. Then followed 80 years of corrupt and inept governments that brought the country to its knees in more ways than one. The nadir was the decision of the Argentine military dictator Gualtieri to invade the British-ruled Falkland Islands, or Islas Malvinas, in 1982. Argentina and Britain had contested possession of these barren, storm-swept South Atlantic islands for two centuries. British colonial and diplomatic neglect combined with Argentinian pride and economic failure to precipitate the two nations into the unsought South Atlantic War. Gualtieri failed to reckon on the character of Prime Minister Margaret Thatcher, who ordered the recapture of the islands with their 2,000 inhabitants and 600,000 sheep. The ensuing Argentinian defeat led to a series of traumatic transformations in Argentina. Not only did democracy replace the dictatorship but also long-needed economic reforms were made and, best of all, was the new openness to God.

For years evangelical missionaries laboured in the land with scant response and slow church growth. Before the war in 1980, Evangelicals were possibly only abut 2% of the population, but by 1990 it was almost 7%. Some reckon that this figure may be nearer 12%.[47] The fact that my nation became embroiled in such a sadly unnecessary war was a grief to me. I was comforted on realizing how such a war helped towards bringing many to a personal faith in Christ.

Afghanistan has long bitterly opposed any proclamation of the gospel. There were many Nestorian Christians in the area a millennium ago, but then came Islam and the Church was wiped out. In more recent times almost every known Afghan convert to Christianity was soon martyred. In 1978 the Soviet Union engineered a Communist coup and subsequently invaded the land. This not only proved to be a major factor in the demise of both Communism and the USSR, but it also gave opportunity for Afghans to come to Christ and the Church to be established. The appalling sufferings of the Afghan people in the 10-year war with the USSR and the subsequent civil wars have given some unique opportunities for the gospel.

At first the Russians sent in Central Asian troops that were culturally Muslim in origin, but so many defected to the "enemy" that they were replaced by those of non-Muslim background. Often evangelical Christians forced to do their obligatory military service were sent as "cannon fodder." Some of these believers were able to witness to Afghans. Over 5 million refugees poured out of the country. Over half fled to Pakistan where Christian aid workers brought a number of Afghans to Jesus through their loving

---

[47] Statistics for Argentinian denominations are notoriously difficult to gather or verify. One of the new post-1982 denominations is the remarkable Pentecostal group named **Visión do Futuro**. They do not keep membership statistics, so estimates of their numbers in 1992 varied between 150,000 and 500,000.

ministry. Other aid workers managed to hold on in Kabul and, at times, elsewhere all through the 20 years of war, and through them others have come to faith in the Lord Jesus. So for the first time in modern history we can speak of groups of evangelical believers in this "closed" land, but which was opened up through invasion and war.

Sudan has known little peace since independence from Britain and Egypt in 1956. The black, animist and Christian peoples of the south were cobbled together in an ill-prepared, synthetic union with the Arab and Muslim culture of the north. War between the two regions has been almost incessant for over 40 years. Who can tell what the true casualty figures have been – especially in the south as the Muslim northerners have sought to subjugate, Arabize and Islamize the unwilling Southerners? Probably 2,000,000 have perished through war or famine. Western media have been denied access to the war zones, so the genocide, slavery and severe persecution of Christians has been little publicized.[48] There have been many cases of the bombing of churches, enslavement, forced conversions to Islam in famine conditions, crucifixion of believers and outright genocide of Christian peoples – especially in the Nuba Mountains in the centre of the country.

Yet there is another side to the story. When most mission work was forcibly terminated in the south in 1964 the percentage of Christians in the South was relatively small – possibly no more than 3-5%. Over these 40 years the great majority of the population has become Christian – predominantly Roman Catholic and Anglican. Many became Christian as a protest, but for many others as a dynamic and liberating experience of conversion. Whole cultures have been revolutionised by the power of the gospel. The Dinka people were long known as resistant to the gospel and reluctant to give up their fetishism and idolatry, but in the last few years there have been dramatic public rejections of all pagan rites and wholehearted embracing of the truth that all power belongs to the risen Lord Jesus. The Anglican Church in the Sudan has many fervent evangelist-bishops, a network of bush Bible schools and vigorous programmes for development in the midst of the most appalling deprivation and suffering.

---

[48] Hammond 1996.

Vietnam's war was vividly portrayed by the media. That famous photograph of a little girl burned severely by a napalm bomb running naked down the street in agony stands out in my memory. It won the photographer the Pulitzer prize in the USA, and helped turn the nation against the war. I never heard the aftermath until I read an article by Charles Colson in Christianity Today.[49] The little girl, Phan Thi Kim Phuc, eventually recovered from her terrible injuries and, for a time, was used by the Vietnam government in anti-American propaganda. The sequel is moving. As an adult she was led to Christ through the witness of a group of Vietnamese believers. Later while studying in Cuba she met another Vietnamese believer. They married and on their honeymoon managed to escape Communism and settle in Canada. In 1996 she laid a wreath in a veterans service at the Vietnam War Memorial in remembrance of those Americans who had lost their lives in the very conflict where she had been so terribly scarred. They now dream of the possibility of Bible school training and Christian service.

This is just one individual caught up in the terrors of war. For most of us it is the negative image that remains etched on our memories. Yet God had a beautiful plan through it all. He is not only the God who works out his purposes on the macro scale, but also on the micro level of individuals, of me. One day from heaven we will see the many individuals, ourselves included, who suffered on earth and see that behind it all was a loving God working out his redemptive plans for us all. No one will say in that day that God was unfair or anything less than omnipotent.

Tyrannies

In Old Testament times, God used heathen rulers to further his Kingdom. One only has to recall the Pharaoh in Moses' day, Ahasuerus in the time of Esther, Cyrus in the time of Nehemiah to see a pattern emerge. Why should it be different today? This century is replete with godless and evil men who became unwitting tools of the Almighty and were often made to look foolish in their striving after fame and power.

---

[49] Christianity Today, 3 March 1997. Chuck Colson wrote this moving article as one once intimately involved in decision making during that time.

Kwame Nkhrumah became the first leader of Ghana at independence in 1957. He inherited a country with a good, viable economy, but by his final demise in 1966, that economy was in tatters and the people impoverished. He had a statue of himself built in the capital, Accra. On its plinth were carved the blasphemous words "Seek ye first the political kingdom and all these things will be added unto you". Is it any wonder that he died an exile in poverty and his country an economic basket case? It is still trying to recover thirty years later. Yet in the economic disasters that befell the nation has come a remarkable movement of the Spirit in the place of spiritual poverty and Christian nominalism. The work of Scripture Union in schools and New Life For All sponsored by the Ghana Evangelism Committee brought a surge of new life to traditional denominations with vigorous outreach to unchurched areas and peoples of the country and also a national strategy for the multiplication of churches.

The Ayatollah Khomeini came to power in 1979 after a vigorous media campaign by Muslim fundamentalists to depose the autocratic Shah of Iran.[50] His tyrannical theocratic rule became a dictatorship worse than the one it replaced. As a result over three million Iranians either fled the country or refused to return to their homeland. At the time of the Revolution it was estimated that in the whole of Iran there were around 150 believers in the Lord Jesus who had come from a Muslim background. Many thousands of Muslim Iranians both inside Iran and among those who fled have since turned from the harshness and hatreds of the Ayatollah's religion to Christ.

I was in Turkey eight years after the Revolution in Iran where there were millions of refugees in or passing through Turkey. Several little fellowships of Iranian believers had come into being in Istanbul. I was told of one Iranian lady who testified, "I praise God for the Ayatollah. All I saw in that man was hatred, yet I was convinced that there must be a God of love." She found that God of love in Jesus. Dare we say that, unwittingly, Khomeini has possibly helped more Iranians to believe in Jesus than any person this

---

[50] The major means for fomenting that Revolution was the humble and widely replicable audio cassette. It was the first important revolution launched by this means. How we Christians need to use this same medium for world evangelization.

century? God chooses unlikely instruments so that the glory may be his alone.

Mao Tse Tung was utterly opposed to all religions, and built a cult round his own personality. What an unlikely man to become the person who, by his actions, has possibly contributed to more people coming into the Kingdom than any person in all of history! The final fall of mainland China to Mao's victorious Communist armies appeared to be the death knell for Christianity once again.[51] In 1949 there were about 800,000 Protestant adult church members with a community of about 1,500,000 and a further 3,000,000 Roman Catholics. The Christians were isolated from the rest of the world, and many forced into government-manipulated "denominations." Even these ceased to exist with the advent of the so-called Cultural Revolution (1966-75). There was not much culture in that revolution, but rather the destruction of anything cultural. In the ensuing terror families were broken up, the economy was ruined and anything religious was destroyed. Church life was extinguished but for two "show" churches kept open for the eyes of prying foreigners.

Many thought that Christianity had died in China. However with the eclipse of Mao's political power in 1975 and the neutralization of his extreme ideology came a great revulsion of the system that had perpetrated such evil. Not only did a vigorous capitalism, albeit greedy, spring forth from within Communism, but also new spiritual life. The secret Church became more open and somewhat freer to gather together and to witness, though still pressured and persecuted. The story of the growth of the Church in China over the past 20 years is still only partially known, but something extraordinary has happened. Many books have been written about this work of God.[52] Various researchers have sought to count the uncountable through careful investigation and by 1992 there were a variety of estimates as to the numerical strength of the whole Church in China.[53] These estimates varied between 25

---

[51] The previous two efforts had been the Nestorians in the ninth century and the Roman Catholics in the sixteenth century. Neither effort had made a lasting impact on Chinese society.

[52] Patterson 1989, Chao 1989.

[53] Jonathan Chao has favoured the higher number of 60-75 million in his book *The China Mission Handbook*. Tony Lambert in his careful surveys for News Network International and others has favoured the lower number of 25 - 30 million. In *Operation World* I consistently use

million and 100 million. It was interesting that when I was compiling the last Operation World in 1993, a report reached me which passed on a verbal "leak" from the inner core of the Communist regime of a secret government survey carried out over two years which gave an estimate for 1992 of 63 million Protestants and 12 million Catholics. Though we have no way of confirming that report, I believe it accords well with other evidence. This would mean a fourfold increase in the Catholic population and a fifteen- to forty-fold increase of Protestants with the great majority being linked to unregistered congregations scattered all over the country. Today we see what is surely the largest growth of the Church in a nation that has ever been known, and one of the factors was the Communist Mao Tse Tung. The Bible has replaced Mao's Little Red Book as the most desired and popular book in China. We are yet to see what the impact of the Church in China on our world will be, but in the twenty-first century it will certainly be significant. Will China become the greatest missionary sending nation ever?

Natural Disasters

The massive increase in the population of the world and rapid urbanization in poorer countries taking place is ensuring that earthquakes, typhoons and volcanic eruptions have a tragic harvest of ever-increasing casualty figures. Jesus himself warned us of these[54] as characteristic of the age between his first and second coming. Below are a few of the many examples in recent years of God working in this way.

Guatemala has seen a mighty turning to God over the past twenty years. The percentage of Evangelicals is possibly nearly 30% of the total population, which is one of the highest in the

---

two figures for the number of Christians - adult believers and the wider inclusive membership or affiliated Christians, which includes catechumens, children, non-member regular attenders and so on. Baptists, Pentecostals and Evangelicals in general would prefer to use the former; Catholics, Anglicans and paedo-baptists would rather use the former. Lambert's and Chao's figures are very similar to my two different categories. I asked Lambert if this was not the way to reconcile the two figures in suggesting that Chao was using the wider inclusive membership and Lambert the more limited adult membership. He agreed that this could be so.

[54] Matthew 24:7.

world. This has been due to intense guerrilla warfare and, in 1976, a devastating earthquake which flattened much of the capital. One of the factors in the growth of the Evangelicals was the loving aid and care administered by both local believers and also international evangelical aid agencies. Hearts became receptive to the gospel as a result. We can praise the Lord for such agencies as World Vision International of USA and elsewhere, TEAR Fund of the UK, Netherlands and Australia and Help for the Brethren in Germany and many others. Their costly investment of resources and loving care have contributed much to the planting and growth of churches in many difficult parts of the world.

Ukraine and Chernobyl. The name Chernobyl is now infamous for the most spectacular and worst nuclear accident in history. This nuclear catastrophe poisoned much of Europe with radioactive waste materials which were spewed into the atmosphere. Large areas of Ukraine and Belarus will remain uninhabited for thousands of years before the radioactivity will have diminished to safer levels. The impact of that contamination on the health and lives of millions of Ukrainians, Belarussians and other nearby peoples will be felt for decades or even centuries to come. This terrible event was so badly handled by the Communist leadership that it played an important role in the discrediting of Communism and the break-up of the Soviet Union.

This catastrophe had an impact for the Kingdom of God. Firstly, the power station was built on the mass graves of Jews massacred by the Nazis in 1942. Secondly, the name Chernobyl is the Ukrainian word for *wormwood*, the very name of the terrible star mentioned by John in Revelation:

> The third angel blew his trumpet, and a great star fell from
> heaven, blazing like a torch, and it fell on a third of the rivers
> and on the fountains of water. The name of the star is
> Wormwood. A third of the waters became wormwood, and
> many men died of the water, because it was made bitter.
> *Revelation 8:10-11*

The parallels are astonishing. I am not thereby claiming that this catastrophe is *the* event prophesied, but it is interesting that of all the 50 nuclear power stations in the USSR, it was the one called Wormwood that was affected. Was God saying something? That is certainly how many in the USSR regarded it. I was amazed to read in the British Daily Telegraph a front page article a few months afterwards entitled *"Russians read the Bible because of Chernobyl."* The reporter described the meaning of Chernobyl and made the astonishing report that all over the USSR spread the bush telegraph message "Chernobyl is in the Bible and speaks of God's wrath on sinners." Bookstores were emptied of Russian-Ukrainian dictionaries, for Bibles could not be purchased openly in bookstores, so many went seeking those who had Bibles to see the words written in Revelation. I wonder how many will be part of that heavenly throng before the Throne because of the Chernobyl disaster? Yet that is the God we serve who could even use Chernobyl for the cause of world evangelization.

Spain has one of the worst drug addiction problems in Europe. Madrid has the highest incidence of drug abuse and addiction in the country. In 1984 God burdened Elliot and Mary Tepper from the USA and Australian(s) Lindsay (and later Myk) MacKenzie for the Madrid drug addicts. They began a work that has become known as Betel.[55] Within 12 years that work had grown dramatically with many wonderful testimonies of deliverance and salvation. Many of the early converts became co-workers and then pastors and leaders in the work. Soon it became apparent that among drug addicts the incidence of AIDS was very high. In 1992 there were estimated to be 300,000 in Spain addicted to heroin or cocaine, but of these 100,000 were carrying the HIV. Many of these were converted to Christ. In that short space of time, over 20,000 have passed through the 20 or more rehabilitation centres. Almost all of those who stayed for the full year of rehabilitation never went back to drugs, and most were soundly converted to Christ.

The results are dramatic in a country that has proved hard soil for the gospel. The total number of adult Evangelical church members is only around 60,000 with a further 30,000 Romany Gypsy Christians. As a result of this ministry a family of churches has sprung up. The main church in Madrid is now the largest evangelical congregation in Spain with 400 members and 700 regularly meeting together. The one sadness is that possibly 30% of the members are HIV positive. So a whole new way of running a church and training of leaders had to be developed. There was an urgency and a passion, for many knew that their lives could be

---

[55] Dinnen 1995.

short. From this work among the dregs of society has come a spectacular missionary movement with Spanish missionaries spreading across Spain and beyond to other countries. Betel is now working among drug addicts and church planting in North Africa, Italy, France, USA, Germany and Britain. God has used even the terrible affliction of AIDS to give a unique break-through for the gospel, and also provide a model for ministry in other parts of the world where AIDS is beginning to decimate whole populations. No wonder Stewart Dinnen gave the title *A Rescue Shop Within a Yard of Hell*[56] to his account of the story of Betel.

I have shared a few examples out of many, but one day in Eternity I am sure God will show us the full pattern of his working in history through the terrible events that have shaken our world during our lifetimes. Without that I wonder whether heaven would be as perfect as it should be! We will have lots more to praise God for than these pale images with imperfect knowledge I have given above.

---

[56] In this he was quoting from the founder of WEC, C.T. Studd who composed this poem:
"Some wish to live within the sound
of Church or Chapel bell,
I want to run a rescue shop
within a yard of hell."

Chapter 11

A Global Army Mobilized

Those of us who live in the West have been long used to the concept of recruitment of new missionaries. The actual number being recruited for long-term missions has not increased, and in many countries has declined. We have also become accustomed to the idea that few ever attend missionary prayer meetings. What is not well known is the extent of mobilization of intercessors and missionary workers in non-Western countries. God is doing a new thing in bringing about a global recruitment of breath-taking proportions.

An Army of Intercessors

Massive global prayer movements – often involving thousands or even millions of Christians across the globe are another source of encouragement. More than that, the impact on the world is immeasurable, with many major advances of the gospel that can be attributed to prayer. The connection between intercession and world events is not so easy to establish here on earth, but one day we will see how mightily prayer impacted our world. As Edwin Orr convincingly shows,[57] the second Great Awakening in the 1790s was intimately bound up with the first great Protestant mission advance in the period 1792-1820, and the second great Protestant advance with the Evangelical Revival that swept North America and parts of Europe in 1858-1860. These great movements were preceded by mighty and importunate prayer movements pleading for revival.

Revelation chapters 5-8 cover the opening of the seven seals. The section begins with that glorious account of the Lamb, the Lion of the tribe of Judah, our Risen Lord who alone was worthy to open those seven seals. The song that was sung round the throne when the Lamb took the scroll was praise for redemption of those from every race, tribe, people and tongue. The opening of those seals represent redemptive acts of God on earth, each one giving a different perspective of his working. The first four seals are surprising and terrible. The first horse speaks of tyranny and

---

[57] Orr 1973, 1975.

oppression, the second of wars, the third of economic stress and injustice and the fourth of massive natural calamities. This list is almost exactly the type of events described in the previous chapter. Yet when we look at this section of Revelation (5:8) mention is made of the prayers of the saints rising up to God. Then in chapter 8:1-5, the seventh seal is a description of fire being thrown down on earth in answer to the prayers of the saints. The whole section of the six seals being opened is bracketed by clear reference to the intercession of believers. God's redemptive interventions, even through terrible calamities, are not only sovereign acts of our Omnipotent God, but are also in answer to the prayers of God's people. Somehow our Almighty God, who does not need us to perform his will, has invited us to participate in his redemption of the world in intercession and witness as his way of achieving that goal. What a privilege! But what a shame that we use prayer so little and feebly when we do.

One of the characteristics of the world of today is the massive mushrooming of globe-encircling prayer movements with thousands and even millions of Christians involved. To mention just a few – the Lydia Fellowship with women around the world deeply committed to a ministry of intercession for world evangelization; the March For Jesus Movement started in the UK and which now involves up to 30 million Christians annually, with a major component of those marches being intercession for world evangelization; the web of different prayer networks linked with Peter and Doris Wagner[58] of Global Harvest Ministries and with the AD2000 Mvt. As well as these are many dynamic and active movements such as the Concerts of Prayer[59] launched and inspired by David Bryant[60] in the USA and then in many other countries, the emphasis on spiritual warfare praying (some might say an over-emphasis!),[61] the exporting of prayer mountain fasting and praying

---

[58] Wagner, Global Harvest Ministries. P.O. Box 63060, Colorado Springs, CO 80962-3060, USA. email <7414.570@xcompuserve.com>

[59] David Bryant latched on to the phrase coined by Jonathan Edwards in New England over two centuries ago in which Edwards advocated concerts of prayer for the conversion of the heathen)

[60] Bryant 1984.

[61] Spiritual Warfare has become a major topic of discussion in Christian circles in the 1990s, with an abundance of books on the subject. This is a whole topic briefly handled in chapter 33 of present volume. Two major views are described in Rommen, 1995.

from Korea, the development of prayer walks and prayer journeys.[62] Though there are aspects of concern over some of these new prayer initiatives, the overall results are extraordinary in generating prayer awareness, involvement and deep commitment.

Never before in history have so many Christians been mobilized for specific prayer for revival, for the Muslim world during Ramadan, Praying Through the Window initiatives of the AD2000 Mvt. for the world's countries, cities and peoples during the 1990s. There is the rising expectation that God is going to do extraordinary things as a result. We see the signs of this. Here I give a few examples of the many.

China was, for over 100 years, the most-prayed for land on earth. Great men of prayer like Hudson Taylor, the founder of the China Inland Mission, travelled round the Christian world pleading for prayer for the unevangelized provinces of inland China. This call generated an army of intercessors and also missionaries for China. For the century before the Communists seized the Mainland, China was the Number One mission field, with up to 8,000 missionaries sowing the seed with tears. The river of blessing was building up behind a mighty dam, but that dam was not breached for another generation. It would appear that the work that God intended for China was too great to entrust to the many mission agencies, so they were removed from the scene in 1949 and 1950. No human agency could now claim the honour for the mighty harvest after 1975, and the one most responsible (as described in the last chapter) would have been horrified to do so! The great church planters of new unregistered congregations were not the mighty preachers of China, nor the watched elders of churches but often pairs of young unmarried women sent out for the task – some even being used of God to plant 50 or more churches in a two year mission tour.[63] Only intercession could have brought the sown seed of the Word to germination and through such unlikely instruments as the means of such a harvest. Would Christians have prayed so fervently for China's evangelization if they had known that it would have to come through the suffering of Maoist Communism and terror? God's ways are above our ways, and his answers are not always in the gentle manner we might have chosen.

---

[62] Hawthorne 1993.
[63] Chao 1989.

The collapse of Communism in Europe and the USSR was probably the most sudden and most unexpected event of this century. Up until the mid-80s it was commonly thought that superpower rivalry could have ended with a Communist triumph. The rottenness at its core was not so readily obvious until the collapse came. This could only have been in answer to prayer. Two men come to mind; men who took to heart this burden of prayer for the collapse of Communism.

Brother Andrew, the writer of *God's Smuggler*, put out a challenge to the Christian world in January 1984 for a seven-year prayer warfare to tear down the Iron Curtain that divided Europe. Within five years the infamous Berlin Wall was torn down and sold as tourist souvenirs, within six years Communism in Russia imploded and within seven years the Soviet Union itself had ceased to exist. What an answer to prayer! It is no wonder that Brother Andrew has now put out the challenge for a ten-year prayer warfare to tear down the barriers to the gospel in Islam. This is the only way it will happen. Islam will crumble before the power of prayer to our omnipotent God!

Professor Zacharias Fomum, a professor of Chemistry, church planter, intercessor and author[64] in Cameroon was burdened in 1987 for the countries under Communism. He called together several hundred Christians to fast and pray for weeks for the collapse of Communism. Before they ended their season of prayer, God gave them the assurance that their prayers had been heard. They prayed through to victory and they waited expectantly for the answer. This was not so long in coming!

Communism was implacably opposed to religion and Christianity in particular. Yet it was Christianity that triumphed. Huge numbers of people in the former Soviet Union returned to the Church of their fathers. This was usually the Orthodox Church. All the years of vigorous propagation of atheism and the cruel persecution of Christians was a signal failure. It was the prayers of God's people who won the victory.

Central Asia has long been a deep concern of my own agency. Since the 1920s we have desired entry into this most inaccessible part of the world. This was the goal of our WEC pioneers from the

---

[64] Fomum 1988.

1930s onwards–to Tibet, Pakistan, Iran, Turkey. We could only nibble at the fringes of the need of the peoples of Central Asia. Even into the 1980s Central Asian peoples represented one of the least reached blocs of peoples in the world. In 1980 Leslie Brierley, the WEC Director for Research and my predecessor and recruiter, launched a prayer campaign in 1980 in his magazine *The Wider Look* for the NAMMECA peoples. NAMMECA stood for Non-Arab Muslim Middle East and Central Asia. This led to many praying specifically for that region, and especially for the Central Asian republics in the USSR. In 1984 God gave us in WEC a new vision for advance, and this included specifically that latter area. In that year we began actively recruiting long term workers for Central Asia. Some mission leaders thought we were crazy, thinking that such an opening would not happen in our lifetime. It did, and it has been fascinating to see how the work of that team has grown to the present and become an effective church planting thrust to those Muslim peoples. It was specific prayer that gave the needed openings.

The World Islamic Conference in Dakar, Senegal was scheduled to be held in 1991. One of the chief points on the agenda of the national leaders of Muslim nations was how to eliminate indigenous Christian minorities in their countries and also how to stop all foreign mission efforts directed towards their nations. In 1990 the leaders of WEC International gathered for our six-yearly International Leaders' Conference in Scotland. During that time the leaders of our Senegal field pled with us for intercession that this conference be cancelled. We had a mighty time of intercession, and as we prayed, our prayers moved from praying about the situation and claiming the victory in Jesus to praise for the coming answer. The answer came in a surprising way – a few months later, Iraq invaded Kuwait and the Gulf War started. This war so divided the Muslim world that the Islamic conference was postponed to the following year. Yet when those leaders did eventually meet, the divisions were still so strong that most of the leaders left before the official ending of the conference with little accomplished. We, as believers, hold in our praying hands the fate of nations, the course of history and the triumph of the kingdom of God.

The Muslim World seems too hard for the gospel, but is that the whole truth? There are so many barriers to a Muslim coming to Christ. This is due to a complex mix of a distorted understanding of who the Lord Jesus Christ really is, the built-in opposition to Christianity for emotional, theological, historical and cultural reasons and the strong pressures from both state and family to anyone who shows interest in Christianity.

More recently there has been the rise of a fanatical fundamentalism which brooks no dissent and has brought tyranny and fear to the majority of Muslims, further limiting open Christian witness. However the savagery and bigotry of extremists in promoting their cause in such countries as Pakistan, Algeria, Egypt, Sudan, Afghanistan, Iran and Indonesia and the glorification of holy war, or *jihad*, has dismayed many sincere Muslims, bringing many to doubt the credibility of Islam and increasing the numbers who are willing to consider the claims of Christ. An example of this is events in Indonesia over the last few years. An increasingly violent extremist Islam has fomented numerous riots and destruction of churches on the island of Java. In 1997 there were many churches systematically destroyed by Muslim mobs. In one case the pastor and his wife were immolated in their church building. The martyred couple died praying for their tormentors. The result was that at least one of the perpetrators came to faith in Christ. May there be many more!

The cost for anyone leaving Islam and coming to Christ is formidable, yet the number of conversions to Christ has soared today to the highest level ever known – though with the rider that the actual numbers are still small. Why? I believe it is the increased publicity about the spiritual needs in the Muslim world and the greatly increased volume of prayer generated. The remarkable fact is that so many of those soundly converted to Christ have come through supernatural revelations of the Lord Jesus or through spectacular and undeniably miraculous healings.[65] Right across the Muslim world we hear accounts of individuals, families and even communities turning to Christ. Prayer is the means whereby the breakthroughs will come.

One day we may look back on the rise of fundamentalism as a fiery trial for the Muslim world that ultimately led to the demise of Islam as a viable ideology. I believe that before Jesus returns there will be ample proof that the gospel is the power of God unto salvation even for Muslims too, with mighty breakthrough, massive

---

[65] Sangster 1984.

people movements and thousands of radiant, witnessing believers who had once been enslaved in the bondages and fears of Islam. Fundamentalism may be the thin edge of the wedge.

An Army of Harvesters

To many Christians it has been long thought that to be a missionary you need a long white nose! For too long Western missionaries were regarded as the elite in mission fields, and had the automatic right to lead. That 'natives'[66] actually become missionaries like them had rarely entered the thinking of far too many. I went out to Southern Africa in the heyday of apartheid. I remember with shame the attitude projected that these poor black people are like children; they can never manage their own affairs effectively and so we, as whites, had the automatic right to lead. This also discouraged the blacks from even expecting that they were capable of doing all that the whites did – and more!

As a young missionary I had to lead a team of African brothers and sisters of my age. Admittedly I had the advantages of background, exposure to technology and finance (even though I was dirt poor!). I began to realize that something was wrong, and then was challenged to change my thinking. I then tried to encourage my fellow workers to participate in decision-making, and doing everything that I did. I laid out a ten-year plan for handover. I expected that everything needed for running complex evangelistic campaigns be done by my co-workers. It was painful and slow; we all had much to learn, but it happened. It became plain to me that, by God's grace, anyone had just as great potential in any Christian work when obedient to the Holy Spirit.

---

[66] How careful we must be with language we use to describe indigenous peoples on mission fields. Almost every term used quickly becomes paternalistic, or even derogatory. Those who live in and originate from Africa have struggled with self-satisfying terms. Think of the depth of feeling in South Africa over such words as *black, native, Bantu, non-white* or even *kaffir*. Or in the USA the struggles of over a century to find neutral terms – even present terms such as *African-American* or *ebonics* may not last more than a decade or so! Even the commonly used term *national* has lost its real meaning and become an indirect way of speaking of those from the mission field – I heard of a *national* preaching in a New York church; I would have thought he would have been American, but no, he was an African!

Through our tent evangelism in Zimbabwe in the late 60s and early 70s, many came to a saving knowledge of the Lord Jesus Christ. Two also went on to become missionaries and eventually mission leaders with YWAM.

Saluh Daka was a transvestite in Bulawayo before the Lord saved him. I well remember him coming to our evangelistic tent to argue. Yet by the end of the month in that area, he was soundly converted. He later joined YWAM and went to Mozambique as a missionary, but was arrested by the Communists in 1975 and spent over a year in prison for handing out Bibles on Independence Day. At one stage he managed to escape from the prison. He found his way to the coast, helped himself to a rowing boat and rowed out to sea to try to reach South Africa. Out at sea he panicked, because he did not know whether South Africa was to his left or right, so he had to come back to shore, and give himself up to the authorities! After release from prison he served in the Philippines and then became the YWAM leader in Cameroon, Africa. Sadly he died from an allergy reaction some years later.

Another was Oliver Nyumbu of Zimbabwe, who was running the YWAM Discipleship Training School at Haywards Heath in England when we returned as a family to Britain in 1980. He invited me to come to speak to the DTS he was leading. He introduced me in a remarkable way, "I am so glad Patrick is able to be with us today! He does not know it, but he is my father in the Lord!" Years before I had preached to a crowd of young people at a camp. After the meeting he and several others had sought the Lord and I then pointed them to the Saviour. The next time I met him was as a missionary in my own country. He continues to serve the Lord in England to this day.

These two men were almost a prophetic foretaste of what would become a major part of my later ministry. The direction of this ministry has been in sowing mission vision in non-Western countries through public ministry and preparing *Operation World* for publication in other languages. There have been many who have come to me with gratitude to share how through these means they had become missionaries. In 1985 Jill and I were visiting our WEC team in Senegal. During our time there we flew in a little New Tribes Mission plane to the capital, Dakar. There awaiting a flight back to the south of the country were two Brazilians. One of them saw me alight from the plane. He ran up to me and gave me a big Brazilian *abraço* (embrace). He delightedly told me that he was now an NTM missionary because he had heard me give the challenge of Senegal several years before in São Paulo, Brazil. The other Brazilian then said, "Oh, you wrote that book did you? That is why I am here!"

Leslie Brierley of WEC International visited Brazil in 1962 with a view to surveying the land as a potential for sending out missionaries. However it was only in 1972-3 that Brierley and another WEC colleague, Bob Harvey, began touring Bible schools giving missionary awareness seminars. It was the start of the massive missionary movement that has matured in Brazil since that time. Bob Harvey became, in effect "Mr Missions, Brazil" together with several other colleagues, including Jonathan Santos, the founder of the Antioch Mission of Brazil.

From this ministry Brierley developed a global strategy for launching mission movements in non-Western countries. Many were touched through Leslie's visits and writings, especially in the magazines *LOOK* and *Wider LOOK* – in such lands as India, Taiwan, Singapore, Japan, Indonesia and in Africa. Some of these recruits formed their own indigenous missions or went with indigenous agencies, some joined WEC. In fact our Field Leaders in Ghana until recently were one of these; they are Indians.

The missionary movement has become global. The early missionaries to the Pacific nearly two centuries ago saw a mighty mission movement start among Polynesians and Melanesians. Most of the island communities and peoples were not evangelized by Europeans but by Islanders – a number being martyred. Sadly this mission vision declined over the years, but it is not surprising that the modern missionary movement of the Evangelical Fellowship of the Pacific uses the symbol of that earlier movement in the name of its structure, **The Deep Sea Canoe Mission**. The same is true for India, China and Africa, but these nineteenth century indigenous missionary efforts have been largely unchronicled.[67]

It is only in the late seventies and early eighties of this century that non-Western missionaries began to be noticed in the West.

---

[67] Tippett 1977.

Various books – by Marlin Nelson, Larry Keyes and Larry Pate[68] highlighted this rapidly growing movement. In some ways a key year was 1984. I do not know what happened in that year in the spiritual realm, but suddenly the number of non-Western mission agencies began to multiply and large numbers of non-Western missionaries joined those largely Western international agencies that were willing to open their doors to them. Agencies such as OM, YWAM, OMF, WEC and others rapidly had to adjust to becoming globally multi-cultural with all the joys and pains that this mixing can bring.[69]

Larry Pate in his book, *From Every People*, made a courageous survey of all the indigenous mission agencies from non-Western countries and cultures he could identify. In it he made predictions that the non-Western mission force would become larger than the Western. There were difficulties with his unequal comparisons of what constituted a missionary and the inclusion of many agencies that were theologically or statistically suspect, but the point was made that the non-Western contribution to world evangelization was becoming so significant that it could not be ignored.

In October 1997 the COMIBAM conference was held in Acapulco, Mexico. It was a specifically Latin American conference and was a proof of the maturity evident in the Latin American Missions movement. Ted Limpic carried out a massive survey of mission agencies in the Hispanic world. This was published for the COMIBAM conference in the Ibero-American Missions Handbook. There were 397 agencies and 3,498 missionaries listed.

For the 1993 edition of *Operation World*, I conducted a global survey of all mission agencies I could identify. There are extant three major definitions of the term "missionary" – the North American (those who leave N. America to work in another country), the European and Latin American (those who work cross-culturally) and the African and Asian (those with an apostolic call who go to evangelize or plant churches where there are none).

---

[68] Nelson 1983; Keyes, 1983; Pate, 1989.

[69] Kuhl 1997. Dieter Kuhl has been the International Director of WEC International, and has had to become intimately acquainted with the strategic, pastoral and structural implications of internationalization in a large evangelical church planting mission. This became the subject of his thesis for his post-graduate degree at Columbia International University.

Using the latter and broadest possible definition,[70] about 31% of the 138,000 missionaries were non-Western. Using the narrowest, this then became 10% of the 76,000 missionaries serving in other lands.

Praise God for the diversity and talent of this large new component in the Mission force. I admire the evangelistic zeal of the Brazilians, the brilliance in handling mission finance of the Chinese, the dogged determination of Koreans in church planting, the courage of Nigerians in evangelizing Muslims. It seems that in the mission force of the future, Westerners will become more the technicians who support the rest; fascination with communication technology is not increasing hours of face to face witnessing! We may one day have to admit that computers speeded every aspect of Christian work except the key ones of evangelism and discipling.

Mission work today has to be a global effort whether we like it or not. The more those countries with a longer experience of missions do to partner with newer sending countries and agencies, the fewer lessons will have to be learnt the hard way. One of the great challenges today is setting up effective missionary training programmes to prepare missionaries from Latin America, Africa and Asia.[71] Informal and formal partnerships and networks on the pioneer mission fields of the world are our future, and despite the difficulties, we have to work hard to make these co-operative partnerships work.

---

[70] Johnstone 1993:643-9 where tables of missionaries for every country of the world are given.
[71] Taylor 1991. Bill Taylor of WEF has tirelessly travelled the world in his vision to facilitate this.

Chapter 12

World Evangelization – in our Generation!

The millennium is a unique turning point in our time. Completing a millennium and entering a new one has a fascination for all of us. It certainly has given every crank and charlatan opportunity to stir emotions and whip up expectations of some magical millennial dawn or some terrible disaster. Many Christians are led astray into fanciful byways, just as the Lord Jesus Christ warned us in Matthew 24. The remaining years of this millennium will surely throw up many more apocalyptic cults, mountain-top vigils for the return of the Lord Jesus, mass suicides and other weird distortions of Scripture teaching on eschatology. One thing we can be sure about – Jesus will come at a time when he is NOT expected![72] It would be too neat for his return to fit dispensational charts covering seven millennia! However there is a justifiably heightened expectation of the soon return of the Lord that is valid, but that may not be in the exact year of the millennium.[73] We can know that the time is near, but not predict dates. The validity lies more in the increasing feasibility of actually seeing the completion of the various commands of the Great Commission.

Ever since the early part of the nineteenth century there have been visions for completing the task, but these only really gained prominence in mission thinking from 1881 onwards. Todd Johnson graphically describes the drama of the effort to evangelize the world in the final 20 years of the last century and also the setting in of discouragement at the failure to achieve the goal in his book *Countdown to 1900*. At the same time David Barrett and Jim Reapsome published their remarkable book *Seven Hundred Plans to Evangelize the World*. For the first time researchers put together a fairly complete picture of the visions and action plans across the entire church and all of history for the partial or full completion of the Great Commission. The number of such plans has proliferated over the past 20 years, and the Barrett database recorded 1,290 such plans in 1998.

---

[72] Matthew 24:44, Luke 12:40.
[73] The actual millennial year may have been 1996. It is widely understood that the selection of 0 AD as the birth-year of the Lord Jesus was erroneous, and was more likely to have been 7-4BC.

I want to share just five global plans here.

1. Radio agencies and the World By 2000 vision

Christian Radio ministries had, for many years, not been known for their close co-operation but rather for competition for scarce resources. Radio is a high technology and therefore a costly ministry. It was a remarkable new day for world evangelization when the presidents of Far East Broadcasting Company, HCJB World Radio, SIM International, and Trans World Radio made a commitment in September 1985 with these words:

> We are committed to provide every man, woman, and child on earth the opportunity to turn on their radio and hear the Gospel of Jesus Christ in a language they can understand so that they can become followers of Christ and responsible members of his Church. We plan to complete this task by the year 2000.

Since then they have been joined by FEBA Radio. Other broadcast-related missions such as Words of Hope, IBRA Radio, Back to the Bible Broadcasts, and Galcom have subsequently joined as Associates. This goal was sharpened to: a daily transmission of a 30 minute broadcast in each of these languages by the year 2000. It is no light commitment because of the effort and resources needed – to find indigenous believers able to broadcast when there are often hardly any native speakers who believe – to maintain a flow of good programmes with the right content and set up effective follow-up mechanisms that lead to churches of indigenous believers.

At the time of making this commitment it was estimated that about 140 of the world's mega-languages (those over 1 million speakers) had Christian broadcasts. This meant that a further 160 language services needed to be developed. With further research a number of additional mega-languages have been discovered.

Between 1986 and 1997 World by 2000 broadcasters had begun transmitting in 75 new languages – and the initiative continues to provide incentive to increase that number as the year 2000 approaches. As of March 1997 approximately 90 remaining languages are scheduled for development. There is much to do, but the goal is achievable. On attaining this primary broadcasting goal it will then mean that over 99% of the world's population would have access to a language they either speak as their heart language, or in a widely spoken language within their area.

2. Campus Crusade and the Jesus Film

The impact of this one film based on the life of Jesus as described by Luke is one of the media miracles of all time. The film was the vision of Campus Crusade's founder Dr Bill Bright from 1950 onwards. A film utilizing both sight and sound to deliver the message of Christ he saw as providing a powerful evangelistic tool that would bring the gospel message alive. Done accurately and faithfully to scripture, Dr. Bright believed the film could be translated and re-recorded into the languages of the world. In 1978, the film was produced at a cost of $6 million. Paul Eshleman became the leader of this project.[74] To date it is estimated that nearly 900 million people have seen the film. Possibly 46 million made some form of commitment to Christ as a result. Follow up ministry has been patchy, so how many have come to a living faith and then were integrated into a local group of believers is hard to measure.

A number of countries such as ex-Communist Russia and Muslim Indonesia have shown the film over national television. The wide use of the film on satellite and through video in the most difficult countries make this dream far more realistic that it might have appeared. The fact that some Muslim countries have banned the film is a big incentive for multiple copies of the video to be made secretly and then widely distributed in those very countries.

3. Bible Translators and Translation goals for AD 2000

We all agree – everyone needs to have and understand God's Word. To make disciples requires the Bible. The goal of a 'church for every people' must include providing that church with the scriptures. Most people can only understand God's Word and indeed any teaching about God or the spirit world or about what is right and wrong when it is expressed in their own language. In the Joshua Project 2000 Peoples List there are 559 languages in which there is no scripture. If the list of people groups needing scripture were extended below the 10,000 population mark then certainly

---

[74] Eshleman 1995. This book gives a vivid account of the story and impact of the film.

another 1,000 would need to be added to this total. So the translation task is still huge.

A forum of agencies involved in Bible translation has set goals for the year 2000 that are also of great significance to world evangelization. These 13 or so agencies are working towards the goal that by the end of the year 2000 the following will have been achieved:

1. All remaining languages spoken by more than 5,000,000 will have the whole Bible in their language.
2. The New Testament be translated into every language spoken by more than 500,000.
3. That there be portions of the Scriptures translated into every language spoken by more than 250,000 people.
4. That translation work will have been commenced in every language spoken by more than 100,000.

Can it be done? The answer is, "Yes and soon." The pace of scripture translation has been accelerating. In the last century 400 languages received some portion of scripture; in this century four times as many, over 1,600 languages have received some scripture. In fact in the last 45 years more languages have received some scripture than in all the previous centuries put together. Yet the "soon" must be qualified. It must be borne in mind that there is an enormous investment of time, people and resources for even one New Testament to be translated – even with the use of advanced computer programming. From start to finish it usually takes 12 to 20 years to publish a New Testament.

4. The DAWN Vision

The vision God gave Jim Montgomery in the Philippines[75] was breath-taking, to say the least. It was for discipling a whole nation by means of the multiplication of churches in every community. The vision was launched in the Philippines in 1974 with the target of a church for every 1,000 Filipinos by the year 2000. This meant multiplying the number of churches from 5,000 to 50,000 in 26 years. The enthusiasm of the churches has indeed resulted in a dramatic increase in the number of congregations, and the goal is well on target for achievement.

The concept was so simple, yet quite effective when rightly pursued, that it is not surprising this has become a global movement. The overarching vision is that there be a living fellowship of witnessing believers within easy access (usually walking distance, but depending on local culture) of every person on the face of the earth. This vision has spread to many countries in the world and the whole philosophy and methodology adapted and developed under the wider concept of *Saturation Church Planting (SCP)* and well articulated by Dwight Smith, the President of SCP International. By 1997 there were 100 national projects encompassing 85% of the world's population.[76] Of these, 30 have DAWN or DAWN-equivalent projects started, and the rest have plans for national congresses to launch one.

Present DAWN/SCP global goals in the launched projects already have yielded a cumulative goal for 3,000,000 new congregations; there are 4,000,000 to go![77]

5. The AD2000 and Beyond Movement

The birthing of the AD2000 Mvt. in 1988 came through the inspiration of Thomas Wang, then the Director of the Lausanne Movement for World Evangelization.[78] He had a vision that God wanted to do something special for world evangelization by the end of the millennium. He wrote a seminal article in the World Evangelization magazine of the LCWE *By the year 2000: Is God trying to tell us something?* This was widely read and stimulated a big response. Thomas Wang is the Chairman and Luis Bush of Argentina/USA is the Director of the AD2000 Mvt.

The goals of the Movement were simple, but very challenging:

> A church for every people
> and the Gospel for every person
> by the year 2000.

---

[75] Montgomery 1975.

[76] Montgomery 1997:vii.

[77] Montgomery 1989.

[78] Thomas Wang noticed the multiplication of separate visions for the year 2000 made prominent by Barrett and Reapsome's research for *Seven Hundred Plans to evangelize the world: the rise of a Global Evangelization Movement.*

My absolute conviction from all the research and gathering of information is that we are in the finishing straight of the marathon for world evangelization. Each of the three ministries of radio, film and Bible translation described above have the potential of providing the message of the gospel for over 99% of the world's population by the end of this century. That is not to say that everyone will turn on a radio to listen, or go to a showing of the Jesus Film or receive a portion of Scripture – or even that the person can read it if he does.

The AD2000 Mvt.'s goal for the gospel to be preached to every person by the year 2000 may not be as fanciful and crazy as had been thought. Added to this is the DAWN vision which aims to make belonging to a live congregation of believers for every person on earth a viable option. We have the structures and strategies to make it happen – if we mobilize. The AD2000 Movement has become a little umbrella to bring together 10 Tracks or Networks[79] which link other large evangelical networks and movements of existing global, regional, national and ministry visions into an integrated whole. The unifying purpose is nothing less than the fulfilling of every one of the Great Commission requirements stated by the Lord Jesus Christ.

World Evangelization – in our generation!

I do not want to minimise the enormity of the challenge of the unfinished task. This will be covered in Part 5 of this book. We cannot ignore the fact that even today an estimated 15% to 20% of the world population has never yet had a fair chance to hear the gospel. This represents around one billion men, women and children. The Muslim, Hindu and Buddhist worlds and their spiritual, ideological and social barriers still need to be broken down by the power of the Lord Jesus Christ.[80] Most of the 62

---

[79] The AD2000 and Beyond Movement has, as of January 1998, the following Tracks or Networks: Unreached Peoples, Cities, Mobilization of Women, God's Word and Christian Literature, Worship & the Arts, Media, Mobilization of United Prayer, Saturation Evangelism and Small Group Leadership Development, Mobilization of New Missionaries, Denominational Leaders and Mobilization of Students.

[80] *Mission Frontiers*, the magazine of the US Center for World Mission, in September 1997 gave some penetrating comments about the need for radical re-thinking if we are to make significant inroads into these big blocs of unreached peoples.

countries of the 10/40 Window still have only a small fraction of their populations that claim to be Christian, and in some of those countries, the majority of those Christians are foreign residents-- not indigenous to the country. There are still over 3,000 peoples in the world where pioneer church planting is still the key ministry, and about 1,000 or more have no known resident witness. We have a great challenge ahead. No one need feel unemployed! Every one of us and every single congregation is vital to the final prosecution of the task Jesus gave us!

I also do not want to minimize the cost involved. We cannot avoid the cross. Technique and technology are aids, but not the method of gaining spiritual victories. How many lives will need to be laid down for the cause of the Gospel, how much travail in prayer, how much sacrificial giving, how much commitment from every Christian? It is not a foregone conclusion that this generation will complete the task. The founder of my own agency made this remarkable statement:

> Let nobody mistake our objective, the devil will seek to drag many red herrings across the scent. Our objective is THE EVANGELIZATION OF ALL THE UNEVANGELIZED REGIONS OF THE WORLD.
> For that we have the divine warrant of God's Word, for anything short of that, however prettily or fancifully expressed, we have no authority nor attraction.
> WE WANT JESUS BACK AGAIN.
> Christ's return will take place the moment the last man hears the witness of Jesus; our object, towards which we press with ever-hastening footsteps, is the evangelization of that last man.
> THIS CAN ONLY BE ACCOMPLISHED BY THE POWER AND LEADERSHIP OF THE HOLY GHOST.
> We care not by whom this glorious end is accomplished. Whether our share is great or insignificant matters not. Only we shall take no rest and give no rest to any till this thing is done. May God bless and encourage every missionary and missionary society, making each a new sharp threshing instrument having teeth![81]

---

[81] Studd ca. 1930. Studd apparently wrote this in a letter from the Congo forests. It was quoted in a leaflet published by WEC in the UK ca.1982.

Conclusion to Part 3

My main aim in this section has been to lift the eyes of Christians away from the local discouragements and look across the world with all its woes, and yet see the mighty hand of God at work, the Church growing and the task being completed. The magnitude of that harvest I have sought to portray is beyond the understanding and knowledge of most. We have much for which we can rejoice in today's world, and we can have a hope for the future.

The Church IS bigger numerically than we had perhaps thought.

We have a finishable task, let us then aim to be the generation that finishes it. Jesus IS coming back, but only when the task is complete. The effort, the pain, the tears, the dying are all worth while for the joy set before us.

Now we must move on to look at the structures needed to sustain that final thrust, and then to look at the unfinished task itself.

Part 4

The Future

The Vision Channelled

Isaiah 54:2

Introduction

Now we come to the heart of the book. Here I open up what I believe to be one of the fundamental reasons for the failure of the Church to implement the Last Command of the Lord Jesus Christ. The reason is structural. All through the history of the Church it is the lack of the right structures or the distortion of existing structures which have crippled our effective prosecution of this fundamental command.

I realize that what I write may be controversial. Some would challenge me by stating that the spiritual dimension is more important than the structural; what about intercession, what about revival and quickened spiritual life? Of course structure without spirituality, mighty intercession, or obedience to God is fleshly and useless in the light of eternity, and even counterproductive. The converse is also true. Revivals which do not impact existing structures and form new ones soon lose their momentum and fruit. The 1904 Welsh Revival blessed the world, but largely missed the church structures in South Wales, so a century later, spiritual life in the churches is at a lower ebb than even in other parts of Britain. The East African Revival (1930s-1960s) revolutionized large and often nominal denominations and the effects are still visible today because the leadership in the churches was involved. Wesley and Whitefield were the two great preachers and revivalists of the eighteenth century. George Whitefield travelled and preached constantly with thousands of conversions in huge meetings but late in life he looked back with regret because little visible fruit remained. John Wesley also preached with great impact, but gathered the converts in structures for edification and evangelism. For a century after his death the Methodist Church was one of the world's most dynamic bodies for extending the Kingdom of God.

I trust that this book will stimulate thinking and provoke further and better work on this vital matter of structures. For only when we understand the principles of kingdom structures will we have the mechanisms for mobilizing and channelling God's people into the Great Commission effectively, and also conserving and maturing the results in missions-committed churches.

It is interesting that Isaiah 54:1 speaks of present harvest and 54:3 speaks of future advance. The structures for harvest we find in Isaiah 54:2. The harvest will not be reaped in our generation if we get our nurturing, mobilizing and channelling structures out of balance.

Chapter 13

Biblical Structures for the Body of Christ

It has taken me many years to understand how important it is for world evangelization that we have the right structures in the Body of Christ. Little attention has been given to this key issue in theology and in writing. It has now surfaced as an area of concern, but with more heat than light being generated. This, to me, is the vital part of what I want to share in this book. We need the right kind of tent (using Isaiah's terminology); structures to channel mission endeavour.

For sixteen years of my life, the focus of my ministry was the use of tents for evangelism. So the symbolism of tents is meaningful to me. As a worker with the Dorothea Mission in Africa we were urban nomads. We travelled with large tents from city to city, town to town preaching the gospel and seeking to bring people in to a living relationship with the Lord Jesus Christ. We knew how to pitch them, repair them, suffer their loss through arson and mobs and even, in one instance, when money was scarce, to make a tent. I can therefore say, with tongue in cheek, that I am one of the very few who can truly claim to be a tentmaking missionary! Of course we use the term "tentmaking" today in a symbolic sense for those missionaries who use their professional expertise as a means for personal support or as a platform for entry into countries to minister to people who need the gospel. I want to use the symbolism of tents in a different way to illustrate my point on structures. We return to Isaiah 54:2 where this is just what the Holy Spirit does for our benefit:

> Enlarge the place of your tent, and let the curtains of your
> habitations be stretched out; hold not back, lengthen your
> cords and strengthen your stakes.

Isaiah has just prophesied about the dramatic harvest that the Holy Spirit was to gather through the Church once the Lord Jesus was crucified and risen. A harvest of such magnitude is cause for great rejoicing. We believers have good cause to break out into singing and rejoicing. In the previous chapter I gave a few examples of what the Lord is doing in the very day in which we live. Such a harvest is a stimulus to believe that there will be further manifestations of the power of God in bringing in the final harvest among those yet to be won for the Kingdom. It is also a challenge that we use the right strategies for hastening the gathering in of that harvest. For that to happen we need the most effective structures.

The 275-year sinful delay of Protestants was now to coming to an end. It was the lack of structures that had limited the impact of those few lone mission promoters and pioneers during that time. William Carey was led to preach to his fellow Baptist pastors on this verse in Nottingham in 1792 and it was the very issue of structures that he addressed. In some ways this sermon preached on Isaiah 54:2 was one of the most world-changing since Pentecost. In his book,[1] *An Enquiry into the obligation of Christians **to use means** for the Conversion of the Heathens,* he clearly states his emphasis that the end of the Christian obligation to obey the Great Commission is only achieved by means (author's emphasis). The means that Carey advocated were explained in his last chapter headed "*An Enquiry into the duty of Christians in general, and what means ought to be used, in order to promote this work.*" It is amazing to see how Carey described what was needed in the Body of Christ at a time when the only examples he could use had to come from the great commercial trading companies of his day[2] and from the multiplicity of religious societies that had been springing up for a variety of aims over the past century. Carey wrote:

1. Prayer

"One of the first and most important of those duties which are incumbent upon us is fervent and united prayer ... The most glorious works of grace that have ever taken place have been in answer to prayer; and it is in this way, we have the greatest reason to suppose, that the glorious outpouring of the Spirit, which we expect at last, will be bestowed."[3]

---

[1] Carey 1792/1988:59-65.

[2] It is hard for us today to understand the power and wealth of the Dutch East India Company in what is today Indonesia, and the British East India Company. For centuries they controlled vast empires, ran armies and held life-and-death control over native populations far larger than their homelands. Netherlands had, in 1800, a population of 2 million ruling the East Indies with 10 million and Britain with 16 million ruled most of India with 185 million.

[3] Carey, ibid. pp59-60.

2. **Missionary Societies** that could service mission teams.

"Suppose a company of serious Christians, ministers and private persons, were to form themselves into a society, and make a number of rules respecting the regulation of the plan, and the persons who are to be employed as missionaries, the means of defraying the expense, etc. ...From such a society a committee might be appointed, whose business it should be to procure all the information they could upon the subject, to receive contributions, to enquire into the characters, tempers, abilities and religious views of the missionaries and also to provide them with the necessities for their undertakings..."

"I would therefore propose that such a society should be formed amongst the Particular Baptist denomination..."[4]

Prayer was the first means advocated. Praise God that this vision for prayer has increased in the past 20 or so years. I sought to give examples of this in the previous chapter. Are we on the threshold of the outpouring Carey prophesied above – or has this already begun?

The second means advocated was the formation of missionary societies. This was a revolutionary concept in his day and it is the human means by which the subsequent astonishing harvest has been won. Before his time the Society for the Propagation of Christian Knowledge (SPCK) had been founded in 1699, but it was not a mission agency in the form that Carey now suggested. The Moravians had, in 1787, reorganized their hitherto rather unstructured mission enterprise into the Society for the Propagation of the Gospel among the Heathen. Carey's agency was the real pioneer of a modern mission agency. Since then, mission agencies have multiplied. In the 1993 edition of *Operation World* we did a global survey of all mission agencies we could identify. We listed over 2,500 Protestant agencies and 4,200 national mission headquarters for sending out missionaries from about 200 of the world's 237 countries.

It is noteworthy that Carey did not develop his theme of "means" from the passage in Isaiah nor from the rest of Scripture but rather from the religious societies and international commercial firms of his day. So even the concept of mission and mission

---

[4] Carey, ibid. 63.

agencies still carries the aura of commercialism, multi-national corporations, colonialism, exporting paternalistic civilization, and, above all, an unbiblicality about it. We have the legacy of this in the commonly used modern term **para-church**. The whole idea of mission then appears **para-biblical** and not part of the true Body of Christ. It is this very point I want to develop here and show the biblicality of a structure to advance mission. Then, further, that this structure must be seen as an integral part of, and accountable to, the wider Body of Christ.

We live in the shadow of the structural distortions in the post-apostolic Church and the subsequent abandonment of such structures in the Reformation. The Reformation led to a healthy reformation of theology but an unwitting, tragic deformation of structure in the biblical model of the Church. In the iconoclasm of the Reformation, the dismantling of monasticism destroyed more than a system, it destroyed the only extant channelling mechanism for initiating and promoting mission. Whatever our misgivings about the monastic system, we must still recognize that for 1,500 years monasticism in its various forms was virtually the only initiator for mission advance.[5]

---

[5] Addison 1936.

Chapter 14

Isaiah's Tent – A Structure for Harvesting

There is something dynamic about a tent. It is flexible, fitting different types of terrain and need because it can be made bigger or smaller by adjusting the number of panels or sections laced together. It is mobile and built for transportation to the places where it is needed. It is temporary; the very nature of a tent is impermanent. We have lost that concept of flexible, mobile and temporary structures as necessary for the Church. Buildings were not constructed, nor seen to be necessary in the time of its early expansion. In the English language we have further confused the issue by verbally equating the gathered people of God with the building in which they meet. The very mention of the word *church* in Britain conjures up images of old, musty buildings, huge restoration bills and graveyards for dead saints rather than vital gatherings of living saints independent of bricks and mortar!

It is interesting that the Holy Spirit gave Isaiah the imagery of a tent that must be enlarged by the people of God. It was to be a tent in which a multitude of spiritual children could be gathered, nurtured, prepared and sent out into ministry. It took a Donald MacGavran, "the Apostle of Church Growth" to awaken the Body of Christ to the concept of church growth[6] as a deliberate strategy for evangelization. McGavran's enthusiasm and dynamism sparked an explosion of research and writing on the numerical increase of congregations and Christians. Many have criticized his emphasis on numbers and belittled the church growth movement, but it is undeniable that a considerable proportion of the dramatic growth of evangelical Christianity around the world in recent years has had its origins in his challenge to the Church. Numbers may not say everything, but they do say something. The Isaiah prophecy of harvest and the need for structures to gather in that harvest has never been so abundantly fulfilled as in our day.

The imperatives are strong – *enlarge, be stretched out, hold not back, lengthen, strengthen.* These are the activities of believers to expedite the harvest. These could be allegorically, but meaningfully applied successively to the ministries of evangelism,

---

[6] McGavran 1970.

discipling, faith in the midst of opposition, supporting missions and intercession, but this is not the main thrust I want to make here. God gives us the charge here to structure for mission. It is our job to make sure that we are strategic in the structures we employ and that they are those best fitted to the task. Sadly that has not been so in the history of the Church.

A Biblical Theology for the Structure of the Church

Can we develop a theology of church structures? By this I do not mean the ecclesiastical empires with their rigidities that have developed over the centuries. I do not believe that Jesus had planned for centuries of delay before the completion of world evangelization and therefore establish long-term structures. The very symbolism of tents used here implies an impermanence and flexibility determined more by pragmatic considerations than by rigid rules that should be applied globally. I think of all the steepled churches together with their medieval customs and robes for the clergy that have been exported to many parts of the former British Empire! I well remember preaching in a parish church in Colombo some years ago. It was a hot and humid tropical climate and the parish priest was putting on all his robes that were designed to keep the clergy warm in unheated medieval church buildings in north western Europe. He swung round to me and blurted out, "It's all your fault I have to wear this!" Isn't this a parable of what has happened so often through the history of the Church? It has held on to the forms and let go the principles.

Right through history there has, however, been an alternative "radical" pilgrim Church that has been marginalized, belittled and persecuted but which held to the original flexibility and vision. Broadbent and John Kennedy[7] give a remarkable history of this stream of witness that has sought to remain true to the original pattern of the Founder. In discussing structures in the Body of Christ we need to discern the principles.

The Structures in the Ministry of Jesus

Jesus gave little information as to how the Church should function after his departure. He did not speak about structures or buildings for the Church except that it would be built on the Rock

---

[7] Broadbent 1931, Kennedy 1965.

and that the gates of Hell would not prevail against it.[8] He spoke more about relationships between his followers than rules and hierarchies. He showed his disciples how to handle those who did wrong rather than describe canon laws or lists of rules.[9] He exhorted them to be servants to those for whom they were responsible rather than to lord it over the flock with popes, bishops and hierarchies.[10] We only have two passages and three mentions in all of the Gospels of the Greek word *ekklesia* which we translate as "church". Jesus did not teach us about the forms in his earthly ministry. He did set an example of how best to go about our ministry. Was he therefore giving the freedom for every age and every culture to be free to express the **form** of the structures best fitted for their situation?[11]

We find that there were three essential structures which Jesus used for his ministry to be effective. This is a pattern which we ought to carefully observe, and in so doing, find that many of the historical and present-day structural weaknesses and distortions in the Church could be addressed were we to apply the same.

First Jesus called the Twelve to be with him as disciples. The Twelve was his **discipling or training structure**. Later he sent out the Twelve, and then the seventy, two by two. These pairs became "sent-ones" or apostles who went out to minister and then report back to the Master who had sent them. While his disciples were itinerating, what was Jesus doing? We are not sure, but Luke 10:18 would hint that he was interceding for them. Here we have **the sending or apostolic structure**. The third structure Jesus used was not his own, it was the synagogue. Every Sabbath, Jesus was accustomed to go to the synagogue and gather with God's people for fellowship, prayer and ministry of the Word. This was the **gathering or ecclesial structure**. The fact that Jesus habitually went to the synagogue even though most of the authorities resented or rejected him and his ministry is important. It is an indication of the principle of the need for such a structure for the Church.[12] It is

---

[8] Matthew 16:18.
[9] Matthew 18:17.
[10] Matthew 20:27.
[11] Peters 1981:168-170.
[12] Winter 1993b:45-57. Winter shows the fundamental importance for both strategy and example of the network of Jewish synagogues in the Holy Land and throughout the world.

therefore not surprising that the synagogue became the model for the local congregations that developed once the post-Pentecost Jewish synagogues expelled the Christians.

These were the three structures in Jesus' ministry. They formed a trinity of interlinking structures that modelled the Trinity of the Godhead; both being a unity yet with a triple internal differentiation of function. There is the one militant Church with three modes of operating for the one goal of world evangelization. This goal could be symbolized by a target with a bulls-eye:

World Evangelization

Each of the three structures are interlinked in the ministry of Jesus. This pattern projected to the future ultimately would have world evangelization as its goal, but this could only be central as all operate together, emphasizing their special giftings and callings. No single structure can function well on its own and keep that over-arching goal central to its ministry. The structure of the Church in the ministry of Jesus could be portrayed like this:

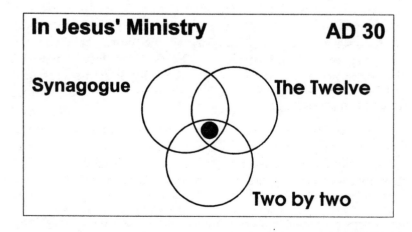

There is a wholesome balance in the way the Lord Jesus Christ integrated these three. The ultimate achievement of his goal for world evangelization could not have been achieved by any one or two of these structures for all were essential.

The Structures in the Old Testament

In embryo we see the same pattern in the Old Testament. Before the Exile in Babylon and Persia the tripartite structure was also discernible.

The first is the gathering and worship structure of the tabernacle and temple with its Priests. After the exile the synagogue system was developed both for the returned exiles in their homeland, and also among the large number of Diaspora Jews scattered across the known world.

Separate from them were the prophets who ministered largely from outside the normal worship systems while still remaining part of the people of God, and yet who ministered into the corporate life of the people of God. In this they approximated to the New Testament apostolic pattern. Moses was the supreme Old Testament prophet or apostle (church planter?!). He was the initiator under God of the whole worship system and appointed the Aaronic priesthood, system of laws and sacrifices and the tabernacle, though he himself was never a priest.

When things went badly wrong in the life of the people of Israel, it was the prophets who intervened and challenged the people to return to God. In the case of Samuel, where the priesthood had failed so miserably, we find that he had to take over many of the functions of priest although he was not a Levite.[13] For the prophets to have an effective ministry they had to be fully identified with God's people as well as being separate from the structures – there had to be both spiritual accountability and structural separateness.

There are few descriptions in Old Testament times of discipling structures, though there are little indications that such existed. Elisha's miraculous floating of the axe-head in 2 Kings 6 was lost in the work of building a school for the sons of the prophets – the first known Bible school? Then after the Exile, we find the

---

[13] 1 Samuel 16:5, et.al.

development where important leaders such as Gamaliel gathered disciples around him whom he taught.[14] That John and then Jesus should have a following of disciples was seen as perfectly normal.

The Structures in the Ministry of the Church in Acts

We find the same tripartite structure developing in the last half of Acts. This was never specifically taught as such, but the Holy Spirit worked in the hearts of the leaders to develop a pattern closely akin to that used by the Lord Jesus himself. In Acts 13 we find the first missionary-sending church in Antioch, and it was the Holy Spirit himself who gave the guidance about a separate apostolic structure:

> Now in the church at Antioch there were prophets and
> teachers, ... While they were worshipping the Lord and
> fasting, the Holy Spirit said, "Set apart for me Barnabas and
> Saul for the work to which I have called them." Then after
> fasting and praying they laid hands on them and sent them
> out.[15]

Many have used this passage incorrectly to 'prove' that the **only** God-given structure for mission is the local church. I would modify this statement to say that the local church is fundamental to mission, but not the only structure for mission. Later in this chapter I want to address this issue more carefully in the light of our present-day experience. In this I am not wanting to demean the vital, fundamental role of the local church in missions, but rather to show that no local church has the structure and gifting to initiate and sustain a successful cross-cultural mission thrust without forming or linking up with an apostolic structure with operational autonomy that is fitted to do the task. Note the following evidence from Scripture here of an apostolic structure emerging:

1. Paul and Barnabas had already been called by the Holy Spirit for the ministry of taking the gospel to the Gentiles. This we also know from the story of Paul's conversion. They were not called by the local church, but the local church recognized the call of the Holy Spirit on them, and they let them go.

---

[14] Acts 22:3.
[15] Acts 13:1-4.

2. Paul and Barnabas were to be set apart (from the ministry and activities of the local church). What is this but another structure? We see that Paul and Barnabas then had to take many operational decisions on their own – they were directed by the Holy Spirit as to where they went. They also decided to take John Mark with them – he soon became the first missionary casualty.[16] Although the Scripture is silent on this, we could wonder if they should have consulted more with the other leaders in Antioch, and possibly avoided this problem!

3. The word used for sending away Paul and Barnabas is instructive. If the Antioch church had been sending them as their apostles, the word derived from the verb *apostello* would have been used, however the word *apoluo* was used. This has more the concept of releasing, setting loose, sending away. In the following verse we see the Holy Spirit taking command by the use of the stronger word *ekpempo*, meaning sent forth by the Holy Spirit. The impression given is of two men being pushed out with an authority and urgency that was not from the local church but from the Lord himself, and the church recognized this in releasing them. They committed them to the Lord with fasting and prayer at that point, and surely thereafter in an ongoing ministry of intercession.

4. The two apostles returned to Antioch to give account of all that had transpired and then re-integrated into the life of the local church. So, though there was a separate apostolic structure, it was not autonomous in principle, but remained accountable to the church from which they had gone yet without an operational control from the church. They were still members and part of that local church with an accountability implied in that relationship and they re-integrated into the fellowship for they stayed "no little time with the disciples". They were never seen as anything but belonging to the church in Antioch even though there were long periods when they were operationally and structurally separate when on assignment by the Holy Spirit.

It was only in Paul's second missionary journey do we find the third structure developing. In Acts 16 we find Paul enlarging his team with Timothy and, by implication, Luke and others. Paul was not only a preacher-evangelist, but also a discipler of others on the

---

[16] Acts 15:37.

team. From a careful reading of the letters of Paul, it would appear that at one time or another there were 40 or so people involved in a team with him. It would be surprising if the apostles had not followed in the pattern of the Lord Jesus in developing new generations of leaders. Paul explicitly advocated this to Timothy.[17]

The evidence is that the early church had pragmatically developed a pattern of ministry and structures close to that used by the Lord Jesus. The diagram below illustrates this. The tragedy is that for the most part we have lost that balance evident in Acts.

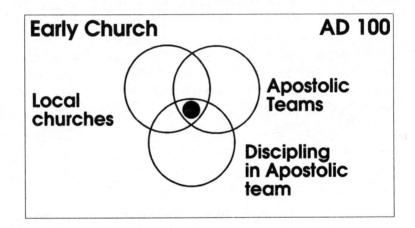

Structures in the teaching of the Epistles

Here I draw upon one significant passage in Ephesians where Paul indicates this three-fold ministry of the Church and the involvement of its entire leadership and the varieties of ministry giftings:

> And his gifts were that some should be apostles, some prophets, some evangelists, some pastors and teachers, to equip the saints for the work of ministry, for building up the body of Christ, until we all attain to the unity of the faith and of the knowledge of the Son of God, to mature manhood ...[18]

---

[17] 2 Timothy 2:2.
[18] Ephesians 4:11-12.

Many translations, including the KJV, RV and others add a comma after 'saints' which imply that the three ministries were for the official appointees of the Church with applauding spectator congregations. What was intended is a total mobilization of the entire membership of the Church for ministry to the world and building up the body, hence the omission of the comma here. The members of the pastoral team were to be facilitators rather than performers.

The three aims of the Holy Spirit's ministry gifting each need a specific structure within which to operate effectively. This passage is an indication that the three-fold structure of the body of Christ proposed has a scriptural and theological basis in the Church.

In this model the structure for equipping the saints is the local church. It is in that fellowship environment that the saints grow in grace and in relationships. The predominant ministry gifting is that of pastor and prophet, but with the other ministry gifts contributing.

The structure for ministry is outreach to the wider world or mission – whether local evangelism or cross-cultural outreach. Here the ministry of the evangelist and apostle predominate, but the implication of the text is that ALL the saints are to be equipped for the ministry. The Bible never divides the people of God into clergy and laity – that is a legacy of an incomplete Reformation and a hierarchical system imposed after New Testament times. In spite of the many books written by Evangelicals on laymen and the laity, the word is never used in this way in Scripture. All God's people should be ministers – some are recognized to have special gifting for leadership roles or for setting apart for specific ministry such as apostleship, teaching, pastoring, and so on.

The structure for building up the body includes the whole range of teaching and training mechanisms. In today's world this could be everything from Sunday Schools to Graduate Seminaries. The predominant ministry associated with this are the teachers.

However these ministry gifts overlap both in individuals, and in structures. There is a complementary wholeness and underlying unity within a flexibility and fluidity in individual gifting and in the basic structures when the Body is functioning under the anointing of the Holy Spirit. This flexibility also opens up the way for not only recognizing the functioning of ministry gifts within a local assembly, but also much more widely. Robert Brow in his book

The Twenty Century Church[19] speaks of **two** complementary structures for the Church and helpfully likens them to the body (ecclesiastical structures) and the bloodstream (mission structures); one is fixed and parochial the other is flexible and for serving the whole Church.

The value of such a perspective of the body of Christ will become apparent as we look briefly at the historical failures which have so limited the effectiveness of the Church in mission. One of the problems with not seeing the Church as a tripartite structure is that all the ministries of the Church as listed above and in 1 Corinthians 12:28 have to be fitted into the one structure, the local church. Where is the place of the apostle or the evangelist or even for a prophet in today's Church? Calvin tried to get round this problem by stating that the function of apostles and evangelists had ceased in the special sense,[20] but with hindsight we see how inadequate that position was. The more likely reason for the disappearance of apostles, evangelists and roving teachers is that there were no longer the wider and more fluid structures necessary within which they could operate. These ministries were too uncomfortable for the rigidities of a static and hierarchical leadership and were eliminated. We still have difficulty in fitting these ministries into our structural model of "church" today.

In the last two centuries movements have sprung up as an effort to remedy that apparent lack of apostles. Specific examples can be cited such as the Catholic Apostolic Church (Irvingites) in the last century and, more recently in this century within parts of the Pentecostal Movement in which the apostles became the leading figures in a theocratic church government. However the real issue is not the need to restore the rank of apostles or prophets to the local churches or denominations, but the need for an apostolic structure separate from that of a local church or denomination.

In recent years the ministry of an evangelist was given wide acceptability by such great men as Billy Graham, but, generally speaking, evangelists are seen to be loose cannons and a law unto themselves. Where do they fit? The nadir of this came in the last few years with tragic examples of televangelists who fell into the sins of pride, greed and immorality because there was no

---

[19] Brow 1968:85-91.
[20] Calvin 1536:Vol 2,319.

accountability structure within the Church of today into which they could fit and play their contributory part.

For the full range of biblical ministries to operate in a biblical way, we need to return to a biblical pattern of structures. I am not advocating a return to the forms of the New Testament Church, which were often more moulded by culture, but rather to the principles that underlie them. The actual structures themselves in any given period of history or in any given culture will have their own appropriate individualities. Even today, the Western mission models that have developed since Carey may not be the best for Brazilian, or Chinese, or Ukrainian missions in the twenty-first century, but the principle of the need for mission structures remains valid. Likewise Western theological training systems have already proved too rigid and expensive in Latin America and Africa, and other alternatives have been developed – but the principle of disciple-training structures is independent of century and of culture.

I have only developed this concept here in relation to one passage relating to the New Testament Church. More could be derived from other passages in Acts, the Pastoral Epistles, Hebrews and Revelation. George Peters in his book, A Theology of Church Growth,[21] covers some of this ground, but in part only. Surely this is an area worth further study!

---

[21] Peters 1981:163-183.

Chapter 15

A 2000-Year History of Church Structures

Church Structures between the New Testament Church and the Reformation

It is astonishing how quickly the concept of mobile apostles who planted churches in hitherto unevangelized regions was changed into settled elders and later territorial bishops. The patterns used by the Lord Jesus Christ and Paul for mission were abandoned and the Church rapidly became institutionalized and more concerned with defence against heresies than aggressive advancement. David Bosch made a pertinent comment,

> There can be no doubt that as early as the late first century, a shift in the understanding of the Church had set in. In fact, some of the New Testament texts already reflect a situation where the mobile ministry of apostles, prophets and evangelists was beginning to give way to the settled ministry of bishops (elders) and deacons. The creative tension between these two dynamics of the Church's ministry gradually collapsed in favour of the second.[22]

Increasingly, over the ensuing centuries, the Church began to be equated with the complex and rigid geographical systems of supranational ecclesiastical empires with archbishops in provinces, bishops in dioceses and priests in parishes. The mission of the Church became less and less that of the Lord Jesus Christ.

It was only in the rise of monasticism in the third century that another mechanism for mission emerged, imperfect though it may have been. The reasons for its rise were rarely mission but more often a desire to escape from the wickedness of the world. It was this desire to be separate from the world that often protected these men and women from the political acquiescence, open carnality and lack of vision that characterized the institutional Church and also allowed a missionary dimension within monasticism. This structure, by default and rarely by design, became the successor to the apostolic structures of primitive Christianity. For the following 1,500 years virtually the only structure that initiated and sustained

---

[22] Bosch 1991:201.

any mission programme was monastic – whether Eastern, Orthodox, Celtic or Roman Catholic. Almost every significant advance beyond the boundaries of the Roman Empire and even consolidation within its confines was due to the dedicated and courageous efforts of numerous individual monks or monastic orders.

It is hard for us in our pluralistic age to comprehend how totalitarian the Church of the Middle Ages had become in lands where Christianity was officially embraced by the rulers. Every part of life in Christian Europe was dominated by the Church. The Church had total control over the educational systems that existed. From the latter part of the eleventh century onwards[23] this included the universities, which were predominantly for the study of theology and preparation of those who would lead the Church. So a discipling structure of a sort also existed, though the content of the teaching and expectations of spirituality were far from the biblical norm.

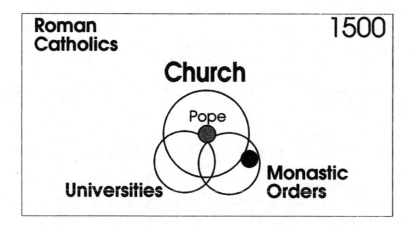

In the Middle Ages in the Eastern and especially the Western Churches, a functioning tripartite structure had emerged that had its parallels to the New Testament model,[24] but had encrusted and

---

[23] The first university was Bologna, which was founded at the end of the eleventh century. Others followed: Oxford 1167/8, Cambridge 1209, Sorbonne 1257, Montpellier 1289, Rome 1303.

[24] The Cistercians (and their mission to eastern Europe) were founded in 1098, Franciscans in 1209 and Dominicans in 1215.

nullified the doctrines of the New Testament with traditions, precepts of men and accretions from paganism. So, though the terminology had changed, the circles used above for New Testament times remain the same even though distorted. Note that the centre of gravity of the Church became that of its leader – whether a Pope (P), Catholicos or Metropolitan; the central aim was not the goal of world evangelization but the accretion of power to the centre of the ecclesiastical empire.

Church Structures between the Reformation and William Carey

Change had to come; yet how hard it was to initiate any change that would not be snuffed out by the political powers of the time. Every citizen had to show outward conformity to the religion of the state. This conformity emerged over the centuries from the teaching of Augustine in his work *The City of God* and led inexorably to the extreme in the founding of the infamous Inquisition in 1215 at the fourth Council of Lateran. In 1232 the Pope gave the Dominicans the control of this terrible instrument of repression. It reached its zenith in the latter part of the fifteenth century. Its power was greatest in the Roman Catholic lands of Italy and France and especially in areas dominated by Spain,[25] which was then the world's major superpower. The survival of the Reformation in the prevailing bigotry and fanaticism of the age was a miracle.

The Reformation was a necessity. Although theology was largely reformed, the inadequate structures then existing were unwittingly deformed. The importance of restructuring did not seem to have been noticed in the effort to get rid of the institutions that had been used for oppression and wickedness. New wine needed new wineskins, but the old wineskins were not replaced.

The ecclesiastical empire model of the Church that the Reformers inherited was hardly touched. The Roman Catholic

---

[25] Initially the Inquisition was instituted to ferret out the "heretic" French Albigensians and Italian Waldensians and later Jews and Muslims who outwardly professed Christianity to avoid deportation but secretly retained their own religions. Later, however, it became an instrument of terror for all dissent to Rome. This gives a graphic and terrible picture of the power of the Inquisition. Once accused a victim had no hope of mercy or escape let alone a fair hearing at a trial. The Roman Catholic

concept of a State or National Church together with the episcopal and parochial system was retained by the Lutherans and Anglicans and the parochial system by the Genevan Reformers. It is this model that still clouds our understanding of the real nature and structure of the Church and wrongly divides God's people into a spiritual aristocracy of clergy and lesser common people known as the laity.

The monastic orders that had so contributed to what expansion the Church had achieved in the previous 1200 years were eliminated in the lands dominated by the Reformation. Their extensive lands and buildings were expropriated by the State or wealthy individuals. The sputtering candle of mission as a component of the Church was largely eclipsed in main-stream Protestant thinking for the next three centuries. As pointed out in Chapter 3, the impetus of the Reformation and also the colonial expansion of Portugal and Spain beyond Europe was a stimulus to the Catholics to retain and develop the monastic missionary orders. The result was a massive growth of the Roman Catholic Church in the New World and many parts of Asia during this time of virtual inactivity by Protestants.

The post-Reformation universities where theology was studied and pastors and ministers trained for the ministry became increasingly independent of the Church. The necessary accountability to the Church as a whole for holiness of life and focus of vision was cut. Under the influence of the Enlightenment they became secularized and theological teaching largely humanized and liberal. One sad outgrowth of this was the prevailing opinion still with us: that theological education is more for attaining academic qualifications and less for training the next generation of godly leaders for ministry in the Body of Christ. That part of the Church which is most concerned with discipling and training was effectually lost to the Body.

The tripartite structure of the Church no longer existed in Protestantism. In the quest for proclaiming a pure biblical theology, the need for a balanced and biblical structural model for the Church had been lost and no one seemed to notice. It is this poor foundation that has contributed to lack of vision for mission and the fragmentation of the Protestant Church. The one overarching and unifying goal of prayer for and action towards world evangelization would have drawn Christians together as nothing else could have done. This, to me, is one of the great tragedies of the half millennium that has passed since the Reformation began. Below is a portrayal of the deficient structures of the Church in Protestantism for those 300 years of ignorance of, or even disobedience to, the Great Commission and caused that sinful delay.

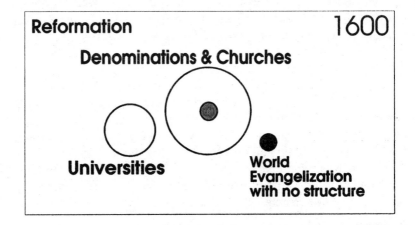

Notice that the goal of world evangelization is outside any of the existing circles of structure, and the discipling circle is an independent entity and a shadow of what it should be. The remaining structures had other subsidiary goals such as stability and continuity or academic excellence. There is no circle for an apostolic structure and so mission in Protestantism, with a few isolated exceptions, enters its nearly 300-year wilderness experience which only began to end just 200 years ago.

The Structural Reformation begun

William Carey advocated *means* for the conversion of the heathen to which reference was made at the beginning of this section. These means were firstly fervent, united and importunate prayer by the churches for world evangelization and secondly "...in the exerting of ourselves in the use of means for the obtaining of those things we pray for..."[26] The exertions to which he pointed were the formation of a missionary society with a committee of

---

[26] Carey 1792:61-2.

dedicated believers and supported by the contributions of churches and individual Christians for sending out missionaries to the ends of the earth.

The only model Carey had to hand were those of the religious societies that had become a part of the Anglo-Saxon cultural heritage of the time and of the secular and highly successful East India Companies of The Netherlands and Britain. He perhaps did not then perceive how biblical was his proposal nor how far-reaching would be its consequences. What he was suggesting was a restoration of that missing circle of structure – not the Roman Catholic monastic model, but more close to the Pauline model of Acts 13 *et seq*. He would have preferred missionary societies supported by all denominations, but admitted,

> "I do not mean by this in any way to confine it (*the society*) to one denomination of Christians. I wish with all my heart that everyone who loves our Lord Jesus Christ in sincerity would in some way or other engage in it. But in the present divided state of Christendom it would be more likely for good to be done by each denomination engaging separately in the work than if they were to embark in it together. There is room for us all, without interfering with each other…"

Wise and prophetic words uttered at a time when no single denomination had even begun such an enterprise. However it was not long before non-denominational societies were begun – The London Missionary Society in 1795,[27] the American Board for Foreign Missions in 1810, the Basel Mission in Switzerland in 1815 and the Rhenish Mission in Germany in 1827. The massive multiplication of interdenominational "faith" missions was still two generations in the future.

The Evangelical Awakening of the eighteenth century and the development of missionary societies proved to be the major contributory cause to the massive growth of Evangelicals in the world today. This I sought to describe in the previous chapter. It is too little known. Far too many Christians have a negative view of missions. The small and seemingly insignificant beginnings are bearing astonishing fruit today. To give one example, SIM

---

[27] The LMS began as an interdenominational society but gradually became more the denominational arm of the Congregational Church. In 1977 it became the Council for World Mission.

International has become one of the largest church planting missions in the world. Through the work of their 2,000 missionaries and their predecessors a family of churches has come into being of probably 4-5 million Christians, which would make it one of the larger evangelical denominations in the world – were they to categorize them in this way! However the historical development of missions, the mistakes made, the lessons learned, the strategies developed are beyond the scope of this book. My aim here is to focus on the structural implications for the Body of Christ.

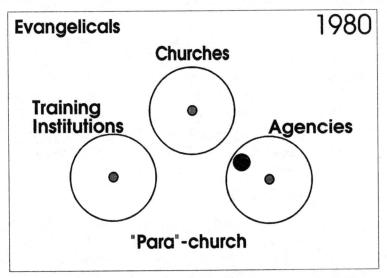

Parallel to the development of missionary-sending societies was the proliferation of evangelical agencies to meet a wide range of social and spiritual needs in society and of the world. Then during the twentieth century an amazing number and variety of Bible Schools and discipling ministries arose which counteracted the tendency to liberal theology, dry intellectualism and spiritual deadness in the existing theological institutions. One only has to look in the Yellow Pages of any English-speaking city in the world, or the *UK Christian Handbook*[28] to see the fruit of that multiplication. Some of these agencies have become global multi-national "empires" with multi-million dollar incomes. The result has been that over these two centuries the three biblical structures

---

[28] Brierley 1996.

have been recovered, but without the needed inter-relatedness based on the unity of the Church which incorporates all three structures as essential for its effective functioning. What has emerged are three autonomous types of structures each with their own subsidiary goals (indicated by the smaller shaded circles). This can be illustrated as follows:

This sad trichotomization of the Church has resulted in a new word entering the English language, **para-church.** A number of unhealthy and inaccurate presuppositions lie behind the use of this term:

1. That the Church consists of the sum total of believers gathered in local churches and denominations.[29] While this is true for all individual Christians, it does not follow that the only valid biblical structures are local churches or groupings of local churches in denominations.

2. That any structure outside local churches and denominations is para-biblical and para-church. The very prefix **"para"** has a negative meaning.[30] This has conferred on non-local church or denominational bodies an unhealthy odour of unbiblicality. One might as well say that local churches and denominations are para-missions!

3. That all para-church agencies should function on sufferance until local churches or denominations get their act together and take over what was really their job in the first place. All para-church bodies should only be tolerated in the meanwhile but should be disbanded as soon as possible.

Later I will show the inherent problems and dangers in individual congregations or clusters of churches taking on the entire responsibility for training and mission. Some of the

---

[29] The net of inclusion varies according to the theological position of the Christian - should Roman Catholics, Mormons, Seventh-Day Adventists, or even Pentecostals and Charismatics be included? What about pluralistic denominations. It is not my purpose to pursue this issue here. I have had some criticisms from readers of *Operation World* because of which groups I counted as Evangelical, Protestant or even Christian.

[30] The Chambers Dictionary defines **para** as *"combining form* denoting beside; faulty; disordered; abnormal; false; ... closely resembling, or parallel to..."

newer streams of church life – especially those with a charismatic emphasis – go further and impatiently dismiss any structures that pre-date their movements as being unbiblical and to be completely by-passed in their apostolic ministries. Such arrogance is sooner or later punctured by the realities of the complexity of far-distant cross-cultural mission work.

4. That para-church agencies have usurped functions which rightly belong to a local church. This is often sadly true and should be put right. This trespassing has often been by default because all too often churches were not fulfilling their biblical role for world mission. There are many examples; to name a few:

- Missionaries have often been 'possessed' by the mission agency; it not being realized that accountability and pastoral care are a shared responsibility.

- Teaching on missions, recruitment and training of candidates is often left to the agency rather than seen as a function of a local church with the help of specialized agencies.

- Furloughs can be almost completely controlled by the agency with inadequate time for relatedness of the furloughing missionary to his home church.

There is a note of polarization and even confrontation introduced between local churches and agencies whenever the term is used. If anyone mentions para-church in my presence or comments that I am para-church because I am a member of a mission agency, I challenge that appellation and suggest a more biblical perspective if there is wise opportunity to do so.

There are real grounds for frustration and concern for all sides in the way that these developments have taken place – often with no prayerful fellowship between those concerned, and without any sense of the need for a unity in the Body in order to train the right leaders effectively and for world evangelization. We flounder, seeking solutions by lopping off dandelion heads rather than tackling the root of the problem. So what are the results?

1. Dynamic and visionary mission agencies with a clear agenda have been frustrated by the lack of vision and parochialism of the churches. They are saddened that there is not more support in the implementation of their vision for world evangelization.

There has therefore been too much independent action in isolation from the wider Body of Christ.

2. Church leaders are dismayed by the multiplicity of agencies competing for the interest and support of their congregations. These importunings are seen as plundering local churches of their best members and scarce finances. All too often they are exhorted to generosity yet with no accountability expected to the donors from the recipients. The para-church bodies are seen as predatory and just "using" the churches as a resource for their own goals which are not necessarily primarily the Great Commission. Below is a view of structures from this perspective where local churches are being used and even abused by the other structures. Sadly there is truth in these allegations.

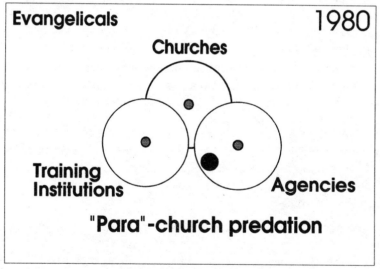

Without fully realizing it, all are victims of centuries of fundamental misunderstandings about the nature of the Church and the three types of interdependent structures required for it to fulfil its destiny as God's means for world evangelization. Just as the Church needs a variety of ministries, it also needs a variety of structures within which those varied ministries can best be exercised. Sadly, independence and competition are more characteristic of today's Christian world than interdependence, respect and co-operation for the one mission God gave us.

We need to recover the basic truth that the Body of Christ is larger than the sum total of congregations and denominations, and that all who are involved in any of the three structures are part of the Church of the Lord Jesus Christ. This requires unity in objectives, accountability in ministry and interdependence in relationships if we are to function as an effective instrument in the hand of God. Without it our overall effectiveness is crippled. Look at these three structures again.

1. Theological education

The legacy of the Reformation period was a theological education system which all-too-often prized academic qualifications above spirituality and the spiritual applicability of the subject matter taught. This separation of theological education from the end-users of those educated has been so large that it is taking a long time to rectify. Academic freedom led to spiritual anarchy. Theological students with little spiritual screening and testing for gifts and calling went for studies in a range of subjects that were not necessarily adequate or relevant for the ministries in which they were later to engage and where world evangelization was perceived irrelevant. It opened up the whole theological education system to formalism, syncretization with the prevailing academic culture and even error. The rise of theological liberalism in the theological faculties of universities in the nineteenth century crippled the spiritual effectiveness of a majority of mainline denominations as this education bore bitter fruit. We still reel from the effects of this apostasy.

Evangelical theological institutions have also not had a good record in the past of making themselves accountable to their end-users: the churches, ministries and mission agencies with whom their graduates will serve. This has been changing for the better in recent years.

Our theological institutions have probably been the greatest factor in the "Sinful Delay"! That is a sweeping generalization that may be unnecessarily unkind, but there is much truth in it. It would be an interesting study to find out which individuals have made the greatest impact on the evangelization of the world, and how relevant was their theological training, if they had any at all. Another revealing investigation would be to find out how many pastors received any teaching on missiology before going into a church ministry. The results would be sobering, and force us to ask the question as to whether theological education in a given school has been a help or a hindrance for world evangelization. David Bosch spoke of missiology in the realm of theology in this way:[31]

> "...missiology acts as a gadfly in the house of theology, creating unrest and resisting complacency, opposing every ecclesiastical impulse to self-preservation, every desire to stay what we are, every inclination toward provincialism and parochialism, every fragmentation of humanity into regional or ideological blocs, every exploitation of some sectors of humanity by the powerful, every religious, ideological, or cultural imperialism, and every exaltation of the self-sufficiency of the individual over other people or over other parts of creation."

Is it any wonder that theological schools do not want such gadflies that irritate and disturb entrenched attitudes, rigid structures and deficient theologies!

There is a commendable change in many schools around the world in seeking to rectify this independent spirit and to actually consult carefully about student selection and suitability and also curriculum applicability for intended ministry. However we need to see a far greater flexibility and adaptability in faculty, curriculum, modularity, transferability of credits, and varieties of routes to qualifications that are fully integrated into the career development of those in Christian service of which mission is at its very heart. This will come as we all see ourselves as important components of the one Body of Christ and serving one another.

During the Global Conference on World Evangelization in Pretoria, South Africa in 1997 a Declaration was issued by the Consultation of 250 Principals and Deans of Theological institutions. This remarkable document, for the first time in history, bound together a large peer group of such leaders to a commitment to put missions at the heart of their vision and teaching curriculum. This declaration is given in chapter 18.

---

[31] Bosch 1991:496.

2. Mission Agencies or Societies

The emergence of religious societies in the seventeenth and eighteenth centuries in Britain and elsewhere was a phenomenon made necessary by the general passivity and lack of appropriate structures in the Church of the time. It rapidly became apparent that these societies or agencies were not just a stop-gap measure to compensate for the inability of the denominations of the time to send missionaries, but that they were an essential component if world evangelization were ever to be advanced. The high level of prayer and financial support given by individual Christians to these agencies indicated their affirmation that such structures were right and valid.

Ralph Winter wrote a seminal article in the Evangelical Missions Quarterly in 1971 entitled *Churches need missions because modalities need sodalities*.[32] He challenged the whole concept that missions are outmoded, anachronistic dinosaurs from a bygone age of church history that should be dismantled like scaffolding as soon as possible once the churches get their act together. He cogently proved the essentiality for the Church of having both *modalities* (structured churches) and *sodalities* (societies, fellowships, mission agencies). Whenever one swallows up the other – whether at home (get rid of mission agencies) or overseas (absorb the mission into the indigenous church) the cause of world evangelization suffers and the vision dies.

It is interesting to observe that denominational mission agencies were successful and innovative to the extent that they were given freedom of action. The tendency over the decades was for the denominational structures in the sending and receiving countries to take control of the mission enterprise and erode that freedom. Many of the older denominational mission agencies today are little more than a channel for fraternal workers or funding to go to those national churches planted on the former mission fields. The same pattern emerged interdenominationally when the International Missionary Council was integrated in the World Council of Churches in 1961 – this subversion or even betrayal of mission

---

[32] Winter, *Evangelical Missions Quarterly* June 1971:193. This article was one of the first good defences of the fact that the Church is more than local churches, but needs apostolic structures as an essential and abiding component for spiritual survival and growth.

virtually ended what had begun earlier in the century as a vital thrust for world evangelization. In no way can an ecclesiastical structure ever manage a mission enterprise without sacrificing the freedom of action essential for the accomplishment of that vision. Mission agencies are not a temporary expedient to be tolerated for the moment, but a vital component of the Church to enable the Church to be what God intended. This is why we have to work towards a deep level of fellowship and mutual accountability for mission in the twenty-first century.

Denominational missions by their very nature are forced into an accountability to the denomination because this is usually the main or sole source of funding and workers. However there is a danger that this support become depersonalized and an obligation for inclusion in the annual budget. Many denominational missions are seeking to rectify this by tying individual missionaries to specific congregations.

Interdenominational missions do not have this restriction, but in their greater freedom from direct accountability to denominational and congregational structures, they can become too independent and secretive. They, in turn, can become an institutionalized and moribund relic of a formerly successful ministry. There are many agencies that should have closed their doors long ago and passed on their assets to others more able to cope with a new mission paradigm. But without that accountability, who is to tell them do this? Our Christian world is cluttered with many such.

The sheer complexity of launching and sustaining a far-distant cross-cultural mission thrust increased the importance of the mission agency to the point that it actually infringed on the ministry prerogatives of local churches. The result was either an abdication of local churches from those responsibilities or a reaction against the apparent predatory plundering of the finances, resources and most useful members of the congregation.

The twentieth century has been notable for the massive multiplication of agencies for home and foreign mission. We began the century with less than 200 known mission agencies, but by its end we will have tens of thousands scattered across nearly every country in the world. The massive accretion of power and finances to such agencies is both threatening to the churches and dangerous to the agencies unless accountability and effective structural links are established.

This had to change. Modern communications, swift air travel between home church and field and the more ready availability of funds are forcing that change. These gave strength to many home churches to expect more say in selection, support, pastoral care of missionaries and even decision making on the field where their missionaries were involved. Some churches went even further and sought to bypass any mission structure by sending their missionaries direct to the field.

Mission agencies that are insensitive to these trends will suffer loss. They need humbly to put right the unwitting independence of action and plundering of local church resources of the past and see the need for a new way of working together with churches with the vision for involvement in obeying the Great Commission.

What about the independent missionary? Why bother with mission agencies at all, and be free of all the red tape and controls? Gordon Olson in his book,[33] *What in the World is God Doing?* gives powerful arguments to show the positives, yet expose the serious inadequacies inherent in missionaries operating independently. He himself went through his first term as an independent missionary. As we have seen, the lone ranger missionary should be the exception rather than the rule. In our mission history we have successful lone pioneers like Mary Slessor of Calabar and George Hunter of Xinjiang, but there are many more who went alone and whose ministries were, at best, mediocre and at worst disastrous for themselves as well as others.. The biblical pattern is working as a team. The independent missionary usually lacks continuity in ministry, supervision, accountability and pastoral care on the field. There are rarely adequate safety nets in the event of sickness, calamities, moral failures, breakdown of logistical or financial support. There is no help in practicalities such as for obtaining visas, representation before the authorities, enculturalization on the field or for finding replacement workers at furlough time. In short, it is a recipe for disaster.

---

[33] Olsen1988:255-256.

3. Local Churches

"The local church is the launch pad for missions" is a slogan often used by Leslie Brierley, my honoured predecessor as WEC's International Director for Research. How true this is, but how rarely is this true in practice. The great majority of churches that preach the gospel have never sent out a missionary, never prayed out labourers into the mission fields of the world and never have any meaningful involvement in prayer. The principle is right but the plain fact is that very few of these launch pads exist, and many that do are deficient launchers. Below are given some Protestant figures from the 1993 edition of *Operation World* which prove this point:

Country	Congregations	Missionaries	Missys. per cong
Singapore	393	567	1.44
Norway	2,341	1,654	0.71
Finland	1,965	1,317	0.67
New Zealand	3,730	1,701	0.46
Sweden	8,332	1,749	0.21
USA	383,328	59,074	0.15
UK	46,262	7,012	0.15
Germany	23,487	3,510	0.15
India	97,796	11,284	0.12
Japan	6,581	407	0.06
Korea	37,985	2,237	0.06
Brazil	148,976	2,755	0.02
Total	761,176	93,267	0.12

Shaded countries are newer-sending countries.

This table shows the astonishing fact that of all the major missionary-sending nations only in Singapore have Protestant churches sent out more missionaries than there are congregations. The major missionary-sending countries listed below have nearly half the world's Protestant congregations, but between them these congregations, on average, are only sending out one missionary for approximately every eight churches. In many cases the situation is much worse: fewer churches actually send missionaries because, those that do, often send out more than one. I would estimate that in the West 90% of all Protestant churches, as a congregation, have no direct commitment to, or involvement with, a real live missionary. Mission has become a vague concept that is so broad as to include almost any activity the church does, or if that activity is overseas, it is little more than giving to humanitarian projects or an annual donation to the denominational mission body.

George Verwer of Operation Mobilization and Pari Rickard of Youth With A Mission lead the "Mobilizing New Missionaries Network." Their passionate message is that we need to recruit 200,000 new missionaries by the year 2000 for the completion of the task.[34] That number seems so impossible, but when one sees how few churches are involved in sending a missionary, the recruitment may not be so unrealistic were they to be mobilized.

The majority of Protestant churches are not involved in the primary task of the church – either through ignorance or lack of vision. Few even of those churches actually involved in sending and supporting missionaries have actually put their act together with a meaningful structure, strategy and involvement that really functions. While writing this book and in travel around the world I have sought for good models of congregations with a well integrated and effective mission programme for local evangelism and involvement in global missions. They are hard to find!

In reading through the book *Churches that Obey, taking the Great Commission Seriously*,[35] I saw that all the 21 examples given of congregations have their good points, but few give a rounded model that I would recommend for emulation elsewhere, and some of those congregations have already changed their policy since the writing of that book. More needs to be written giving examples of successful mission-minded churches from around the world.

Even with those local churches that have had a good mission record, it is rare to find long term consistency. Great mission-minded churches of the past have not always maintained that vision, or have been diverted into specializations such as only supporting nationals or placing exclusive emphasis on a particular region or type of ministry. It is astonishing to find out how few congregations have been successful and consistent over decades and several generations of pastors. Sudden changes in mission policies, arbitrary changes in missionary support levels that

---

[34] The Acts 13 Vision of George Verwer has been actively promoted by him since 1996 as a workable model for sharing out the responsibility among Protestant congregations around the world. Contact the OM base nearest you for more details.
[35] Forster & Richard 1995.

accompany leadership changes or local problems often precipitate missionaries on the fields into a crisis in which they are powerless and voiceless, but which fundamentally affects their futures.

Some of the most assiduous efforts at sending missionaries are to be found among Jehovah's Witnesses, Mormons and others who claim that their own group alone has the "truth." To our shame, such involvement is rare in evangelical congregations. How is it in your own congregation? There are many books and resources that could help you.[36] In chapter 17 I list a number of different ideas for implementation.

---

[36] Beals 1995; Pirolo 1991; Stearns 1991:160-194.

Chapter 16

Who Sends the Missionaries?

This is a key question. Is it the local church, the denominational leadership, the mission agency, the Bible school, or is it really God's responsibility? Many examples of each could be given – both mission endeavours that were highly successful and that were ghastly failures. More recently there has arisen a strong voice promoting one model as the correct one – for the local church to be the only biblical structure. This has been a reaction to the historical fact that all too often the mission agencies were not only perceived to be the sending structure, but also, in practice, had become the only sending structure with the local church ignored or spurned.

At the outset it must be stressed that there is no one single **form** of sending structure for the Body of Christ – either in the Bible or in history. It is astonishing to see the variety of structures that God has used to further world evangelization. Before 1700 there were apostolic teams, wandering monks, papal envoys, mendicant orders, military orders, Jesuit 'commandos', colonial expansion for mission, migrant mission communities for spreading Christianity to non-Christian areas and peoples. After 1700 came the rise of missionary denominations like the Moravians, denominational, interdenominational, non-denominational, faith missions, direct-sending churches and so on.[37] All have their relevance for the time and culture in which they operated; all had their weaknesses and deficiencies – some very serious indeed, but the gospel, or some of it, was proclaimed, and the Kingdom of God extended in spite of these. However the **principle** of the need for a mission structure alongside that of congregational and denominational structures and undergirded by effective leadership training structures at home and for the emerging churches was basic to the lasting success of any of these models. The degree to which this tripartite partnership had developed to further that mission thrust determined the fruitfulness of that mission movement.

Who, then, actually *sends* the missionaries? Is it the local church, or the mission agency or even the training school? Have we

---

[37] Barnes 1902:436.

been polarized by a deficient view of the Church? A good case could be made from Scripture for any one of the three:

1. **The discipling/training structure.** Jesus sent out the 12 and then the 70 from the context of his discipling. Paul did the same. Thus it was in many cases of missionary sending by monastic orders through the ages. In modern times there have been some significant mission thrusts launched directly by training schools – for instance the Bethany Fellowship in Minneapolis, Minnesota, USA; Betel Brasiliero in João Pessoa, Brazil; and the Indonesian Missionary Fellowship, Batu, Java, Indonesia. This often resulted in the formation of a new mission agency and then a national denomination in lands where church planting was undertaken. The negatives:

   - a tendency for central control to be exercised by the leader
   - inadequate links with local churches at home
   - inhibition of the development of team and church leadership and innovation in ministry
   - subordination of the national churches to the aims and financial needs of the founding institution

2. **The church structure.** The Church in Antioch is the biblical example in which they sent away (*apelusan*) Paul and Barnabas and later the two teams of Paul with Silas[38] and Barnabas with Mark. However it must be stressed that the Greek word *apoluo* here is not a strong verb like *apostello* – it has more the meaning of releasing, setting loose or permitting to depart. It has more the picture of an impatient horse in a stable, which gallops out into the field when the door is opened. There is implied in the word a greater inner sending which comes from God. The Moravians were a direct-sending denomination for most of the eighteenth century, only finding that a mission-sustaining structure apart from the Church was necessary. In the nineteenth century a number of fellowships of churches developed a sophisticated system of direct sending of missionaries to the mission fields – notable examples being the Brethren movement and the Churches of Christ. In recent times an increasing number of churches in Singapore, USA and Britain have become direct-senders, but with mixed fortunes,

---

[38] Acts 15:40.

and with many painful failures. What are the weaknesses of this model?

a. Home church leaders are overburdened with the cares and complexities of mission work *and* home church problems. Either one or the other suffers. Usually an internal crisis at home distracts from the mission thrust and the effort is crippled and even collapses. Setting up an adequately gifted missions committee or board that operates largely autonomously from the church leadership can alleviate problems – effectually becoming a mission sending structure within the church.

b. Directive leadership from home results in decisions that are painful to mission personnel or damaging to the development of the work on the field.

c. There is usually inadequate cross-cultural gifting and experience both for the home leadership and for the training and preparation of missionaries.

d. Pastoral care for those on the field is rarely sufficient or timely in a crisis.

e. Church politics and culture of the home country imposes unnecessary restrictions or cultural patterns on the emerging churches.

f. The narrow, parochial support base limits exposure to the world-wide Church in all its complexities, and can inhibit advantageous partnerships emerging on the field with other missionaries and agencies.

g. There is rarely a strong enough team to provide a support structure on the field in a crisis situation.

3. **The apostolic structure.** It is interesting to see how once the church had laid hands on Paul and Barnabas, the team was augmented by the apostles who recruited Mark.[39] Later Paul recruited numerous others – Silas,[40] Luke, Timothy, and so on. We also find that Paul sent (Greek word: *apostello*) fellow workers to Corinth and Tychicus to Ephesus.[41] However this word is used only twice in the whole of the New Testament when referring to the sending by men. It is interesting that in

---

[39] Acts 13:5.
[40] Acts 15:40.
[41] 2 Corinthians 12:17; 2 Timothy 4:12.

Dutch and Afrikaans the word *mission* is rendered as *Zending* or *Sending*. Again this pattern of sending was common in the monastic orders – especially the Franciscans and Jesuits, and then with the interdenominational missions from the mid-nineteenth century on.

The Greek word *apostello* is used about 130 times in the New Testament, and all but two of those instances refer to God's action in sending, and in those two remaining instances, it was used by the Apostle Paul, as a mission leader, in the paragraph above. It is never used of a local church. Many push the Antioch church model to the point that they advocate that the leaders in a congregation should actively seek missionary candidates, recruit them and then send them. This is a laudable vision, but a dangerous one, and certainly not what happened in Acts 13 where it is the Holy Spirit who had given the initial call.[42] If there is not the stronger and deeper certainty of the Holy Spirit calling and sending the missionary, the pressures and trials on the field could lead to failure and tragedy. Recently I was in a Middle Eastern country where I was told of a church which had sent missionaries to plant a daughter church in that unresponsive field. A number of those sent were actually enlisted by the church and sent as their missionaries without those chosen having first had a prior specific leading from God. I was not surprised to hear that of these called in this way, hardly any of them lasted longer than a year on the field before returning home crushed.

Ultimately we must affirm that it is God, the Holy Spirit who calls to apostleship – as Paul testifies at the beginning of nine of his 13 letters.[43] The church becomes the hearer of the voice of the Holy Spirit and the secondary sender.

Yet the Church as a whole has a vital role in the sending of missionaries. Should we not rather see the sending as a function of all three structures of the ONE Church working in a mutually accountable partnership? This is the plea I make here. Any one structure that takes it upon itself to be THE sender is sure to find out that the negatives usually outweigh the positives. It is not a

---

[42] Acts 13:2.
[43] Romans 1:1;1 Corinthians 1:1; 2 Corinthians 1:1; Galatians 1:1Ephesians 1:1; Colossians 1:1; 1 Timothy 1:1; 2 Timothy 1:1; 1:11; Titus 1:1.

case of either/or, but of all three being part of the sending, each part of the Body having a different contribution to the sending. No one structure can be an adequate and completely self-sufficient sender of missionaries. I give a few examples of such inadequacies:

1. **Interdenominational Faith Missions** have been strong on pioneering and church planting, but very often weak on ecclesiology for the churches planted. My own agency shared in this weakness. Our membership was drawn from a wide variety of church backgrounds from Episcopal to Brethren and with theologies ranging from Reformed to Pentecostal. For too long we lived with a level of church government that was the lowest common denominator on structures and in theological teaching. The results were mixed. By 1984 we had WEC-related churches (we didn't call them 'denominations' – though that is what they were!) formed in many of our fields and a total constituency of possibly 300,000 people. In Liberia we planted churches that became the United Liberia Inland Church. On the coast among the Bassa the early missionaries planted churches that had pastors and deacons like a Baptist congregation, but inland among the Gio and Mano, were churches with elders and no pastors like the Brethren, and the whole related to a structure that was a hybrid of Presbyterian and Baptist! In 1984 we began the long and painful process of developing principles and adequate guidelines for church planting and development that would result in well-taught and well-led churches with evangelistic and mission outreach.[44] We should have done this long before, but we had not had a high enough view of the importance of the Church and its structures.

2. **The Christian Brethren** is a remarkable movement that began in Britain in the 1830s. The names of J.N. Darby, George Müller, Anthony N. Groves in Iraq (1828-1832) and India (1832-1853) and Fred Arnott in Central Africa are famous representatives of this movement. The Brethren, especially the Open Brethren, generated a large and vigorous movement of missionaries sent directly from their assembles. Even today, with a global constituency of a little over 1,000,000 believers, they have about 1,400 missionaries on the field. The results

---

[44] Woodford 1997. Brian Woodford, a leader in WEC International, wrote his doctoral thesis on the basic principles for planting churches by non-denominational mission agencies.

have been patchy to say the least. Direct sending with little adequate cross-cultural training before leaving for the field, and fields where there was little lateral accountability within a missionary team were the negative. The result was some brilliant successes, many agonies and not a few casualties. In only a relatively few countries did a strong network of indigenous assemblies arise. All too often the missionaries thought they were planting New Testament churches, but much of what developed was a caricature of Victorian Anglo-Saxon Evangelical Christianity with all its quirks and foibles.

3. **Celtic Christianity in the early Middle Ages** had a dynamism and commitment to scholarship and training, but a poor ecclesiology. When the crunch with the hierarchical structures of Roman Catholicism came, the Celtic uniqueness was swamped and ultimately vanished. This is not an endorsement for the strong hierarchical Catholic structure, but a recognition that the Celts had little hope before the immense organizational power and resources of Rome *because* they had no stable structure.

Singapore's mission force has grown significantly. Evangelicals have made their city state the premier mission-sending country in the world. The uniqueness of this mission force is that about 60% of these missionaries are sent directly from their churches. I was privileged to hear Lawrence Khong, pastor of Faith Community Baptist Church in Singapore, testify from his heart at the Global Conference on World Evangelization in Pretoria 1997. His congregation is one of the better known Cell Churches with a visionary programme for planting Cell Churches around the world. He started by asking forgiveness from mission agencies for his arrogance and pride in dismissing them as traditional structures that were outmoded and making the decision to go it alone in directly sending their own missionaries to other lands. Things began to go wrong, and in their pain this made them all the more determined to succeed in this effort. It was moving to see Avery Willis, one of the Southern Baptist International Mission Board leaders come to Lawrence and embrace him and pray for him. This then sparked off a response from mission agencies as they repented for a corresponding independence and insensitivity to local churches in treating them as milch cows for money and recruits and refusing to be accountable for their further use of what they took or inviting them to be partners in mission.

This was a good beginning on the long road back to a real trust and partnership in mission between the three God-given structures for the Church. There will need to be a lot of humblings, repentances, and earnest fellowship between the three structures if trust, co-operation, partnering, mutual accountability, eternal fruit and the completion of world evangelization are to be obtained.

Reference has already been made to the local church as the *launch pad for missions*. The local church is the fundamental structural component of the Church for mission. Without local churches actively committed to mission, world evangelization is not possible. The launch-pad concept is good, but too limited; it is passive. Today the cry from many concerned congregations is that they want to be more involved in the actual process of mission. This is right and proper, and mission agencies need to heed this. We should rather state that the analogy should be of a three stage rocket to launch an earth-encircling satellite. In this analogy, the local church is both the launch-pad *and* the first stage of the rocket. The training structures then are the second stage and the mission structures the third. The satellite, or the mission force must continue to relate to the ground for any meaningful results from the mission to flow. The analogy breaks down when we realize that the communication from the satellite must be with all three structures – each continuing to have their part to play in the maximizing of the ministry and gifts of the missionary in a life time of service. However this analogy may, in fact, be a representation of the truth. How many missionaries have come home shattered by a hard term on the field only to find that communications with the home church had not been circulated to the membership, and knowledge of and prayer for their ministry negligible?

Mission is a close partnering of the whole Body of Christ, not just one of it parts. One of the most significant trends today in pioneer evangelism is the paramount importance of partnerships and networks on the field between ex-patriate workers and agencies and also the emerging leadership of indigenous churches. The next step is to ensure that partnership is made even wider and involve sending churches and training structures as essential components in the whole. We are all needed if we are to finish the task.

We need to be practical too. Once we understand the principle of the unity of the Church, but that it has a tripartite structure, it helps us to understand the rights, privileges and limitations for each component in practice in the sending and supporting of missionary activity. In the next three chapters I will make a number of practical suggestions for each.

Chapter 17

How Can a Local Church become Mission-minded?

There is no perfect model! Many churches with an interest in obeying the Great Commission are docile spectators in a sport played by others. Yet the local church is pivotal to the whole mission enterprise, and it should be the "seed-bed for missions."[45] How far we have fallen short of this ideal! How can churches regain their rightful place as fundamental to world evangelization?[46] Only as the local church sees its reason for existence as mission – whether local, national, trans-ethnic or international – can it really be a truly biblical church.

It must involve re-education across the board from the pastor to the youngest member of the Sunday School. There must be intense dialogue with leaders of mission agencies and theological institutions. There must also be a vigorous assertion of the rights and responsibilities of the local church in every aspect of the preparation, pastoral care and ministry of their missionaries.[47]

For this to happen, there needs to be another leadership team within the structure of the church that operates separately from the pastor-elder-deacon model that is common in most denominations. This is commonly called a Missions Committee. There are some good case studies of local churches from around the world that have re-structured to make mission central to the life of the congregation in the publication *Churches that obey – taking the Great Commission seriously*.[48] In Bill and Amy Stearns' book, *Catch the Vision 2000*, there is a helpful list of ideas and suggestions for action to raise the mission vision of a local congregation.[49]

---

[45] Borthwick 1985:272.
[46] Beals 1995. *A People for His Name – A Church-based Missions Strategy*. This is one of the best books I know for giving a comprehensive yet readable coverage of practical steps to restore missions as central to the life of a local church.
[47] Gaukroger 1996. His book *Why Bother with Mission?* is one of the simplest and best books I know to introduce mission to a local church. It is written in simple modern language and has helpful discussion group questions after each chapter. Also very good for young people.
[48] Forster & Richard 1995, especially 172ff.
[49] Stearns 1991:169 ff.

The most successful mission-sending churches with a missions committee are constantly finding the need to change and adapt, to discard what does not work and to take on board what might work better. However I suggest that there are certain basic elements that should be present in a local church structure if a successful long-term mission strategy is to be implemented. Below are some key components. These are so important that I have boxed them to draw attention to them. This list is by no means exhaustive:

1. **Is there a clear vision statement on mission?** Every member should be fully aware of the motivating vision of their church. If mission, both local and global, is not part of this, the church is not really a biblical church. Clear vision gives direction, motivation and commitment to all involved.

2. **Is the pastoral team committed to a global vision?** If the leadership ignores or belittles world evangelization or, at the most, passes on responsibility in the church for mission to others who are not part of the inner core of leadership, the vision for mission is doomed. The pastor must be totally committed to world evangelization and enthuse his congregation to follow his lead – otherwise do not select him as your church pastor. This attitude must be shown in commitment to private and public intercession for missions, preaching content, allocation of time for world vision in Sunday services, active support of the missions committee, involvement in the selection, preparation, pastoral care and ministry on the field of missionaries from the fellowship. The fellowship should encourage pastoral visits to their missionaries and provide the budget for such visits, in consultation with the agency, to missionaries on the field where and when appropriate.[50]

3. **Is there a mission structure within the church?** This could be a mission committee or mission board. The pastor cannot do the job of leading this, nor can any single individual – but in many churches this is often what happens. The chairperson should be one of the inner core of the leadership team, but with the pastor *ex officio* as one of the members. Beals has an excellent summary of the composition and duties of a mission committee.[51] ACMC, Advancing Churches in Mission

[50] Beals 1995:71-78.
[51] Beals 1995:115-122.

Commitment,[52] is a North American organization that has built up a solid reputation for helping churches to set up a viable mission structure within congregations through seminars, excellent materials on setting up missions committees, fund-raising.

4. **Have you a mission Policy Statement** which also includes a job description for the leader/chair-person, secretary, and members? This Policy will need constant re-assessment and development. Its purpose is to set measurable goals for educating in missions, raising and allocating funds, growing and supporting missionaries and two-way communication with their missionaries.

5. **Is there a systematic teaching programme on mission for the whole congregation?** This should include Sunday services, Sunday School, house groups, youth and children's groups.

6. **Mission should be an integral part of every department** in the congregation. Is it? Mission is not just an activity of those who might be interested and a department of church activity on a par with the young marrieds group, ladies coffee mornings or the choir. It is fundamental to the functioning of every department. It is the Mission Committee that will seek to develop this involvement. It is tragic to me to find how many congregations assume that missions is not for children and young people. Young people can reach adulthood in many of our evangelical churches and never once hear a missionary message or meet a missionary in their lives! I once was asked to minister on vision for the world in a church in Australia, but to my dismay, I found that the pastor had arranged an alternative programme for the young people that he thought would be more interesting for them. Most missionaries on the field were first stimulated and even called into missions during their youth. We need to give vision rather than entertainment to our young people – and older!

7. **Is a high publicity profile for mission** and the church's commitment to projects, agencies and individual missionaries provided? This should not be just at an annual missions

---

[52] ACMC: Address: P.O. Box ACMC, Wheaton, IL 60189-8000
　　Tel:1-800-798-ACMC, FAX: 1-708-260-0285.

conference, or special week-end, but through the year and with many different methods of exposure – notice-boards, world maps, missionary speakers, entertaining furloughing missionaries, short term involvement in mission activities, prayer walks, field visits and so on.

8. **Is there a definite commitment to regular prayer for mission?** This should not be just the traditional mid-week meeting where a few faithful gather, but woven into the entire life of the congregation – during the Sunday service, and in every gathering of the fellowship.

9. **Is there a recruitment and training programme** for prospective workers and missionaries? The Lord Jesus Christ commanded us to pray for labourers.[53] How many congregations actively do this? Not only should such prayer be made, but also there should be the follow-through with discipling and in-service training to prepare those who respond to become effective missionaries. Few churches do this, but there are some excellent examples.

10. **How realistic is your policy on giving** in support of mission and missionaries? To take the gospel to distant lands is expensive even if missionaries live close to the poverty line. Travel, education of their children, equipment (within limits!) are costly to provide and maintain quite apart from the cost of the ministry itself. Any congregation that sends out a missionary should be realistic about the cost and ask the right questions of the missionary and of the channelling agency, but how many congregations do this?

Here is an exercise in realism! Think through what it actually costs to send a missionary couple overseas and support them to the point that they become mature cross-cultural workers on the field. It would actually take, on average, 11-13 years! Broken down into three years theological training, one year orientation with the agency, one to two years raising support, one to two years language study and then five to seven years acculturalization on the field. Let us suppose that a low average level of support over these years through their training at home and establishment overseas were US$35,000 (for many the

---

[53] Matthew 9:37-38.

needs are higher). That works out at around $420,000 over 12 years, and then probably come the big expenses for missionary children's secondary education (often prohibitively expensive) and the parents are forced home for lack of funds just at the point when they are beginning to reap the fruit of their years of preparation. It would be more realistic to double support for a few years to cover the higher expenses in order to maximise the years of time and money invested in the preparation, but few think in these terms in home churches.

11. **Is there a good balance in mission involvement** between pioneer and development, spiritual and social, foreign and local outreach? There should be a rounded wholeness in the mission involvement of the congregation.

12. **A real commitment to pastoral care of missionaries and their children.** This is both on the field, during furloughs, for further in-service training and also when the missionaries return from the field for furlough, re-direction or retirement.

There are many books that have been written to help local congregations gain and develop a mission programme.[54] This is too big a subject for me to tackle here. Neal Pirolo[55] gives a long list of books, teaching materials, videos, seminars, possible short-term overseas exposure trips and so on.

Finally I want to ask a hot-potato question.

Can a local church directly send their missionaries overseas? There are whole streams of evangelical Christianity that strongly maintain that this is the right way (see Chapter 16). My response is a cautious affirmative, but with some warnings that should be heeded. There have been too many courageously foolhardy experiments in this that have caused more damage than good to the kingdom and the individuals involved. The frustrations experienced by local churches with mission agencies could be then avoided, but at what cost?

1. **Check on the motivation** for sending missionaries direct to the field. Is it pride, a desire to extend the ecclesiastical empire or a desire to prove that we can do it? Sadly those who do this are

[54] Mays 1996; Beals 1995.
[55] Pirolo 1991.

rarely students of mission history – even rejecting the past as old-fashioned and seeing the new patterns as 'of the Holy Spirit', but thus condemned to repeat the tragic mistakes of the past. Is it the clear leading of the Lord?

2. **Are there the cross-cultural skills and experience within the church** for selecting candidates, preparing them for the field, and giving adequate advice, support and care on the field? Most churches who have tried this route have ended up disappointed and frustrated because the gifting available was not adequate for the demands. Directly-sent missionaries are often home-trained too; is that training of the quality and breadth required in today's world? Missiological training is complex and important.

3. **Is there a separate mission structure** in the church with its own leadership and commitment to the mission enterprise? Without this, the sending will surely fail. Sending missionaries today is a highly complex operation – information, visas, travel, relations with other Christian bodies on the field, pastoral care and oversight half way across the world. Then there is the need for field research, development of viable strategies and planning of ecclesiology. All these need both time and expertise. Few congregations could confidently handle all these.

4. **Has the prospective field been adequately researched?** We have very few countries and peoples left in the world where no Christian outreach is happening. The need to send missionary apostles to where the Church is not should be paramount. A number of apostolic direct-sending efforts have been little more than visiting a country where English is widely used (less need to learn languages or cultures) and where there are usually already many churches. The "mission" becomes a redistribution of existing saints so that they become followers of an overseas church empire – sometimes with funding to lubricate the redistribution.

5. **Has there been adequate networking** with other Christian agencies at home and abroad? The day of the lone pioneer missionary or isolated apostolic team has gone for ever. Most of the least evangelized parts of the world are not in the major cities, where there are usually other indigenous and ex-patriate Christians already ministering. Direct sending will only be effective and survivable for most missionaries if there is a

network of accountability on the field with others often of many other agencies.

6. **What kind of church is envisaged?** Direct sending churches are often the least culturally sensitive in planting churches in another country. There is often the strong desire to reproduce the patterns of the sending church with all its theological foibles, worship-patterns, approved Bible versions, leadership styles and attitudes about women, dress, use of time which may be at best irrelevant and at worst extremely offensive to the local culture.

7. **How much control is exercised from the home church** in the day-to-day operation of the ministry? The autonomy of action which Paul and Barnabas, William Carey and Hudson Taylor sought and expected is ignored. The lessons of hundreds of years of mission history and experience is spurned.

This takes us a step further to ask: **should** a local church send missionaries direct to the field without any partnering with mission agencies? I personally doubt it if it means ignoring the vast range of skills, advice, experience and expertise available. It is a denial of the unity of the Church in mission. No one can go it alone today; we need each other. Church planting is a team ministry – usually of the same sending or channelling body, but increasingly also multi-agency or church teams too. Sadly the behaviour of mission agencies has often repelled those who could have been helped, and for this agencies need to repent – the subject of a later chapter.

Chapter 18

How Can a Bible School or Seminary become Mission- and Church-minded?

In July 1997 I had the privilege to be involved in a rather special conference of nearly 5,000 Christian leaders – the Global Consultation On World Evangelization or GCOWE-97. The main body of the Consultation was three intense days in 10 autonomous consultations of specialists, all with the aim of furthering the goal of the AD2000 Mvt.: *The gospel for every person and a church for every people by the year 2000*. I participated in the consultation of Principals and Academic Deans of theological institutions around the world. I believe this was the first time such a consultation had ever been held, and the basic theme was how to mobilize theological training institutions to have a greater impact on world evangelization.

Dr. David Kim, of the Torch Centre in Seoul, Korea was one of the leaders of this consultation, and his message opened with the striking words, *"We are dangerous people."* He explained the double meaning. Many theologians have been a danger to the Church through their erroneous teachings that have corrupted generations of pastors, but others have had a deeply beneficial impact on world evangelization through mission vision imparted in intense discipling to students in their seminaries and Bible schools. The history of theological schools in Europe and North America shows that denizens of these institutions can be the most gullible section of the Church for swallowing false teaching. Apostasy in the places of theological learning suborned first the churches, then whole denominations and subsequently the mission field.

Earlier we traced some of the history of the emergence of theological training and how it became divorced spiritually and academically from the churches into which their students returned for ministry. Probably the root cause of the marginalization of missions over the last few centuries has been our system of theological education. Spirituality and mission were sacrificed in the name of academic freedom and academic standards. Accountability for the range of subjects taught, the theologies espoused and the quality of spirituality of students to the end-users was lost.

This has had a further negative impact on those whom God has raised up for new pioneer initiatives. They have often turned their backs on a rounded theological training because of the perceived spiritual deficiencies and practical irrelevance of training offered. This has then frequently led to blinkered vision, superficial evangelization and a stunted ecclesiology with the result that the emerging Church is the poorer and less able to withstand the malice and wiles of the devil. The emerging non-Western mission movement is just as affected by these attitudes. A far more flexible and broad approach is needed to make theological education more user-friendly. Bill Taylor of WEF has been tirelessly promoting the need for cross-cultural training to be adapted to the real situations where mission movements are developing around the world.[56] A theological education that truly serves the cause of mission is of incalculable benefit for the Kingdom.

The key to the mobilization of local churches for mission lies in our theological training, and the pastors trained. It is more than tragic that the whole discipline of missiology has been relegated to a minor and supplementary role in most schools. It is a sinful neglect. Once a pastor is immersed in the busyness of ministry with all its demands, it needs a miracle of revelation to open his life to missions if the seed were not well sown and germinated in seminary. To me, changing the seminaries seemed an insurmountable task, for there was no academic peer-pressure grouping extant in the world that would put pressure on the average theological school to change. I well remember being part of the leadership of a conference of selected leaders from all over Europe. A number of us were determined to include in the conference declaration that theological training should have mission at its heart, and as an essential component of every discipline. I was on the drafting committee, but so was a President of a very well known European evangelical seminary. He fought tooth and nail to water down that statement. We laboured through the night on the draft with this being the chief sticking point. Sadly we ended with a statement that had to be a compromise, but the power and cutting edge of the challenge had been blunted.

I was under no illusions about the challenge to see changes. However at the Pretoria GCOWE consultation I believe it

---

[56] Taylor 1991.

happened when there was unanimity among all the delegates in wording the following declaration which I include in full, for it spells it out in the words of 250 theological leaders in a manner far better than I could express!

Declaration with the 10 Theses

RESOLUTION

Two hundred and fifty Presidents and Academic Deans (PAD) representing theological schools from 53 nations gathered at the Doxa Deo Church in Pretoria, South Africa, July 1-3, 1997 to consider ways in which the schools they lead can further the goal of "a church for every people and the gospel for every person." Theological educators have tremendous potential to bless, but also to damage the church; to enhance but also to hinder the fulfilment of the commission.

Out of the worship, plenary addresses, workshops, testimonies, prayer, discussion, and informal fellowship the following ten theses have emerged:

1. The primacy of missiological concern for world evangelism must be recognized and focused in the total curriculum of ministry training.
2. Partnership at all levels and in multiple forms is essential for reaching the unreached people of the world.
3. Formal, non-formal and relational approaches to learning are to be seen as complementary rather than competitive.
4. The content of ministry training must uphold the uniqueness of Jesus Christ and the necessity of personal faith in Him as Lord and Saviour. This is especially imperative in the light of the increasing pluralistic environment which has been brought about by the resurgence of non-Christian religions hostile to the advance of the gospel, by the erosion of historic Christianity in the West, and by the increasing prevalence of secularism almost everywhere.
5. Ministry training must aim to produce practising supernaturalists who minister effectively in the power of the Holy Spirit, relying on prayer and complete trust in the Word of God.

6. Basic to all ministry training is spiritual and character formation in the life of the student, in part facilitated by the example of the teacher.

7. Approaches to ministry training must reflect concern for the whole counsel of God wisely contextualized and sustainable by local and national resources.

8. Academic accreditation may serve to guarantee quality control and encourage institutional effectiveness. At the same time it should not be allowed to impede the spiritual and missiological thrust of theological education. Every effort must be made to assure that accrediting structures affirm and promote commitment to world evangelization.

9. Serious consideration should be given to the training of both husband and wife for their mutual effectiveness in ministry, and accessibility to ministry training broadened to include all who can benefit from it.

10. A permanent PAD track should be incorporated into the AD 2000 Movement and another Consultation convened.

Looking to the future, we call upon college Presidents and Academic Deans and commit ourselves to put the vision of "*a church for every people and the gospel for every person*" at the heart of ministry training. We resolve to explore together new paradigms of partnership in theological education that training schools share their distinctives and resources to accomplish the goal of global evangelization. We shall continue to press the claims of the kingdom as we move towards the consummation of history and the coming of our Lord in the glory of God.

I was thrilled to hear this; an answer to prayer. For the first time in history a significant and representative body of theological trainers set up a peer-pressure accountability structure to ensure their schools become Great Commission-centred schools. I pray that it may become as powerful a defining instrument in the theological world as the Lausanne Covenant has become for Evangelicals since 1974. It would be significant if this declaration therefore became a measure of a school's commitment and mentioned in every advertisement for the school. May that come about.

As I look through this Declaration I miss one important feature – that of accountability to the Church for theological institutions. This is implied in the second Thesis concerning partnership. This needs to be more strongly stated. Administrators and faculty need to be accountable to those to whom their students will go – the denominations, local churches and agencies. This has been the tragic lack in the past centuries. There needs to be a definite paragraph in the purpose statement of every place of theological learning that they are servants of the Church and accountable to it for the quality and content of their teaching and the godliness of both faculty and students.

The time for the independence of seminaries is gone for ever. It must be recognized that they are not para-church bodies, but part of the Body of Christ, and therefore accountable to it. The whole curriculum, discipling and internship programme needs to be sensitive to the envisaged ministry of their students. This will mean radical changes from the old pattern of academia with an ivory tower seclusion during the time of study. It will be uncomfortable and untidy, but there needs to be more flexibility, wider transferability of credits academically and globally, a combination of periods of study interspersed with spans of ministry, with the subjects studied geared to the next stage of ministry. A new paradigm in theological education has arrived in which we move into a lifetime of study for a lifetime of ministries. This will only come once we see the wholeness of the Church and the essential partnership between its component structures. The time of single-career workers in both the secular world and in Christian ministry has gone for ever. There will be the far easier transfer of pastoral staff to the mission field and to the world of theological education and vice versa. Are we willing for the wrenching changes in our institutions to permit this? Are we willing to slaughter our sacred cows of tradition, academic freedom and pride for our own ways of doing things? For Christ's sake and for his expanding kingdom we should.

As in the previous chapter I give a check list for you to measure the mission commitment of a theological institution. It is not comprehensive, and could be further developed. My desire is that this be both helpful and challenging.

1. **Has the School a Vision or Purpose Statement with a strong commitment to Mission?** Unless mission be placed at this high level, other agendas will force it to the periphery.

2. **Is there adequate accountability to peers in the theological world to ensure commitment to mission is maintained?** My prayer is that from 1997 onwards the GCOWE-initiated PAD Network provide such. Starting a missions committee that is a vital, central body for the school would be a good start.

3. **Has there been recognition that the School is part of the Body of Christ** and therefore accountable to the churches and mission agencies for not only theological purity, but also in curriculum development, accreditation route sought, spiritual life of faculty and students and envisaged ministry of the student?

4. **Does every full course offered also include a component of missiology as an essential for completion of that course?** Not every student will be called into cross-cultural work, but every student needs to be fully conversant with missiological issues for effective ministry whatever that may be.

5. **Have all invited onto faculty been asked about their commitment to mission**, and desire to ensure the discipline taught has at its heart, God's heart for mission? Any subject taught that has no relevance for mission is not Bible-centred.

6. **Has the School actively promoted mission as a noble and viable avenue of service for graduates?** There is often an unstated elitism that those who cannot fit into a pastoral ministry at home ought to consider mission service, and that all who become missionaries are second class. This attitude is often why men often stay at home and more women go overseas.

7. **Is the spirituality of faculty and students the top priority?** People who know God, the power of prayer, the anointing of the Holy Spirit and are not afraid to confront the enemy and expect miracles are needed for the ministry at home and abroad.

8. **How willing is the school to broaden out the routes to qualifications** to include formal and informal learning, home and overseas ministry and a greater transferability of credits?

Chapter 19

How can a Mission Agency become Church-Minded?

The mission agency is a biblical structure in concept. However, as we have seen, the practice of how agencies operate may be far from scriptural. Over the years our unbiblical understandings have been reflected in the way mission agencies have developed. They have taken on many of the functions that rightly belong to the local church. Wrong attitudes have led to misunderstandings and a spirit of confrontation between churches and agencies.[57] How can we recover the right balance as partners for world evangelization?

There are some basic principles on which we need to agree:

1. **The Church is God's agent for world evangelization.** By this I mean the Church Universal. The Greek word *ekklesia* means both the Church Universal, and also the local assembly or church. If one takes only the latter, the implication is that the local churches alone should shoulder the full responsibility for world evangelization.

2. **The Church consists of three operational structures** that are mutually interdependent and in partnership for world evangelization: local churches, training structures and mission sending agencies.

3. **The apostolic team, or mission agency, is God's means for planting churches in unevangelized areas.** As shown above, the complexities and level of commitment to the long-term goal of cross-cultural church planting demands such to exist and be recognized even if the type of structure can vary widely according to culture, time and ministry.

4. **The primacy of the local church for world evangelization is fundamental.** The local church is the only provider of the basic resources for mission – funding, manpower, intercession, support. A recent WEF survey on mission attrition[58] showed that one of the main causes of missionaries returning

---

[57] Palmer June 1984, EMQ article p 244. Makes an eloquent plea for partnership between local churches and missions. The title itself is a message! *The homeland church – partner or pawn.*

[58] Taylor 1997. WEF published the results of a conference investigating the causes of missionary attrition with the title *Too Valuable to Lose.*

prematurely from the field was because they were not rooted and grounded in a local church. George Peters comments:

> We believe we are not out of line with New Testament thinking if we state that the local congregation of believers stands in a unique relationship to Christ and that the local assembly becomes the mediating and authoritative sending body of the New Testament missionary. This is a vital biblical principle and we dare not weaken, minimize or disregard it.[59]

However there are limitations on a local church in cross-cultural mission, for it can only impact the world beyond its own locality in partnership with other structures for both training and channelling – whether within its own congregation or, better, in partnership with other churches or agencies.

5. **The mission agency is both the servant of, and partner with, local churches** in world evangelization. It is this servant spirit and sense of accountability to local churches which has been lost. In the process the idea of partnership has also been lost.

If we agree on these principles, then there are a number of follow-through steps that can be taken.[60] Again I am enclosing these in a box to show the importance I attach to these:

By the local church in relating to mission agencies

1. **Be prepared to take the initiative.** For too long local churches have been passive in expecting the agencies to take the lead in recruitment and training. For many churches their involvement in missions is that of spectators. Local churches should have a far bigger role with a missionary recruit in the initial approach to a mission agency and then in the furtherance of his or her ministry.

2. **Expect accountability from agencies.** If your money and manpower are needed by a mission agency to fulfil their function, then accountability at every stage is obligatory. However the converse needs to be stated that there is also an accountability of the congregation to the missionary and the mission agency which cannot be ignored.

---

[59] Peters 1972:218.
[60] Beals 1995:133-154. Beals has two superb chapters on the mission agency and its responsibilities to the sending church.

3. **Insist on partnership.** This means making time for representatives of the agency to sit down with the local church leadership to discuss expectations, requirements, mutual areas of responsibility, finances, doctrine, standards, pastoral care, etc.

4. **Ensure that the final acceptance of the missionary recruit is a combined local church and agency exercise** with complete consensus expected on both sides as to the acceptance and subsequent steps towards field service.

5. **Determine the degree of involvement of the local church in the field ministry of their missionary.** Too many missions expect that the sending church relinquish all say in the ministry and pastoral care of their missionary. It is right that operational control be in the mission team, but that does not end the need for accountability of the individual members to their own sending churches. Some mission agencies have committed themselves to be a channel for, and an umbrella to, a local church team committed to cross-cultural church-planting in an unreached people. This has its merits, but I personally wonder how workable it is in practice.

6. **Recognize the resources, giftings and abilities of the agencies** in areas beyond the gifting of the members of local churches. There should be a recognition that their authority as a church has been delegated to the agency for the time of their service on the field. However this means that the agency needs to recognize its continuing accountability to the sending church.

By the Mission Agency in relating to Local Churches

1. **Be humble** in recognizing that, even by default, agencies have usurped functions that belong to the local church. Be determined to rectify this – even in costly confessions of failure in the past.

2. **Recognize the pivotal role of the local church in mission.** In all possible ways help restore that role through consultation with the relevant leaders, show willingness to serve the church in teaching and ministry on principles and in practical areas such as setting up a missions committee and handling finances for missions.

3. **Aim for a servant role in ministry to local churches.** The aim should be to impart a blessing in ministry rather than expecting

to receive a financial or manpower blessing! The contributions of an agency in information, opportunities for short and long-term service, experience in working cross-culturally can be vital. Ministering life to others is the best way to ensure adequate support.

4. **Challenge with tact and wisdom** those congregations which are either not committed to evangelical theology or not convinced about the present validity of missions. We have to be realistic and admit that most of these points in this section are directed to evangelical congregations where there is already an awareness of and commitment to missions. Large numbers of European congregations are in this situation. Antagonistic extraction of members to become missionaries or missionary supporters is not likely to endear the agency to the unsympathetic leadership of the congregation.

5. **Defer to the local church** in matters pertaining to the recruitment of their members for mission service. No agency should pursue application procedures without being sure that, where possible, the sending church is actively involved in the application. No missionary should be accepted for candidacy without ensuring that there is harmonious understanding in all areas of potential breakdown – such as financial support, funding of home office expenses, use of time before field service and on furlough, compatibility of doctrine and standards and mutual accountability between the local church and agency leadership.

6. **Discuss areas of sensitivity** – in such as personal pastoral problems, sensitive issues within the team of missionaries on the field, the level of involvement of the church with field matters, how to handle field visits by church leaders. The whole issue of security and confidentiality of information in countries not completely open for mission activity has to be faced.

7. **Value the partnership of the local church** in any action by the agency that affects the life and ministry of their missionary. Quick and effective communication from mission leadership on the field or at the home base to the local church in any urgent or serious situation is an obvious expectation, but how often is it done?

8. **Seek to ensure there is adequate home staff** for good accessibility and communication between local churches and

the mission agency. I realize that to follow through with this there could be an increase in administration and costs, but the long-term results for the local churches, mission agencies and the missionaries themselves would make the effort worthwhile.

George Peters wisely said:

> The mission agency ought to be the church's provision, instrument and arm to efficiently expedite her task. It can neither displace nor replace the church, though it may be called upon to act in the place of the church.[61]

Mission agencies need to be aware that the potential for breakdown with local churches is great if lines of communication are inadequate, leadership unapproachable or secrecy too tight. I remember speaking at a pastor's seminar about the need for mission agencies to be more open in cases of pastoral need, and one pastor sprang to his feet and with great feeling shared his concern about one of their missionaries. The missionary was one day dumped on the doorstep of the church office a physical and emotional wreck and in desperate need of pastoral care. He then went on to say that it was like trying to get into Fort Knox to find out from the leadership what had actually happened. The pastor was rightly indignant. He had every right to expect to be brought into the picture right from the very beginning, but this was not done.

One of the encouraging signs of progress towards world evangelization today is the extent to which local churches around the world are wanting a more active role in mission – whether it be in intercession for specific countries and peoples, personal involvement in specific projects or outreaches, close involvement in sending their missionaries and in their ministry. All this is made more possible by the ease of travel and communications. Who would have thought 20 years ago of e-mail or long distance telephone calls enabling missionaries half a world away speaking in the Sunday service of their sending church? Mission agencies need to change and change fast to have a cutting edge in the twenty-first century. This cutting edge will, of necessity, be one of close partnership with local churches.

---

[61] Peters 1981:206-239.

Conclusion of Part 4

This whole section has dealt with structures for world evangelization. We have seen that there is biblical warrant for a plurality of structures within the one body, the Church. We have also seen through history how distortions have occurred which have impaired the effectiveness of the Church in its mission. We need to restore that wholeness to the Church so that world evangelization be accomplished.

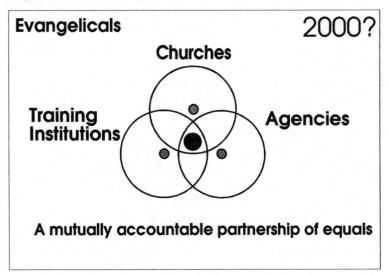

The model proposed is shown above. It is a tripartite inter-relatedness between three basic structures – churches, theological training institutions and apostolic sending agencies. Each is a valid biblical structure and each has its individual strengths and giftings to contribute to the whole, but none can keep central the accomplishment of the Great Commission without the other two.

What is advocated is a partnership in servanthood each to the other so that the Church become what God always intended – a perfect Bride for his Son to co-reign with him through all eternity. We have fallen far short of that ideal, therefore every effort must be made to repair broken bridges of understanding and fellowship, and establish practical working relationships at every level so that we, the Church, might be one in love, the power of the Holy Spirit and vision for a lost world.

The Church IS bigger than we had thought – in structures too.

Part 5

The Consummation

The Vision to be Realized

Isaiah 54:3

Introduction

We have good reason to be encouraged because of what God is doing in the world, but that must be balanced by the solemn reality that so much remains to be done and that the forces opposed to us are so formidable. The finish of world evangelization is in sight, but there are huge barriers to jump and strongholds to break down before the end when Jesus returns.

Isaiah foretold the massive spiritual harvest in verse 1, and then exhorted us to have the right structures and strategies for what remains in verse 2. In verse 3 he gives the promise:

> For you will spread abroad to the right and to the left, and
> your descendants will possess the peoples[1] and will people the
> desolate cities. *Isaiah 54:3 RSV*

Isaiah uses language understood in terms of the Old Testament people of Israel, but as seen in the earlier verses of this passage, the significance of the words is far wider and even New Testament in tone. World evangelization is foreshadowed. Many English translations such as the NIV use *dispossess* rather than *possess*, which unfortunately restricts the application to the Old Testament context of Israel taking the Promised Land; I am convinced the application is wider and also of application to the times in which we live.

---

[1] Nearly all English translations give the word nation. This miscommunicates today because we think of a modern political state. Isaiah was not so much speaking about political entities as about ethnic entities or peoples.

The three phrases in this verse point to three major missiological challenges we face if we are to complete the task of world evangelization. These are **geographical** – reaching every inhabited part of the world, **ethnic** – reaching every people, and then **urban** – the very modern concept of reaching cities. To these I add three other challenges which are indicated later in chapter 54 – the **ideological, sociological** and **spiritual**.

These six challenges I apply in the following six chapters to the unfinished task ahead of us in the twenty-first century.

Chapter 20

The Geographical Challenge

The promise is that God's people will spread abroad to the right and the left, or we could equally say, to the north and the south, the east and the west. Every inhabited part of our world must be exposed to the gospel of the Lord Jesus Christ. This is a geographical challenge. There are tough challenges, but for missionaries to reach them:

- no valley is too isolated – like the remote unevangelized Kingdom of Mustang on Nepal's northern border,
- no island is too distant – like the yet-unreached Maldive Islands in the Indian Ocean,
- no forest is too dense – like the Congo jungles where the Pygmy people live,
- no mountain is too inaccessible – like the remote and harsh Tibetan plateau of central Asia,
- no city is too fortified – like Mecca where no Christian is allowed to set foot, and
- no desert is too hostile – like the Saharan oases in Algeria where the Mzab Berber peoples live.

Here are some of the geographical challenges:

The 10/40 Window

Great swathes of the surface area of our globe are still without a significant indigenous Christian witness. The maps in chapter 9 give the extent to which the Gospel has already spread. In the 1995 map the major gaps are clearly seen. This is predominantly in North Africa and Asia where Islam, Hinduism and Buddhism are usually the dominant religions. The map on the following page highlights this challenging part of the world. This must be the area of major focus for pioneer mission in the next decade or more. However it has been the area of greatest neglect until recently.

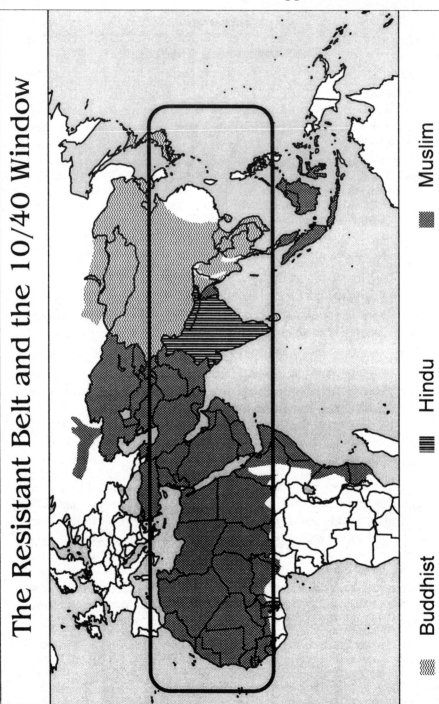

The Resistant Belt and the 10/40 Window

Muslim ▨　　Hindu ▦　　Buddhist ▧

For years I called this *the Resistant Belt.* Since 1990 the phrase, *The 10/40 Window,* coined by Luis Bush of the AD2000 Mvt.,[2] has become widely known. This is the area between the latitudes 10° and 40° north of the equator and between the Atlantic and Pacific Oceans. The concept is good and the publicity impact brilliant – even if this rectangle only approximates to the areas of greatest spiritual challenge.[3] Basically the countries in or near the 10/40 Window that are under-evangelized have only 35% of the world's surface area, but 65% of its population. The map opposite includes both the 10/40 Window concept shown by the rectangle and the Resistant Belt with the shading.

The sheer number of people living in the Window area is daunting. Of the 6 billion people in the world in 2000, I reckon that 1.2 – 1.4 billion have never had the chance to hear the Gospel,[4] and over 95% of these individuals reside in the Window area. How can we smugly ignore such a huge number facing a Christless eternity with no opportunity to hear the Good News and experience the love of God as revealed in the Lord Jesus? What a challenge to faith, intercession and action – we are obligated to **do** something about it for the love of Christ constrains us.[5]

To add to the challenge, over 90% of the world's poorest and most deprived, the children that are most abused and most of the world's illiterate live in the Window area. This is where diseases such as AIDS, tuberculosis and malaria rampage largely unchecked and untreated. It is also these areas that are the least accessible for any overt mission endeavour either because of antagonistic political and religious systems, geography or lifestyle. For instance, almost all of the word's nomads live here. We face our biggest challenge yet in world evangelization. The tide of the gospel has risen and flowed over two thirds of the earth, and is lapping at the one third where the final bastions and citadels of Satan's kingdom

---

[2] AD2000 and Beyond Movement publications.

[3] Indonesia, Mongolia, the Muslim republics of Central Asia, Sri Lanka, Maldives and Somalia should be included but are outside the Window. Countries in the Window with significant, often nominal, Christian populations such as South Korea, Philippines, Eritrea and many European Mediterranean countries should perhaps be or are omitted.

[4] Johnstone 1993:27 (est. 20% unevangelized, 47% non-Christians living where they are likely to be evangelized and 33% professing Christian), Barrett, 1987a:85 (est. 17% unevangelized).

[5] 2 Corinthians 5:14-15.

have yet to be broken down. Let us not minimise the size of the remaining task, but also not be discouraged by its magnitude.

The following diagram shows the number and proportion of Christians, non-Christians with opportunity to hear the gospel and the totally unevangelized non-Christians in the 10/40 Window and rest of the world.

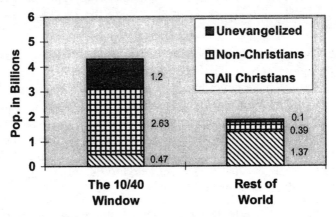

World Evangelization & 10/40 Window

Unevangelized Countries of the World

The colonial and territorial empires of 80 – 100 years ago hardly exist any more. Where are the Chinese, Japanese, Russian, Ethiopian, Dutch, British, French, German, Italian, Portuguese, Spanish, Danish, Austro-Hungarian, Turkish and even the American Empires[6] today? Yet in 1914 these 15 powers controlled or dominated, directly or indirectly, all but a handful of states in the world[7]. Almost all of these came to an end or became a shadow

---

[6] Why has this quintessentially republican and freedom-loving nation been listed? One only has to see the confirmation of this in the territorial acquisitions of Puerto Rico, Philippines, Guam resulting from war with Spain in 1899 and the vain Filipino attempts at gaining their independence 1899-1902. In that war 4,200 Americans and 220,000 Filipinos were killed.

[7] In the whole of Africa there was not one truly independent state with the exception of Ethiopia, which was, to all intents and purposes, an Empire in its own right. In Asia there were only a few such as Thailand, Maldives, Iran, Afghanistan, Mongolia; some only nominally so. Maybe

of their former selves in the twentieth century cataclysms of two world wars and the collapse of Communism. The multiplication of independent nation states and the growth of the membership of the United Nations is one obvious result. Whatever our embarrassment at our national arrogances or resentments because of political and cultural subjugations our own nations perpetrated or suffered, some of these empires opened the way for the penetration of the gospel.

The rise of ethnism and global communications in the past decade have lessened the hold of ideologies and begun to erode the powers of nation-states. Yet the modern nation-state still remains an important fact of life today and will be for many years to come. It is these states that raise such complex restrictions on trade or movements of people and permit corrupt bureaucracies that make life so difficult for travellers and for the servants of God. As a young missionary I travelled in 1963 the 4,200 Km from Pretoria in South Africa to Nairobi in Kenya. All I had to do at the four border crossings was show my passport. This was impossible 20 years later because of apartheid, sanctions, visas and war. Today missionaries have to live with the cliff-hanging suspense of obtaining visas in Indonesia and Europe, the hostile obstructionism to travellers of some former Communist nations, or the frequent road-blocks and border delays caused by bribe-seeking soldiers and immigration authorities in Africa.

It is the national, religious, economic and cultural policies of these nations that largely determine the complexity of entry and range of ministries available for those who want to live and witness for Christ. The nation-state is not going to fade away before the vigorous or violent ethno-nationalism of such as the Karen in Burma, the Kashmiris of India, the Basques of Spain, the Celts of Northern Ireland, the Tuareg of Mali and the Quechua of Peru and Ecuador. There are too many vested interests and personal egos of leaders involved. How important it is for us to pray for the rulers of this world as Paul advocated to Timothy.[8]

In 1998 there were 237 countries and territories in the world. That was the same figure when the 1993 edition of *Operation World* was published. However there have been a few changes –

Liberia should be added, but the USA had retained a paternalistic control despite nominal independence.

[8] 1 Timothy 2:1-4.

Nevis has declared itself independent from St Kitts in the West Indies, and Hong Kong has returned to the rule of China, but there has been nothing like the extraordinary changes that took place between 1990 and 1993 when 23 new countries came into being![9]

How far has Christianity become the professing religion of these countries? The next graph shows the rather startling situation in 1998 which is explained below:

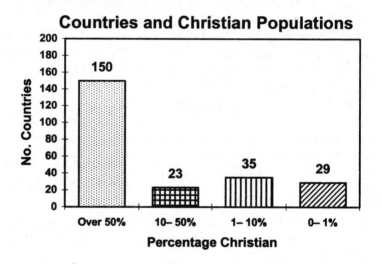

Countries and Christian Populations

Note the following:

1. There are 150 countries that have a majority of their inhabitants professing Christianity in one form or another. This number looks high, but is quickly explained. About 70 of these countries are 27 island territories or mini-states in the Pacific, 25 in the Caribbean and 18 elsewhere, their total population being less than 10 million people. One of the smallest being the 34 inhabitants of Pitcairn Islands, which has at least four claims to fame – it is Britain's last colonial possession in the Pacific (looked after by New Zealand); it is the world's only Seventh-day Adventist country, its main source of foreign exchange is postage stamps and it is the world's most isolated country!

---

[9] For instance the USSR became 15 states, Yugoslavia 5, Czechoslovakia and Ethiopia 2 each, but Germany and Yemen united.

2. The other 87 countries are almost all within or near the 10/40 Window. In the second column are 23 countries, some with very significant numbers of very active Christians such as Nigeria, Chad, Sudan, India, South Korea, Singapore, Hong Kong, China; all of which are within the 10/40 Window but not in the Resistant Belt [please map on p226]. It is probably in this category that there are the largest number of dynamic Christians and where the most significant growth of the Church is occurring. In most of these lands there are still significant areas where Christians are very few indeed, which is shown in the next section.

3. The 35 countries in the 1-10% Christian category contain some of the world's largest such as China, India and Pakistan. These three countries alone have 2,250 million people, or over one third of the world's population! The large Christian minorities in some areas must not blind us to the huge numbers of individuals in these lands who have never had a chance to hear the gospel.

4. It is amazing that there are only 29 countries with resident communities of Christians where they comprise under 1% of the total population. Here are some of the most challenging:

Difficult or dangerous for foreigners	Some tent-making ministry possible	Some scope for open Christian witness
Algeria	Afghanistan	Cambodia
Bhutan	Bangladesh	Mongolia
Iran	Comoros	Nepal
Maldives	Mauritania	Niger
North Korea	Morocco	Thailand
Sahara	Tunisia	Turkey
Somalia	Yemen	
	Libya	

This small number may be surprising for many. In some lands there are many expatriate Christians but few indigenous believers – such as in the Arabian Peninsula and Gulf and this raises the national Christian percentages above 1%.

The amazing fact of our time is that not one of the 29 countries in the final category is without a group of believers already seeking to live for Jesus. I must qualify this statement, for in Libya, the Maldives, Sahara and maybe Afghanistan that group of believers is predominantly expatriate and indigenous believers very few. We have run out of countries which are totally pioneer lands. This was not so 20 years ago, but it is today. The implications are immense. It means that all mission activity must be planned in fellowship with or, at least, with sensitivity to the believers already in the country. Here are several examples:

Certain Muslim countries have been targeted for short term "blitzes" with open-air preaching and handing out tracts in the streets. These Christians were prepared to take risks – but the risk of a few days in prison and expulsion from the country did not compare to the impact on local believers. There have been times when leaders were arrested and badly treated and the careful work of years severely disrupted because of such activity. The foolish insensitivity of foreigners can lead to severe persecution and even martyrdom for national believers.

Many European countries are spiritually needy today. Large proportions of their populations have never been inside a church, and have no concept of the true gospel. However if North Americans come over with the image of "pagan" Europe and no concept of history and the past impact of Christianity, Europeans are hurt. The Reformation started in the Czech Republic, Calvin was a Frenchman, the Waldensian Church in Italy was founded before Luther nailed his Theses to the door of the church in Wittenberg. The German Church has produced some of the greatest theologians of the Church (also some of the worst!). Nearly every culturally Catholic country of Europe has had a history of believers being hounded to death for their faith.

The Collapse of the USSR opened an astonishing door of opportunity for foreigners to fill the ideological and spiritual vacuum left by Communism. In 1997 there were about 6,000 Protestant missionaries in the former USSR and many thousands more have gone for short term ministry or visits. However the gross cultural insensitivity and lack of humility by some to listen and learn from believers who had borne the long years of Communist oppression have harmed the Kingdom. The subsequent backlash against such spiritual imperialism has brought in an imposition of laws banning foreign mission activity in Russia and elsewhere and the imposition of severe restrictions on indigenous evangelical believers and their witness.

Whatever the need of a country, it is essential that any foreign mission that enters that country seek fellowship and, as far as possible, partnership with the indigenous Church – whatever the differences in world view and understanding of the Scriptures. However, sometimes a small, introspective group of believers may be unaware of, or unwilling to face up to the great need in parts of their own country, and their attitudes cannot be the only determinative factor for the entry and ministry of foreigners. In 1990 I made a survey trip to Bulgaria, for it was on our heart to see a WEC ministry launched among the million or so Turkish speaking minority. I was surprised at the strong negative note from some of the Bulgarian Christian leaders who were dismissive of any outreach in a language other than Bulgarian as being unnecessary, yet a people movement among the Millet Turks was just beginning. There are reckoned to be over 16,000 new Christians among them today. Praise God, despite this a fruitful ministry began in co-operation with other Bulgarian Christian leaders.

The list of countries in the table above represents a formidable challenge. Please pick up a copy of *Operation World*, and go through that list, looking up the relevant sections, and may your heart be touched. Here I can only give a little taste of the challenge by listing some with their spiritual needs and challenges:

Bhutan is a hermit Buddhist kingdom in the Himalayas that strictly limits the number and activities of foreigners in the country. The few Christians are largely among ethnic minorities, and these minorities have often been harried, pressured and even chased out of the country. There are just a handful of indigenous Bhutanese believers.

Libya is ruled by the maverick Colonel Ghaddafi, who for decades has been a thorn in the flesh of many nations. Yet his land is one of the most closed for Christian witness, and there are probably less than 10 indigenous believers, with not yet a single church where Libyans can worship and find fellowship.

The Maldive Islands is a small Muslim republic in the Indian Ocean. This is one of the most closed countries in the world. The 150,000 Maldivian population has little opportunity to hear the gospel in any form, being poor, with little available technology and no Christian broadcasts. Any attempts at distributing Scriptures on the islands has been followed by the police immediately seizing every copy. There are known to be only a handful of Maldivian believers in the whole world.

North Korea is a pariah nation gradually starving to death under its crazed Communist leadership.[10] No real witness or any open Christian church life has been possible for 50 years. The groups that survive are underground. Yet many, especially South Koreans, have plans to help and evangelize the country as soon as it opens for the gospel.

Sahara is a Muslim desert nation fighting for nationhood, but ruled by Morocco. Almost the entire indigenous population lives in refugee camps in Algeria. Few have ever had a chance to hear the gospel. Where are those preparing to reach them as soon as the opportunity arises? Praise God, there are some.

Saudi Arabia could be the biggest challenge of all. It is the headquarters of Islam with its two most holy cities, Mecca and Medina. It is vigorously hostile to any Christian presence or witness, with the large ex-patriate community strictly watched and controlled. Saudi believers, if found, are executed. Foreigners caught gathering with other believers or accused of witnessing are expelled if Western, but possibly beheaded if Filipino. Yet there are those who are praying for the land to open and looking for ways and means of bringing the gospel to Saudi people.

Somalia is strongly Muslim, but torn apart by internal strife between rival Somali clans. Also it is the scene of the humiliation of the UN peace-keeping forces in 1994-5 as well as the destruction and scattering of the only significant group of Somali evangelical Christians which once met in the now looted and destroyed capital, Mogadishu. Who is prepared to risk all to take the gospel to this proud, warlike people?

---

[10] A press report in September 1997 estimated the death toll to date from famine as between 500,000 and 2,000,000.

Other countries could be added to this list, but this does not tell the whole story. Many larger countries have significant numbers of Christians and churches, but there are often whole areas of the country still unevangelized. Here are a few examples:

India could become the most populous nation on earth by the year 2025. It is also the most diverse with its races, languages, castes and also its concentrations of Christians. Nagaland and Mizoram States in NE India are possibly the most evangelical states in the world, but the vast Ganges plains of North India contain the greatest concentration of unevangelized people in the world. For instance, the number of people in Uttar Pradesh in North India is about 180,000,000 and the Christian percentage is 0.1% and falling – this is about 180,000 people. North India will probably be the touch-stone of our success or failure in completing world evangelization in our generation.

Russia is the largest country in the world. It is also extremely diverse. Generally speaking, the Russians are probably no more than 0.5% Evangelical Christian; the majority are Russian Orthodox, but church attendance is only around 2% of the population. However many of the regions such as the North Caucasus, Northern Siberia and autonomous republics such as Tatarstan, Tuva, Buryatia and Kalmykia (the homeland of Europe's only indigenous Buddhist people) have little or no evangelical presence, and what witness there might be is usually that of migrant Russians.

Turkey, straddling Europe and Asia, was once Christian, but now Muslim (with the Turks replacing or absorbing the earlier peoples, the Galatians, Bythnians, Kurds, Armenians, Georgians, Greeks, etc.). The country has nearly 100 provinces, but less than 15 have any on-going evangelical Christian witness, and even fewer a live fellowship of Turkish-speaking believers.

Europe is nominally Christian, but for most, Christianity is a faint cultural backdrop for a highly secularized society. Maps showing the concentrations of evangelicals reveal how many areas of Spain, Portugal, France, Italy, Greece, Poland, Serbia, Macedonia, Germany have scarcely any groups of witnessing believers.

Nigeria and Chad are lands that have seen dramatic growth of the Church, but this growth has been almost entirely in the south

and centre of these countries. Many peoples in the Muslim north
are unevangelized.

Sudan has been torn by civil war for 30 years; a war in which
over 3 million are believed to have perished. The war was to
impose Islam on the non-Muslim south. The attempt failed, and
helped in provoking most of the southern population to embrace
Christianity despite the suffering. However the North and Darfur
province in the west are some of the least evangelized areas of
Africa.

Vast regions in the area of the 10/40 Window are still awaiting
the message of life. Our job is far from done, at which point we
could say that the gospel is available for every person. The many
media ministries may give us openings, but basically there need to
be believers on the spot witnessing and discipling for effective
church planting to be done.

Chapter 21

The People Challenge

Isaiah also challenges us that: *"Your descendants will possess the nations (peoples)."* Here is an ethnic or linguistic challenge. Jesus clearly stated that we must make disciples of all peoples in the great Matthew 28:19 statement. It is not enough to have a Christian presence in every **place**, but also to have followers of Jesus in every **people**.

In Chapter 8 I described the growth and development of the vision for the peoples of the world. We saw the breath-taking progress that has been made in reaching the world's peoples. We not only dream of discipling every people, we could actually see it realized in our lifetime.

There are various important ministries that must be strengthened for this discipling to be effective and lasting.

Research

We must know the facts if we are to disciple every people. Research information is therefore vital. There has been research carried on all through this century. The momentum for research on the world's peoples has accelerated over the past 20 years. We need to know who the unreached peoples are, where they live and what their evangelization status is. The Global Consultation on World Evangelization in Pretoria in June 1997 was an opportunity to present a fairly complete overview of unreached peoples at the end of the twentieth century.

For the months prior to that gathering, much work was done on the list of the peoples of the world. It had been decided several years before that for the remaining years of this millennium we needed to make a strategic limitation of the peoples to those over 10,000 population and under 5% Christian or 2% Evangelical, and also to limit our listing to peoples defined by ethnicity or language.[11] The cut-off points were reasonable, but arbitrary. The

---

[11] Further research and field responses indicated that some of the 1,500 peoples were not ethno-linguistic, but ethno-cultural. This came to light at the same time as a plea from Indian Christian leaders that the ethno-linguistic categories did not fit the ethno-cultural realities for church

difficulty in obtaining accurate information on the smaller peoples was a major consideration.[12] This reduced the number from about 3,000 to 1,500 least reached strategic peoples. Further investigation into which mission agencies were committed to specific peoples in this latter list revealed from responses that there were only about 500 peoples in the 1,500 without **known** outreach activity.[13] From other sources I know that there were a number of these peoples with mission outreach, but for which we had not received questionnaire responses.

We also realized that a long list of 1,500 peoples is a daunting challenge to read, understand and act upon in a meaningful way. We therefore grouped the peoples in two categories:

Affinity Blocs – of which we defined 12. Into these 12 we grouped every one of the 1,500 listed peoples. On page 240 is a map of 11 of these.[14] The 12th Bloc is for the Jews[15] who are global and therefore not represented on this map. The 13th grouping is hardly a 'bloc', but a catch-all category for unrelated peoples all over the world which did not fit into the other 12. These 11 regional Blocs are grouped by affinities of language, history, culture, etc. All these 11 are located within or near the 10/40 Window. It is interesting that nearly all the least reached peoples elsewhere in the world are actually migrants from these 11 blocs who now live in Europe, the Americas and Australasia.

People Clusters – Within each of these affinity blocs are other smaller groupings of peoples, often with a common name or identity, but divided by political boundaries, dialect differences,

---

planting among the caste groups of India. We therefore had to draw up a parallel list containing these categories for where it was more relevant in a church planting situation.

[12] By the year 2000, we plan to have a full list of all less-reached peoples including those with populations below 10,000.

[13] The full list is available in book form from the AD2000 and Beyond Movement office, 2860 S. Circle Dr., Suite 2112, Colorado Springs, CO 80906, USA.
Also on the WWW: <http://www.ad2000.org/>.

[14] A good coloured map of these Affinity Blocs has been published by Global Mapping International. 7899 Lexington Drive, Suite 200A, Colorado Springs CO 80920, Email: <info@gmi.org.> WWW <http://www.gmi.org/>.

[15] Fischer, 1997. *Intercessor's Prayer Guide to the Jewish World*. 1997: USA: YWAM Publishing.

etc. We have identified about 150 of these People Clusters, which include nearly 80% of the 1,500 peoples on the Joshua Project list. Here are 50 better known examples of these less-reached People Clusters in the various Affinity Blocs:

African Sahel: Fula, Mandingo, Wolof, Hausa, Kanuri.
Cushitic: Nubian, Somali, Beja.
Arab World: Algerian Arab, Kabyle, Riff, Libyan Arab.
Iranian: Kurd, Farsi, Tajik, Pathan, Baloch, Luri.
Turkic: Turk, Azeri, Kazak, Tatar, Uzbek, Uighur.
S. Asian: Bengali, Bihari, Hindi speakers, Urdu, Gond.
Tibetan: Lhasa Tibetan, Amdo, Bhutanese, Khampa.
East Asian: Hui, Mongolian, Japanese.
S.E. Asian: Burmese, Thai, Zhuang, Laotian, Dai.
Malay: Minangkabau, Acehnese, Sundanese, Madurese.
Eurasian: Chechen, Cherkess, Bosnian, Siberian groups.

These peoples are categorized in the table below.

Affinity Bloc Name	No. of People Clusters	No. of peoples in Bloc
African Sahel	19	395
Cushitic	4	37
Arab World	19	271
Iranian	12	181
Indo-Iranian (S. Asia)	30	449
Turkic	12	256
Tibetan	5	197
East Asian	6	70
S. E. Asian	14	93
Malay	18	175
Eurasian	5	44
Jewish	1	56
Totals (approx)[16]	145	2,224

[16] These figures must be seen as approximations, for further research is showing that some peoples are more reached than realized and therefore omitted, and other peoples are added – usually because migrant communities of larger peoples are discovered in other lands.

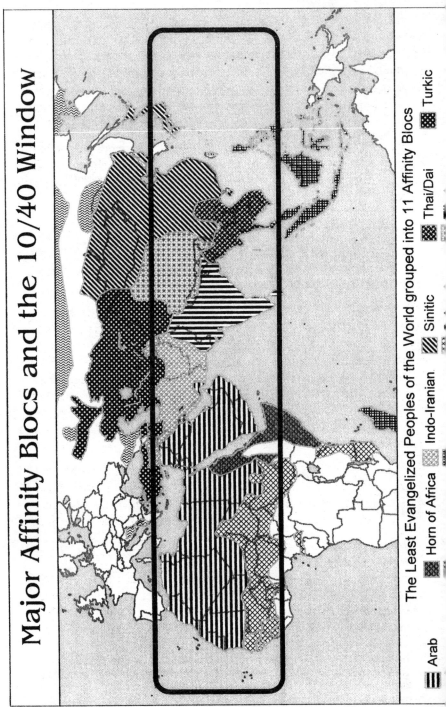

Major Affinity Blocs and the 10/40 Window

The Least Evangelized Peoples of the World grouped into 11 Affinity Blocs

Arab   Horn of Africa   Indo-Iranian   Sinitic   Thai/Dai   Turkic

A book was prepared for the October 1997 Praying Through The Window III[17] initiative containing a short description of, and prayer items for, 128 of these People Clusters.[18] It has been estimated that up to 50 million Christians around the world used these materials for prayer during that month – probably the largest prayer initiative the world has ever seen. God will give the breakthroughs among these peoples that appear so hard to reach!

For the first time in history we have a reasonably complete listing of the world's peoples and the extent to which they have been evangelized. This is why the next stage of church planting is possible.

Church planting

Can we really see church planting initiatives launched for all peoples within our present generation? Some might question that. In answer I report on what transpired in GCOWE-97.

Luis Bush, the Director of the AD2000 Mvt., made a great effort during GCOWE to encourage mission agencies represented and the various national delegations to commit themselves to reaching each of these remaining 500 peoples. By the end of GCOWE only 172 were left without any commitment from those present. However it must be added that we know of many smaller peoples (possibly around 1,000) with populations less than 10,000 who are just as worthy of attention, and part of Jesus' discipling command which are not included in these totals.

The implications of this are immense and exciting. It means that we are also running out of peoples where there is no pioneer work already in progress or in planning. To have reached this point is a very special moment in the history of missions! It also underlines the need for wise networking and partnering with others to ensure that the most effective way to achieve this is pursued.

Planting one congregation of believers in a small tribe of 1,000 can be significant, but one church among the 6 million Tibetans or a few churches among the 200 million Bengalis is less than a drop in the bucket. Our aim should be at minimum a church for every

---

[17] The AD2000 Mvt. sponsored annually from 1982 an annual global prayer emphasis, each focusing on a particular category of the world's population.

[18] Hanna 1997. *Praying Through the Window III.*

people, but this is only a beginning. This is where the Discipling a Whole Nation vision of Jim Montgomery is so valid. We need to ensure that there is a vital, worshipping group of believers within easy reach of every man, woman and child in the world. I reckon that there are now about 3,000,000 congregations of all kinds in the world today. Montgomery has written a challenging book *7,000,000 Churches to Go!* to highlight the task ahead of us.[19] The DAWN Movement founded by Montgomery has made a significant impact in many countries around the world in setting country-wide, multi-denominational goals for church planting to achieve that vision.

Church planting has been greatly enhanced by many support and media ministries which are people and language-sensitive. Immense efforts are being poured into these ministries, all of which have the potential of almost completely covering the world's population and peoples. Here I briefly describe the possibilities and goals of some of these mega-ministries.

Scripture translation

It is almost impossible to conceive of a strong church within a people that has no word of the Bible translated into their own language. The lack of the Scriptures for the Berber languages of North Africa was a significant factor in the surprising disappearance of the once-large North African Church between the coming of Islam in 698 and the twelfth century. The same was true for the Nubian peoples of the Upper Nile, who eventually succumbed to Islam after being Christian for 1,500 years; the Bible was never translated into their Nubian languages.

William Carey saw Bible translation as so important that it became the main thrust of his mission work. He wanted to lay the foundations for strong Indian churches through the labours of his missionary successors. The impact of the translation of the Bible is shown by the pioneer work of the London Missionary Society in Madagascar. The LMS made it a high priority to translate the New Testament into Malagasy. Soon after terrible persecution broke out

---

[19] Montgomery 1975, 1989, 1997. Montgomery's challenge as to the need for church multiplication applies both to areas not yet evangelized and to areas that have been evangelized, but where accessibility to churches is inadequate.

under Queen Ranavalona. The missionaries were expelled, but in spite of this the Church survived and even multiplied.[20]

We can only praise God for the remarkable ministry of the Bible Societies around the world who have multiplied over and over the number of languages that now have Scriptures. More recently God raised up the Wycliffe Bible Translators with the specific vision to provide a New Testament for every language without the Scriptures. WBT is now one of the largest cross-cultural mission agencies in the world. Their workers had, by 1997, translated the Scriptures into 420 languages, and have teams working in a further 965. The rate of increase of Bible translations into new languages is shown in this dramatic diagram.

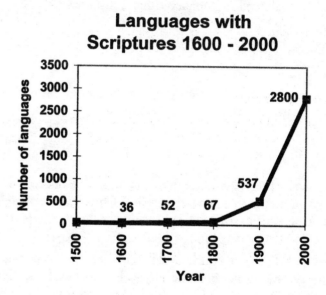

A Forum of Bible Agencies was formed in 1992 linking together the efforts of 17 Bible translation and distribution agencies. The aims are courageous and need to be covered in prayer. In 1993 these were :

1. The whole Bible translated into all languages spoken by five million or more by the end of 1999. There were 33 languages in this category that needed to be translated.

2. The New Testament translated into all languages spoken by over 500,000 people by the end of 1998. This meant a commitment to 77 languages that needed to be translated.
3. Some Scriptures in audio or written form for all languages spoken by more than 250,000 by the end of 1997.
4. Translation begun in all languages spoken by over 100,000 people by the end of 1997.

Of the world's 6,703 languages, at least 925 and possibly over 2,000 languages still have a need for New Testament translation work. The majority of these languages are in the African Sahel and Horn of Africa, the Iranic peoples, Central Asia, the Caucasus, China and India. We should be urgently recruiting many more dedicated and talented missionary Bible translators in order to see this task achieved. There is much work to keep an army of translators busy for another generation or more.

Literature

The power of non-Christian literature in corrupting millions is well known, for one only has to think of the pernicious evil that came through Hitler's racist *Mein Kampf*, or Marx's warped theories in *Das Kapital*, and Mao Tse Tung's poisonous diatribes in the *Little Red Book*.

The power of Christian literature should not be underestimated. Some reckon that over half of evangelical Christians attribute their conversion, at least in part, to Christian literature.

Today there is a prodigious volume of Christian literature produced and distributed quite apart from, and complementary to, the work of the Bible Societies – such as The Bible League, Scripture Gift Mission, the Gideons, Pocket Testament League and many others. Here I will only describe what I regard as the most globe-covering literature vision the world has ever seen – that of Every Home for Christ. The vision is very simple, but its outworkings have had extraordinary coverage and impact.

That vision is to prayerfully distribute a simple, relevant gospel presentation to every home and institution in each country of the world. Every Home for Christ has systematically distributed almost two billion multi-page gospel messages globally, each with a decision card, in languages spoken by 95% of the world's population. Illiterate people are reached with audio messages and the blind are provided messages prepared in Braille. Over 19 million of these decision cards have been returned to 80 global offices where each is followed up with a four-part Bible Correspondence Course. The aim is that every contact be introduced to a worshipping group of believers.

Other statistics are equally impressive. In 1997 almost 2,000 full-time nationals were employed in 80 countries, who co-ordinated as many as 10,000 volunteer distributors in the field during any given week. On average, these workers physically take the Gospel to 350,000 new families every seven days, or approximately 50,000 families a day. Based on a global average of 5.2 persons per household, this means that as many as 250,000 persons are provided reasonable access to the message of salvation through EHC activity every day.

In areas of EHC activity where there are no Bible-believing churches of any kind, converts are encouraged to come together for fellowship, Bible study and worship in small groups called "Christ Groups." These sometimes develop into well-established congregations. To date, some 15,000 Christ Groups have been established world-wide with the majority being in such regions as India, Indonesia, Nepal, Africa, the South Pacific, and the former Soviet Union. According to a report received recently from Africa, just one Christ Group near Kinshasa, Congo Republic, has grown to become a well-established church with more than 2,000 members in less than two years. In a city in the Ukraine another Christ Group grew to more than 3,000 in only 18 months.

Since the first EHC was launched in Japan in 1953, systematic every-home distribution has been carried out in more than 166 countries. Seventy-five have had at least one complete nation-wide coverage. Others, like Singapore, Hong Kong and Taiwan have had multiple coverages. Some countries, like India and the Philippines, have had two coverages and are being covered for the third time. The EHC ministry is currently active in 80 countries including many new works in the former Soviet Union, French Africa, Asia, and the Pacific. By 1997 EHC activity world-wide had been responsible for distributing over 1.78 billion pieces of gospel literature in hundreds of languages.

One cannot but be impressed with the breadth of this vision and the above results – even if the magnitude of such figures obscures the disappointments and failures. Yet by this means we have to admit that even in such a large and complex country as India, with the largest concentration of unevangelized individuals in the world, it is likely that nearly all the homes have been visited twice!

Audio Ministries

The story of Joy Ridderhof and Gospel Recordings, the mission she founded, is one of the great missionary sagas of this century.[21] It was a brilliant innovation to devise the means for painstakingly recording simple gospel messages on to records, and later, tapes and CDs even in languages where there were yet no believers or missionaries. The medium also lends itself to being able to fairly quickly produce gospel messages for a multitude of languages and dialects. This linked with simple play-back devices such as the Card-talk for records or manually operated play-back machines for cassettes enabled missionaries to leave an audio message that could be played over and over again. Illiteracy, lack of resident believers or lack of missionaries speaking their languages did not prevent the truth being given to unevangelized peoples. This tool has often been the first means by which totally unevangelized peoples first hear the gospel.

Gospel Recordings has grown into an international network of missions organizations under the title Global Recordings Network with bases in 30 countries. They produce and distribute **audio evangelism materials** in many of the tongues spoken in every country on earth. In 1997 GRN succeeded in preparing a gospel message in their 5,000th language.[22]

One of the advantages of this medium is that the resources and time needed are small enough to enable recordings to be made for the smaller peoples that could not otherwise be served with radio broadcasts or Bible translation for many years to come. A Bible translator would need to think carefully before committing all the effort and the 10-15 years to translating the New Testament into a language spoken by 300 people, but there is far less hesitation for

---

[21] Barlow 1952, Thompson 1978.
[22] Gospel Recording Network have an email address at
     <GloReNet@aol.com> and a web site at
     <http://ourworld.compuserve.com/homepages/GloReNet>

preparing a recording, or series of recordings for a people of 50 speakers.

GRN have a programme called *Tail-enders* -- those who are the last to get served, if they **ever do** get served. Gospel Recordings/Global Recordings Network is committed to finding and providing for the evangelization of Tail-enders, who are being ignored and neglected. The ultimate aim is to have a recording for every living language and dialect on earth; possibly a total of around 16,000[23]

There is not the space to tell of many other worthy agencies that specialize in producing audio materials for evangelism and discipleship – Scriptures on tape, teaching, and so on. Here I simply want to show the power of this medium in contributing to the evangelization of the least reached peoples on earth, especially those bypassed by other ministries because of smallness of size or isolation. This further enhances our potential to reach every race, tribe, people and tongue within our lifetime.

The Jesus Film and Videos

The Jesus Film Project has already been mentioned on p 154. This literal portrayal of the life of Jesus according to the Gospel of Luke has become one of the most powerful evangelistic tools of recent times and the most-watched film in history.[24]

The year 2000 vision is that at least all of the world's 300 languages spoken by more than one million people and at most all languages spoken by more than 75,000 people, and many of the smaller ones, will have a version of the film available and in use by then. The intermediate goal was 271 translations ready by the end

---

[23] The latest WBT Ethnologue total for known languages of the world is 6,700. However the Ethnologue also lists known dialects of these languages. This adds almost 10,000 dialects to the language list. The difference between language and dialect is hard to determine, but decided not only on linguistic, but also historical, cultural and social factors. If one group of people dislikes their same-language neighbours, a few words that differ, or shades of pronunciation are all that are needed to make a dialect into another language and another New Testament preferred!

[24] Eshleman 1995. This book tells something of the history, struggles, triumphs and fruit of this extraordinary gospel tool.

of 1993. By August 1997 this total had reached 417 translated and a further 226 in production.

The effort, planning and resources needed to produce this film in so many languages is staggering. Many thousands of Christian workers in many agencies are working hard in preparing new language versions or extensively showing this film. It has become a significant contributor to world evangelization.

Radio

Christian Radio has had an extraordinary history with some thrilling results in gradually breaking down long-held prejudice against the gospel. It has also made a pivotal contribution to providing teaching to Christians and their leaders especially where no other teaching resources were accessible.

The most dramatic evangelistic results have been where regular culturally-relevant broadcasts have been beamed into areas closed for most overt mission outreach. Justin Long of the Global Evangelization Movement and working on the *World Christian Encyclopedia* reckons that there are probably around 3 million people who have come to faith in Christ as a result of radio and television broadcasting, of which possibly 400,000 of these are isolated, often secret believers in areas where no church exists. Such figures are almost impossible to verify, but amazing stories have emerged from Russia, China, India and many parts of the Middle East of large numbers of churches being planted and nurtured almost entirely by Christian radio. The ministries of HCJB in Ecuador, Trans World Radio, Far East Broadcasting Company & Association, Radio IBRA, and many others have borne fruit beyond all that earlier detractors would have expected.

In recent years many of these large global ministries have come together to form the *World by 2000 International Network*. The aim was the Gospel by Radio to all Peoples. To be more specific, the aim was to provide the gospel by means of radio to every mega-language (this is a language spoken by more than 1,000,000 people) with a daily half-hour broadcast. This means that over 99.5% of the world's population would have the potential to hear the gospel in a language they could understand. The logic behind this is that nearly all of the people who speak a language of less than 1,000,000 would be at least partially bilingual and know sufficient of a more widely spoken language to understand the message. Of course in many areas radio listeners would be few, but in others many. For instance it was reckoned a few years ago that 15% of the population of the southern part of Muslim Yemen listened to the Christian FEBA station on Seychelles in the Indian Ocean.

At the time the World by 2000 Network made the commitment (mentioned in more detail on p.152) to broadcast daily for at least 30 minutes to every language of over one million speakers, it was estimated that about 140 of the world's mega-languages had Christian broadcasts. This meant that a further 160 language services needed to be developed. With further research a number of additional mega-languages were identified.

Since its inception World by 2000 broadcasters have added 75 new languages – and the initiative continues to provide impetus as the year 2000 approaches. There are now approximately 90 remaining languages which are scheduled for development.[25]

It is astonishing to see the progress towards this goal. However with many of the remaining peoples, the difficulties look almost insurmountable, and will need a large investment of expertise and funds, development of scarce or non-existent follow-up ministries, and a sufficient pool of native-speaker Christians with the maturity in the Lord to make the programmes. Just a few examples of the challenge:

- **The 3,000,000 Luri people in Iran** are one of the least reached peoples in the world. There are no known Christians in Iran directly involved in reaching them, and there are few Luri communities in other countries where they are more accessible. How, then, can broadcasts be made when no Christians are available to speak into a radio microphone?

- **The 4,000,000 Kanuri of Niger, Nigeria and Chad** have been evangelized by SUM, SIM and other missions for decades, but after all this effort, the Christians among this Muslim people can be counted on fingers and toes. There are no viable churches and few Christian leaders to recruit for radio ministry,

---

[25] The World By 2000 Network has a web site where more details may be found of languages broadcast, and languages for which broadcasts are needed: <http://www.wb2000.org/>.

and even if there were, those vital workers would probably have to leave another key ministry to do this. To prepare a daily 30 minute broadcast with the content and necessary appeal is a challenge that needs a team of dedicated workers for broadcasts and the essential follow-up ministries to be maintained.

• **The 1,500,000 Kham Tibetan people of China** have no broadcasts in their language, and the Christians among them are few. Most of these are also in the far west of China straddling the borders of the Tibetan Autonomous Region. Much of the Tibetan area is in turmoil because of Chinese attempts to quell separatist unrest. Were any Kham Christians able to help with preparing broadcasts, where could they do this, and would they bring trouble to themselves and their relatives were their voices recognized by the authorities?

Satellite Communications

The rapid development of satellite TV broadcasting and the widespread distribution of ever-smaller receiving dishes has radically affected our world – sadly often for the worse with ubiquitous programming that panders to the basest instincts of man. Yet even this medium is proving a remarkable means for proclaiming the gospel in lands hitherto almost inaccessible for the gospel.

For some nations, the advent of satellite technology is a boon for avoiding the need for provision of expensive cables for both national telephone systems and also a network of ground-based television transmitters. This means that even the less-developed countries could leap-frog into twenty-first century technology. Poverty is no longer necessarily a major factor in accessing high-technology communications. We can therefore expect that prayerfully launched and wisely managed Christian TV broadcasting could have and is having a significant impact on large numbers of peoples that are otherwise very little exposed to the gospel.

There are a number of Muslim countries that have been very aware of the subversive and corrupting effects to existing morals and religious beliefs by widely accessible programming over which they have no control. Some countries have tried to ban satellite receiver dishes, but to no avail – the dishes get smaller by the year and more easily concealed. It is reckoned that by 1997 about 80% of all homes in Saudi Arabia had satellite dishes, and in Tehran, Iran over 100,000 dishes were being set up every month. The desire for such is accentuated by the boredom induced by unimaginative Islamic programming; when a Muslim scholar sits in front of a camera and chants the Qu'ran, it is a strong encouragement to channel surf!

There has been a rapid rise in Christian investment in this medium. In 1997 the Christian broadcasting organizations, **SAT-7** (Cyprus), **The Bible Channel** (UK) and the **Miracle Network** (Norway) were all started using the AMOS satellite with a footprint covering the whole Middle East. The response to Arabic broadcasting by the end of 1997 was far beyond the expectations of the producers. By September 1997, 25 million people a week were hearing about the Gospel in India by satellite TV, but this will increase to more than 50 million in 11 languages by January 1998. There are big plans for such satellite networks for Latin America and East Asia.

The rapid expansion of "bandwidth" available is enabling more broadcasting with the possibility of interactive discipling programmes, whether by email, sound or TV with computers and satellites. This opens up the way for individual discipling in any language over satellite links. All closed borders become increasingly irrelevant and less of a barrier for any ministry. It is hard for us to imagine in 10 years time what might become reality – a missionary based in Germany discipling Mantsi believers in northern Siberia, a Korean intensive TEE course run for Mauritanians in Arabic based in Seoul or a group of refugee Hmong in French Guiana having fellowship with their fellow Hmong believers in Laos! This all opens up the potential for significant mission work to the ends of the earth to be run from a local congregation's own facilities.

This also opens up the possibility of continuity of ministry even if continuity of residence is denied the missionaries of the future. Are we ready to fully exploit these amazing technologies?

Conclusion

We must not be dazzled by the wonders of technology and think that the need for mighty intercessory prayer is obviated, the need for the cross and suffering nullified, or the value of real life acculturation and incarnation of expatriate missionaries within the culture lessened. Technology lessens our sole dependence on physical nearness and direct personal contacts, but does not lessen its value. Every people on earth must be reached with the gospel and discipled for the kingdom, but the flexibility and variety of tools and possibilities have multiplied. Let us use them where appropriate.

Each medium provides another layer of global coverage. Not every layer will affect every person equally, but the cumulative multiplicity of media layers does give us grounds to give greater expectation that the task can be finished if we mobilize the resources of the Church.

Chapter 22

The Urban Challenge

Isaiah's words in 54:3 are powerful; *"...and will people the desolate cities."* The third section of this verse gives the urban challenge. Many times we read in the Old Testament of cities being utterly destroyed. The broken hearted cry of Jeremiah over the destruction of Jerusalem at the hand of the Babylonians is the most poignant.[26] The physical Jerusalem was subsequently rebuilt and inhabited again by God's people. Yet, as we have seen, this verse has a New Testament and world evangelization connotation to it.

The massive urbanization of the past century has occurred in the midst of and even because of terrible desolations through wars, earthquakes, ecological degradation through population growth and human sinfulness. It is the desolations due to the sins of society today that need the healing of the gospel. The crime, drug trade and abuse, alcohol, prostitution and the desolations they have caused, have root causes that only can have a spiritual solution.

The great cities of the world are the key challenge for mission in the twenty-first century. We ignore the cities to our peril. The great cities of our world are the source of most of our wealth and misery, wisdom and depravity, innovations and sin. The engine for societal change is in the cities, but, if used wisely, it could be the dynamo for the growth of the Kingdom. Consider the following:

The Growth of urbanization

The twenty-first century will be an urban world, just as the previous 20 centuries of Christianity have been a rural world. The end of the second millennium is also the end of the rural majority with just over 50% of the world's population urbanized. The graph on the next page tells the story of the last two centuries with projection to 2100.

Two centuries ago the world was rural, with an urbanization of 4% and only one megacity in existence – Beijing with 1,100,000.[27]

---

[26] Lamentations Chapters 1-5.
[27] Barrett 1985. Barrett defines a megacity as one with 1,000,000 population, super-cities with 4,000,000 and super-giants with 10,000,000.

By 1900 these had increased to 14%, 18 megacities and 2 supercities – London and New York. By 2000 these will have reached 51% urbanized, about 20 supergiants (only one of which is in Europe or North America), 79 supercities and 433 megacities. That trend will continue so that by 2100 the number of rural inhabitants may be only 10% of the world's population. The cities are even more vital for mission strategy than they were in Paul's day.

**The growth of city dwellers
1800-2100**

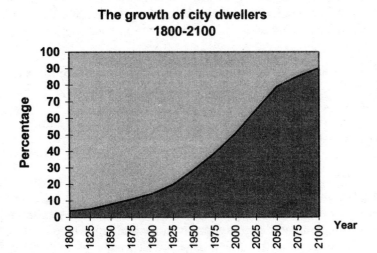

The growth of the urban unevangelized

Pioneer missions in the twentieth century have been characterized by the need to reach unreached peoples; a process within sight of conclusion. The twenty-first century will be characterized by the need for pioneer missions in the great cities of the world – a much more complex and multi-layered kaleidoscope of needs. Mission frontiers in the twentieth century were perceived as rural, but we must switch our thinking to the urban challenge as the frontier of the future.

The last two centuries of mission activity have, to a great measure, been a rural success story, but a partial failure in the cities of Africa and Asia – the areas that most need pioneer evangelism.

We have been winning the countryside and losing the cities, and all the time our rural constituency has been draining away to the cities. The graph below with figures from Barrett's challenging book *World-class Cities and World Evangelization*[28] shows how the massive migration of rural people in the developing world is steadily increasing the number of megacities. This trend must be reversed by far more attention and resources being directed to the evangelization of the cities. The glamour and romanticism associated with the jungles, mountains, deserts and remote islands seem like "real" mission work to the home constituency, but living in a concrete jungle, or squalid slum is far less attractive, and undesirable as a place of ministry. The developing world had 55% of the megacities of the world in 1980, but by 2050 this will have risen to 81% of the cities indicated in the graph below.

The growth of World Class cities
1900-2050

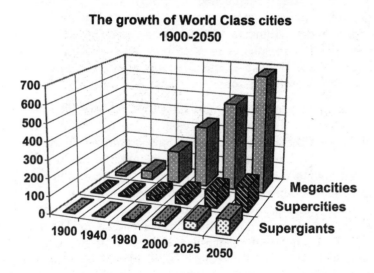

Cities in the more developed and affluent part of the world with their urbanization largely complete have inner city hearts that have died and been surrendered to squalor, crime, prostitution, drugs and violence – as well as providing a sort of home to indigenous or immigrant ethnic minorities. Then in the developing world where

---

[28] Barrett 1987:16.

urbanization is going on at a explosive rate, the cities have been ringed by vast squatter communities in shanty towns.[29]

There has been a tendency for Western missionaries to miss the importance of the massive urbanization now taking place. Most of those migrating to the cities have been driven by economic necessity from their impoverished rural homes to a poverty often greater than that which they left. A vast, receptive, desperate, barely surviving people need help, and the Christians are not there to offer hope with a vital spiritual message and a future as an alternative community. In the past, middle and upper classes were often targeted, and most of the churches were planted among these upwardly mobile people. The theory was that as these movers and shakers came to Jesus, the gospel would trickle down to the poorer people.[30] It rarely happened. Wealthy Chinese Christians in Bangkok, Thailand, or prosperous Ghanaian Christians in Accra were no more willing to welcome poor urban migrants into their churches than middle class Victorian Methodists welcomed the converts from William Booth's labours among the down-and-outs of London a century before.

The urban poor are the most receptive, but also the most under-evangelized. It is strategic to reach them, for the gospel has an uplifting effect when the gospel takes hold of individuals and communities. The great people movements into the kingdom have started among the poor. This was true from the time of Acts,[31] in the Roman Empire, the people movements in India and Pakistan over the past two centuries, the turning to God through the Pentecostal movement in Latin America, and so on. The pattern has generally been first the outcasts and the downtrodden, but this has percolated up through society until eventually impacting the structures of society. The cutting edge and spirituality of the Church is often blunted when the rich and powerful become Christians!

---

[29] These slums go under different names in different parts of the world. *Shanty towns* in South Africa, *Bustees* in India, *squatter areas* in Philippines, *bidonvilles* in Francophone lands, *favelas* in Brazil, *barriadas* in Mexico, etc.

[30] Grigg 1992:14.

[31] 1 Corinthians 1:26-29. Here Paul shows that the Corinthian church was made up of a majority of uneducated, low class, 'foolish' and despised.

One of the most powerful advocates of the need of the urban poor is Viv Grigg. When I first met him, he was living in a squalid slum in Manila. We walked though the smells and noise of the area where he lived. We had to climb up a ladder, through a trap door to sit with him and drink tea. His meagre possessions were scattered round this hot, stuffy little room. I felt he had earned the right to speak with passion as a prophet on behalf of the urban poor. His books have been a provocative means to the Church to take up the challenge.[32] Through his ministry he has helped birth four specialized "Servant" missions to the urban poor. He does not mince his words in speaking about the challenge to missions:

> …we must thrust out groups similar to the devotional communities of the twelfth century preaching friars, or the wandering Irish monks that converted Northern Europe between the fifth and ninth centuries… In our case we must send communities of men and women, married couples and singles, with commitments to live as the poor among the poor in order to preach the kingdom and establish the church in these great slum areas…[33]

and

> God is offering Western missions the chance to return to a biblical commitment to the poor and to incarnation as the primary missionary role model. The need is urgent: several thousand catalysts in the slums of scores of third-world cities who can generate movements in each city. Two billion people cry out.

It is interesting that when Mother Theresa, the Roman Catholic missionary to Calcutta, died in 1997, the Indian government ordered a State funeral for this remarkable woman who dedicated her life to alleviating the last months of the dying among the poorest of possibly the poorest population of any city in the world. In a remarkable way the quiet witness of that work opened the hearts and touched the consciences of the rich and powerful of that great nation.

Viv Grigg has compiled some sobering statistics to show the mushrooming growth of the urban shanty towns over the past 60 years, for it is basically in this period that these squatter

---

[32] Grigg 1984, 1992. His book *Companion to the Poor* tells his story.
[33] Grigg 1992:16-19.

communities have become significant. The whole process was triggered by World War II and the massive spread of industrialization to many non-Western countries. Over these 60 years to the year 2000 the urban poor in decaying inner cities and massive encircling squatter settlements has risen to about one billion people – almost as large as the entire Muslim population of the world. Of the two billion people living in Third World cities in 2000, it is reckoned that 40% will be the very poor.

Grigg has also demonstrated the disparity between the rich and poor in terms of spiritual neglect. I give three examples:

1. **Manila, Philippines** in 1988 had a population of 8,500,000. Of these, 30% lived in squatter areas. There were then 677 evangelical churches in the city, but only 51 church planting efforts directed to the squatter areas.

2. **Bangkok, Thailand** in 1986 had a population of 5,400,000 with well over a million living in 1,020 slums. Of Bangkok's 97 evangelical churches only three of these were in the slums.

3. **Calcutta, India** in 1988 had a population of 12,000,000; families that occupied one room were 66% of the whole. 3,000,000 lived in slums and an estimated 1,000,000 lived on the streets. In the city were 132 churches, some with poor people as members, but only ONE church of the poor reaching out to the poor.

Over the past twenty years there has been an encouraging new emphasis on holistic urban ministries, The writings of Roger Greenway, Harvie Conn, Ray Bakke,[34] Ed Silvoso and many others have raised the profile of urban church planting and given both hope and workable models for ministry which impact the multi-layered complexities of our cities. I have been encouraged by the number of young people today who are committing themselves to urban ministry among drug addicts, street children, prostitutes and the homeless. I believe a new day for urban ministry is dawning. As we look to the twenty-first century what are some of the salient points of strategy that we need to highlight? David Barrett gave a

---

[34] Greenway 1979; Bakke 1997. *Urban Mission* is an excellent publication edited by Harvie Conn, for those interested in church planting in urban contexts.

long list of proposals. I list a few, but draw from Barrett and other sources:

1. Organise corporate prayer for the city and for one another by Christian leaders from all ethnic and denominational backgrounds. This is a ministry strongly and persuasively promoted around the world by Ed Silvoso of Argentina[35]. The strong emphasis on reconciliation and unity for the purpose of reaching their cities has been with evident fruit in co-operative outreach.

2. Do city-wide research which highlights unreached sections and areas of the city population, and motivates congregations to specific action for their evangelization. In recent years some notable research has been done into major cities such as Mexico City, Lima in Peru, Nairobi in Kenya, Singapore and others.

3. Initiate city-wide outreaches that bring together congregations and agencies across the denominational spectrum. These should make use of every appropriate medium such as radio, TV, video, literature, and a wide variety of specialized ministries to the poor, disadvantaged, culturally isolated and those involved in the structures of sin in the cities. I have been impressed with the insistence of Evangelist Billy Graham that the churches in a city unite to invite him and to work together before he would agree to come to hold an evangelistic crusade.

4. Link up leaders of churches from every stratum of society, from upper/rich to lower/poor for meaningful relationships that provide economic uplift, training and the tools for self-help among the poor, and also provide a ladder of spiritual home congregations for the upwardly mobile as they begin to escape the poverty trap. It is difficult to get this right without appearing to be patronizing.

There is a danger with the "homogenous unit"[36] principle that targets a specific unit to the exclusion of all others, especially if it is the more wealthy section of the population. While this can help in the initial gathering of the first converts to be disciples, it can be dangerous when this is theologized and institutionalized to the point that it becomes introspective and

---

[35] Silvoso 1994.
[36] The homogenous unit principle was defined by Donald MacGavran in his book *Understanding Church Growth* p198-215. See also Winter, 1993: B41.

centripetal – drawing like people from other churches around to
their impoverishment, and limiting the vision for evangelism to
other sections of the city.

5. Make a vigorous effort to reach ethnic minorities in the cities –
   especially those who are increasing by immigration. Those first
   five years are the window of opportunity for reaching them.
   Abidjan in Cote d'Ivoire has experienced a massive influx of
   immigrants from all over Francophone West Africa to its
   relative wealth. Though this city is in the forest area, and with
   very few indigenous Muslims, over half the four million
   population is Muslim today. Most of the immigrants arrived as
   Muslims, but many others became Muslims within six months
   of arriving because when they arrived homeless and without
   help in the city, the Muslims invited them to stay temporarily in
   the mosques until they found some other place to live.
   Christians were missing the opportunity because they were not
   there to help these migrants in their time of need.

6. Form Incarnational mission teams to work together in needy
   areas with a specific vision to plant indigenous churches with
   their own leadership and level of functioning that is compatible
   with their surroundings. The danger is always there that these
   workers with their relative affluence, even if living simply,
   become a straw to be clutched at for escape from the poverty –
   and even a visa to study or live in the West!

7. Christians must determine to co-operate to change sinful
   structures of their society which so degrade, impoverish and
   exploit the poor.

8. Build into every programme of urban Christians a mission
   outreach to other cities and countries. This programme should
   be integrated into every department of the congregation.

9. Set definite goals for outreach and church planting and set up
   mechanisms that monitor interim goals.

Our desolate cities are an immense challenge. The Lord
promises us that these cities will be populated with his people.

Chapter 23

The Social Challenge

Isaiah has much to say about both the individual sins and the sinfulness of the people of Israel. Whole chapters are filled with stern warnings of God's judgement on both individual and societal sin and degeneration into violence, drunkenness, corruption, immorality, oppression and idolatry.[37] Even the passage highlighted in this book brings out the two levels of sin – of the individual in Isaiah 52-53 and those of society in 54. The latter shows the marks of a society whose structures have been corrupted, urban desolation in verse 3, dysfunctional families in verse 4, oppression in verse 14 and organized violence in verse 15. The Scripture shows that both must be addressed. In the twenty-first century the agonizing social evils in society will have to be faced as an essential component of mission, and not just the proclamation of personal salvation.

Great evangelical awakenings in the past have been accompanied by a multiplicity of evangelical social initiatives that transformed conditions of the less privileged of society. This was especially true in the wake of the eighteenth century revival of the Wesleys and Whitefield and of the Great Awakening in the mid-nineteenth century. The whole legal system was overhauled, prisons reformed, slavery banned, the poor children protected, universal education promoted and workers' rights established. The major factor for introducing these improvements in Europe and North America was the social consciousness of Evangelicals.[38] Missionaries in the last century strongly emphasised education, social reforms and bringing health programmes to Western colonial territories as an essential component of bringing the gospel message.

The sad truth is that for much of this century Evangelicals have retreated from linking mission with any specific social programme, mainly as a reaction to the overemphasis by churches and missions that became liberal in theology and where proclamation of the

---

[37] Note specifically Isaiah chapters 1 and 5.
[38] Many examples could be given – Evangelicals such as Wilberforce and the fight for the banning of slavery, Elizabeth Fry and the reform of prisons, George Müller and the care of orphans and so on.

gospel was eclipsed.[39] This was derisively called "the social
gospel." It must be affirmed that right through this century,
evangelical missionaries have said little, but done much in
education, medicine and social welfare as an essential part of their
mission activity, but not said much about it.

The turning point in the perception of Evangelicals came with
the great International Conference on World Evangelization in
Lausanne, Switzerland in 1974. The Lausanne Covenant
formulated at that Conference has proved a major rallying point for
defining the faith and mission of Evangelicals in evangelical
churches and structures and those in conciliar, pluralist
denominations. The fifth of the fifteen statements stated:

Christian Social Responsibility

We affirm that God is both the Creator and Judge of all men.
We therefore should share his [God's] concern for justice and
reconciliation throughout human society and for the liberation
of men from every kind of oppression. Because mankind is
made in the image of God. Every person, regardless of race,
religion, colour, culture, class, sex or age, has an intrinsic
dignity because of which he should be respected and served,
not exploited. Here too *we express penitence both for our
neglect and for having sometimes regarded evangelism and
social concern as mutually exclusive*. Although reconciliation
with man is not reconciliation with God, nor is social action
evangelism, nor is political liberation salvation, nevertheless
we affirm that *evangelism and socio-political involvement are
both part of our Christian duty*. For both are necessary
expressions of our doctrines of God and man, our love for our
neighbour and our obedience to Jesus Christ...[40] [*my italics*].

For much of the twentieth century social change had been
regarded as just a *fruit* of the gospel rather than an *essential
component* of that gospel. This understanding of the Great
Commission had not included both the evangelistic and social
responsibility, thus the latter was side-lined. Subsequently
evangelical understanding went through further change. In 1983

---

[39] Bosch 1991, 381-389; 400-408 gives an excellent history of this
development across the whole Church spectrum from Catholicism to
Evangelicalism.
[40] Douglas 1975:4-5.

there was a World Evangelical Fellowship conference where a balance was struck between evangelism and social involvement. From this came the *Wheaton '83 Statement*. In Paragraph 26 was stated:

> Evil is not only in the human heart but also in human structures... The mission of the Church includes both the proclamation of the Gospel and its demonstration. We must therefore evangelize, respond to human need and press for social transformation.

With this declaration, Evangelicals were more free to launch into what has become an amazing variety of mission initiatives in which facing up to the social evils of society was seen as part of the essence of the Great Commission. This is not to say that the discussion or even the arguments are ended, but a new sense of social responsibility has brought a greater wholesomeness to the mission thrust of the Church. In hindsight we can see that evangelical hesitation to social change was a temporary reactionary aberration. The danger of the pendulum swinging too far must always be watched.

Over the past two decades we have seen the multiplication of mission efforts in famine relief, orphan care and the growth of such agencies as World Vision, TEAR Fund, Help For The Brethren (*Hilfe für die Brüder*). This was followed by major initiatives and networks emerging for drug addicts, prostitutes, AIDS victims, children in need, the urban poor and landmine victims which have received much publicity. The twenty-first century will provide even greater challenges that will stretch our ingenuity and resources and test our love and commitment to the limit. I only mention a few here as areas in which Christian ministry could and should play a major role.

Children at risk

Looking back over the twentieth century it is astonishing to see how little ministry to children has featured as a major concern for mission agencies in recruitment, in discussion at international conferences and in deployment of resources. The great Lausanne Congress of 1974 issued the milestone declaration of the Lausanne Covenant. It has no mention of children or young people other than that mankind is *made in the image of God regardless of...age*. The

LCWE Consultation on World Evangelization in Thailand in 1980 had 23 tracks, 18 of them for specific witness to refugees, cities and the major religious blocs, but nothing for the 35% of the world's population under 15. Praise the Lord for the rectification of this at GCOWE in Pretoria in 1997. At that event, one of the ten tracks was specifically for ministry to children and two others had a high youth component.

Since the middle of the century the work of such missions as Child Evangelism Fellowship and Scripture Union has become well known, but peripheral to the thinking of most Christian churches and agencies. Even more astonishing has been the low profile given to children in their millions who have been exposed to the most horrific conditions of war, famine, urban squalor, abuse, exploitation in labour and in the infamous sex "industry."

Only in the past decade has this begun to change as people began to be concerned for the vulnerability of marginalized and poor children. News coverage of terrible events and situations such as massive child sex-abuse cases by child-carers in the West, massacres of street children in Latin America, the cruel exploitation of indentured child labour in India and Pakistan, the tragedy of the drugged child-soldiers of the Liberian and Sierra Leone civil wars or the criminal abuse of the child prostitutes of Bangkok and Manila in sex tourism. A new word has come into our vocabulary *children at risk.* How did we carry on our preferred ministry to adults and not notice that so little was being done for the next generation and how many were under threat – some reckon that the total number in situations of present risk as over 800 million children.

Just consider the following facts:[41]

Abortions: Every year 40 million or 29% of all children conceived are never born but aborted [*United Nations*].

Child prostitution: An estimated 10 million children suffer forced prostitution, and 1,000,000 children a year become prostitutes [*World Vision*].

Malnutrition kills 35,000 children under five every day [*World Vision*].

---

[41] These facts were published in the Oxford Statement concerning Children at Risk on 3 Feb 1997 as a product of a consultation in Oxford, England in Jan 1997.

Street children number over 100,000,000. These are defined as those who live and/or work on the streets of the world's cities [*UNICEF*].

Victims of war – over 1,500,000 children were killed in war between 1984 and 1994, a further 4,000,000 were disabled, maimed, blinded or brain damaged by wars and 12,000,000 lost their homes. During that period 35 nations are known to have forcibly recruited children into their armed forces [*Save the Children 1994*].

AIDS victims – over 1,500,000 children were known to be infected with AIDS in 1993 [*UNICEF 1994*]; the number has since risen markedly.

Slavery and child labour: between 100 and 200 million children are estimated to be involved – often in very bad conditions [*UN Children's Fund*].

A new mobilization is taking place to rectify this. The Viva Network[42] has emerged as a co-ordinating hub for an amazing variety of ministries speaking out on behalf of these millions of marginalized children. By 1997 it was reckoned by Viva Network that there were over 110,000 Christian workers involved in 20,000 separate projects directed in outreach to over 1,000,000 children on a daily basis in high social risk situations. Both Latin American Mission and SIM have made children one of their priorities in the years to come.

Phyllis Kilbourn, one of my WEC colleagues, was so moved by the effects of the 1990-1997 civil war in Liberia, her former field of service, that she has written three sobering and challenging books on children at risk[43] published by MARC, World Vision. Out of this has been birthed a new ministry entitled Rainbows of Hope specifically geared to children at risk around the world.[44]

At last the children of the world are becoming a major focus of mission. This gives greater hope for the Church of today as well as the Church of tomorrow.

---

[42] Viva Network. P.O. Box 633, Oxford OX1 4YP, UK
    email:<100423.2255@compuserve.com>
[43] Kilbourn 1995, 1996, 1997.
[44] Rainbows of Hope, PO Box 1707, Fort Washington, PA 19034-8707, USA, e-mail:< 75573.3070@compuserve.com>

Ministry in the twenty-first century will be in a more pressurized, crowded world with the urban poor multiplying exponentially. The implications for children are grim; the number that are vulnerable will grow even faster. Christian ministry should and will have a major emphasis on these children.

Drug addiction

The massive increase in the cultivation, manufacture, and trade of narcotic drugs has become one of the largest, yet illegal, global industries. Whole nations such as Afghanistan, Myanmar, Colombia and some Caribbean states have become almost completely dependent on and corrupted by the income from drugs. Vast legions of police and military forces are deployed to limit this evil, but all too often they themselves become corrupted by the massive profits which accrue from colluding with the purveyors of these drugs. Multi-billion dollar transference of funds stimulates organized crime, corrupts financial institutions and destroys countless lives – not only in the West, but in the producer countries too. In many Western countries today, the majority of young people have used drugs illegally at least once, but sadly many have also become addicted and worse.

The mission enterprise of the twenty-first century cannot ignore this problem. It will continue to become a problem in our cities so engulfing that it will become a major ministry and, if tied effectively to a church planting vision, also fruitful. It may prove a major source of breakthrough for the gospel in many parts of the Muslim world, and Asia as well as the West.

Disease

Major medical advances during this century have bred a false optimism about the ability of modern medicine to master every disease. Massive immunization programmes have eradicated smallpox, and reduced such killer diseases as polio, leprosy, measles and scarlet fever from being a major scourge to a rarely seen, preventable sickness. The discovery of penicillin and the widespread use of antibiotics magically reduced life-threatening infections, making pneumonia and meningitis curable sicknesses. Major parasitic diseases such as bilharzia and malaria were in retreat. Many forms of cancer were becoming more treatable and the survival rate of those afflicted was rising. It only seemed to be a matter of time and research before all viruses, cancers and even genetic diseases would become a fading memory.

That was not to be. The last twenty or so years have seen an alarming come-back of many old diseases and dramatic appearance of new diseases. We have become aware that doctors are fallible and limited in what they can achieve – even when they appear to have virtually unlimited resources.

1. **Tuberculosis** was a major cause of death a century ago, but in many parts of the world TB had virtually been eradicated. The gradual evolution of resistant strains of the TB bacteria was hastened by the advent of the HIV in the 1980s. AIDS patients became a major incubator for TB. It has made a frightening comeback, but this time the long-trusted drugs are of little avail as the TB bacillus has developed new forms resistant to them.

   a. Over 30 million people contracted the disease in the '90s – most in the less developed world. Over 26% of avoidable deaths in the Third World were caused by TB, and about a third of these were AIDS-related.

   b. In 1997 it was announced in Russia that 400,000 prisoners were to be released from prison in an amnesty, but it is estimated that 70% of the prison population have the disease. Already the Russian medical system is in a state of collapse with lack of funding and resources to cope. The coming impact on the general population is frightening. Many other nations face similar problems. Who but Christians are going to provide the long-term love and care such patients need?

2. **Malaria** has long been a scourge in tropical and even some more temperate lands. It was one of the main reasons for the late development of Africa, and the high casualty rate among missionaries in West Africa in the nineteenth century. The little jingle "Beware, Beware the Bight of Benin, where few come out, but many go in" was a grim reality. The advent of quinine and a range of anti-malarial prophylactics and widespread efforts to control the mosquito carriers of the parasite gradually rolled back the boundaries of areas prone to malaria and greatly reduced the incidence of the disease. Since independence came to many countries, malaria has bounced back with vigour when many governments relaxed the efforts at control by the colonial

powers. Strains of the parasite have become resistant to every known prophylactic.[45] It was because of less efficient control in economic crises, global warming and movements of population that once more the disease is spreading to areas once freed from it, and has begun to invade countries free for centuries. Over 105 countries have resident malaria infestation today.

In 1996 over 3 million died of the disease, including one million children. It is estimated that the incidence of malaria will double between 1994 and 2010. This gives us two great challenges – are we willing to take the risk for the Lord Jesus to serve him in a malaria-prone climate, and are we willing to be part of the solution in preventing the disease or alleviating the lot of those who are afflicted?

3. Cancers

At present in the Western World one in every three deaths is caused by cancer. By 2010 this will rise to one in two. The uneven geographical incidence of the cancers point to diet, pollution and nuclear radiation as significant causes. It is astonishing that the powerful tobacco companies are making such efforts to export their deadly products to the less-developed nations as resistance to them in the West increases. Our world faces pollution and ecological disaster on an increasing scale, and this will be reflected in the incidence of cancer and other diseases. Efforts to control ecological degradation will be the least in the poorer and developing countries; the very areas that are also more likely to be spiritually needy.

4. Coming Pandemics

In the fourteenth century the Black Death or bubonic plague killed possibly 40 million people which was nearly a third of the population of Europe and Asia. Cholera killed millions in Asia in the nineteenth century, and influenza 18 million in 18 months in 1919-20. Could we see terrible new pandemics that decimate populations again? Maybe.[46] Both the cholera and influenza viruses mutate; some forms could be more virulent than any now known.

---

[45] *Journal of the American Medical Association*. Jan 7, 1996. Vol. 275 No3.
[46] A recent book written by Laurie Garrett became a best seller with its evocative title: *The Coming Plague: Newly emerging diseases in a world out of balance.*

The over-use and misuse of antibiotics have helped to hasten the development of "superbug" bacteria against which there are now no known drugs.[47] The astonishing ability of bacteria to develop resistant strains, and even to pass on that resistance to unrelated bacteria is truly nature's fight-back.[48]

The emergence of new and exotic killer diseases gives no grounds for complacency. One only has to recall the lurid reporting associated with Legionnaire's disease, Ebola, the flesh-eating bacteria that acts too quickly for any drug to combat it.

The Mad Cow Disease, or Creutzfeld-Jakob Disease, mainly in the UK, is caused by a body even smaller than a virus, called a prion. So little is known about this type of disease. Is this a warning of worse to come? AIDS is one such.

AIDS

AIDS and HIV, the virus that causes it, has spread with frightening rapidity. This is astonishing for a disease that was unknown in 1980, with such a long incubation period, and largely caused by sexual promiscuity. AIDS is highly emotive because of its link with the basest of behaviour in society, the sex industry, and because of its insidious challenge in the prevailing rejection of any moral standards.

Accurate figures are hard to come by; firstly because many countries have passed laws banning compulsory testing for the virus because of this emotive reaction; secondly, in many countries the social stigma of admitting to having the virus leads to official silence, and; thirdly many of the worst afflicted countries cannot afford either the finance to test victims or to provide any medical care for them. A low estimate for 1996 was 30 million carrying the virus, 10 million with the AIDS disease, and 6.5 million already dead from the disease. About 25% of all deaths are of children infected with the disease at birth. It is estimated that there were 1,500,000 deaths attributable to AIDS in 1996, and 2,300,000 in 1997 – one can only speculate how many more died, the real cause not divulged or known. Here are just a few further observations:

---

[47] The staphylococcus aureus bacteria has recently been found to have developed immunity to the last known antibiotic left in the medical armoury.

[48] See Geoffrey Cannon's book, *Superbug: Nature's Revenge.*

1. **The West, especially USA and Brazil**, has seen large numbers of homosexuals afflicted. Wide publicity and massive funding for research into remedies have caused the rate of increase of reported HIV cases to drop and the development of AIDS from those with the HIV to be slowed. The medical improvement has been achieved but with high costs – $10,000 to $15,000 on drugs annually. This cost is way beyond the reach of those in other parts of the world where the incidence of the disease is so much greater. Russia, on the other hand is in the grip of a massive pandemic of AIDS with 1,000,000 likely to be infected by 2000.

2. **Africa** has seen the worst incidence of AIDS with nearly 20 million known to be infected with the virus in 1996. Officially, countries such as Botswana, Zimbabwe, Malawi, Zambia and Uganda are reckoned to have had 12-18% of their populations that were HIV+ in 1996. The unofficial figure is likely to be higher. Only in Uganda has the incidence started to decline because of the government campaign against AIDS and the efforts of Christians in promoting the only way to eliminate the disease, i.e. total abstinence from sexual activity outside marriage, and total faithfulness in it. In Malawi 6 people an hour die of AIDS, which is over 50,000 a year. The economic devastation is horrific with deaths most prevalent among the most economically active part of the population and with an expected 10 million AIDS orphans in Africa by the year 2000.

3. Soon **Asia's** HIV+ population will surpass that of Africa. Widespread prostitution has spread the disease like wildfire through the populations of India and Thailand and surrounding nations. Estimates for the numbers infected in India by the year 2000 range from 15 to 50 million.

The horror of the above statistics are mind-numbing. However, when in contact with the real people whose lives have been devastated by the disease or by bereavement, it becomes even more heartrending. The plain truth is that the average person cannot cope and face the realities of AIDS. We Christians have the message that can give eternal hope to those afflicted, and the moral alternative to bring this awful pandemic to a halt. In the next 20 years there will need to be a multiplication of new ministries and agencies to minister and plant churches in AIDS-devastated societies.

I referred to the Betel ministry in Spain linked with WEC International on p127-8. This ministry to drug addicts has developed into a full-orbed church-planting and missionary effort while grappling with all the pastoral and personal pains and uncertainties of AIDS as a constant companion. It is a foretaste of a new type of community of Christians for the twenty-first century. May there be many more.

Conclusion

I have only been able to highlight some of the challenges for social ministry. Other vital areas of ministry could have also been described such as ministry to prisoners,[49] orphans,[50] Christian aid to the deprived, ecology missions, education, literacy, and so on. My aim has been to show these as a vital component of the Great Commission in the twenty-first century.

What, then, are the probable directions for evangelical mission agencies in the twenty-first century with regard to social ministry? I can only point out a few:

1. There will be a multiplication of specialized ministries launched by Christians as public and governmental programmes disintegrate before their sheer size and expense.

2. Medical missions will multiply, but with a greater emphasis on supplementing government programmes, expanding preventive care rather than the traditional mission hospitals, loving care to those who become ostracized by dangerous diseases such as AIDS.

3. Only those agencies with a social agenda that is tied to a successful indigenous church planting ministry will be able to generate the finances and work-force to sustain and expand the ministry. Giving from outside the country is finite, and will not expand at the level of expense of these ministries.

---

[49] The remarkable ministry and high profile given to Christian outreach to prisoners owes much to the ministry of Chuck Colson and the Prison Fellowship he founded.

[50] The ministry of World Vision cannot be left unmentioned in this regard, but today there are many other ministries seeking to minister to orphans.

Chapter 24

The Ideological Challenge

The Future of Political Ideologies

The two hundred year infatuation with revolutionary ideology as the driving force in the affairs of humankind is basically over. The infatuation was triggered by the French Revolution with the storming of the Bastille in 1789. The spirit of revolution flowed like lava from a volcano across the world and reshaped society.[51] Ideology became the primary factor in world political movements – whether revolutionary ideologies such as Nazism, Fascism, Communism, or evolutionary ideologies such as democracy, capitalism or liberalism. Its death-knell came to an end in 1989 with the tearing down of the Berlin Wall which divided the two Berlins. Those 200 years were but a blip, an aberration in the history of the world. This is shown in the student world; for what do they demonstrate today? In the 1960s and 1970s it was ideology, nuclear weapons, Vietnam, apartheid, but today it is about grants, food and examinations. Widespread disillusionment with political systems, parties and cynicism about politicians themselves are also manifestations of this.

The Collapse of Communism

Communism threatened our world over much of this century. It had gained an aura of permanence and invincibility that concealed its rotten core with its flawed economic theories and unworkable, hate-driven social engineering programme. Even in 1986, who could have predicted that within five short years, that ideology would no longer exist as a viable political system and those countries where it survived would have either reneged on the basic economic tenets of Communism or simply become crude dictatorships with Marxist-Leninist fig leaves to cover their ideological nakedness. Christianity, so long oppressed and even suppressed in these lands, has survived, re-appeared and blossomed in vigorous new life.

---

[51] One fascinating spin-off was Napoleon's promotion of the metric system and enforcement of driving on the right on roads in all countries

We must not ignore the continued presence of militant atheism in those lands where Communism, even modified Communism, continues to dominate. About a quarter of all humankind is still living under such governments that hate the very existence of the true Church – a hate that appears so irrational and counter-productive were we not to know the satanic origin of that ideology. The ongoing persecution or shackling of the Church in China, Vietnam, Laos, Cambodia, North Korea and Cuba is still real and painful. Ministries to strengthen those believers are still important. Prayer is still needed for the persecuted church in such lands.

The Discrediting of Capitalism

The sudden collapse of European Communism led to unhealthy gloating by capitalistic societies. Many have written about the victory of capitalism over Communism. Market forces may be more efficient than the command economy demanded by Marxist theory, but unredeemed sinful human beings control both systems. Both are easily manipulated by those who are selfish, greedy and cruel, and who fiercely protect their own privileges and conceal their manipulation of the system from the majority.

Christians have too often thought of capitalism as basically "right," but the '90s have revealed the grave deficiencies of a flawed ideology. The prevailing philosophy is hedonistic and seems to be, 'Money is good and for my pleasure and I could not care less about the less privileged, the environment or any moral code (if I can get away with it).' The new mafia capitalists of Latin America and the former Communist world as well as the sleaze, massive financial scandals and ostentatious wealth in the West have not been a good advertisement for capitalism.

The Reformation brought about a revolution in society. Politicians became accountable to those they ruled, individual and property rights were respected, honest work was honoured and Absolute Truth recognized as to be found in a loving Creator, Redeemer God. It was on this basis that capitalism thrived. Capitalism with these underpinnings removed becomes just another avenue down which human greed and selfishness drives. So today

---

conquered or directly influenced by him. Hitherto, horsemen rode on the left to better defend themselves with the sword in the right hand.

the prevailing world-view of most Westerners this century has become profoundly secular and indifferent to spiritual things.

The Future of Religious Ideologies

Massive global change is not only affecting political ideologies, it is also affecting religious ones too. Islam, Hinduism, Buddhism and even Christianity, as a socio-political force, are under threat as never before. We will be surprised and shocked by the massive disruptions and upheavals that will affect all of these ideologies in the twenty-first century. We close our eyes to these coming events at our peril and to the detriment of the whole mission enterprise. People are desperate, hurting, leaderless and without hope for this world or the next because the religious straws at which they clutch are failing them. They still need the gospel, but stripped of its non-biblical clothing. World evangelization will continue until the coming of Jesus, but is that evangelization process to be brought to consummation by our present presuppositions and methods? How relevant will we be for the challenges of the next century? Here is a brief look at the four main religious ideologies which present the greatest challenge to mission.

The End of Christendom

Christendom itself as an ideology is flawed and failing fast too. The rapid marginalization of the Judeo-Christian cultural heritage and also the failure of Christians to preserve their privileged position are patently obvious in the Western world. We are being compelled to return to a much more biblical and radical position – that of being a minority in the world but not of it. Few Christians are aware that the 1,700 years of a politicized Christianity as the ideology of the ruling elite are rapidly drawing to a close. Whether we like it or not, the concept of the **imperial Church**[52] dominated the thinking of Roman Emperors from Constantine onwards through the papacy, the Reformation and the nineteenth century mission movement. Its marks are also visible in the largely Protestant Moral Majority or Religious Right in the USA and the

---

[52] Hall 1997. Hall eloquently warns Western Christians of the ending of their long-held privilege of holding the reins of power, and the need to rethink the nature of the Church and its role in society. His thesis is that the Church must regain it prophetic voice by its separation from the world and yet being in the world as salt, yeast and light.

efforts of Russian Orthodoxy to eliminate every alternative religious opinion today. The era of Constantinian Christendom is ending. A Church deprived of political power is freed from the burden of trying to use human power to dominate and influence the world. The time for a more effective mission to the needy world is dawning. We need to recognize this, adapt and seize the opportunities offered. Our reference point is not territorial or church growth aggrandisement, but building a kingdom that is not of this world, yet which will fill the earth as a contrasting alternative society. We need to return to the concept of a **pilgrim Church**,[53] a Church that will be hated, rejected, despised, persecuted, yet be an incisive, decisive, victorious minority which, one day soon, will be ready for its Heavenly Bridegroom as the perfected Bride. The twenty-first century may be the time when the alternative Church becomes recognized as the real Church.

Christendom is doomed, but the future of biblical Christianity is bright. It is taking us a long time to perceive this. We need to stop mourning the decline of Christianity in Europe and many parts of the West, and realize that the coming of Christianity did not convert Europe, but "baptized" the paganism that still has to be adequately confronted with the claims of Christ. The Europe of today has reverted to attitudes that prevailed in the time of the early Church. Europe's secularism, unashamed sinfulness, infatuation with neo-Hinduist New Age thinking and occultism needs to be confronted once more, as in the first centuries of the Church, by a Christianity unafraid to love and win those who persecute it.

The Disintegration of Islam

Samuel Zwemer, the great Apostle to the Muslims, wrote a book in 1916 with this heading.[54] Certainly 80 years later that disintegration has not taken place and looks unlikely as we watch the geographical spread and the economic power of the Muslim world and the fierce willingness of Muslim fundamentalists to sacrifice their lives in the violent elimination of their perceived enemies. Yet was he prophetic? Are there signs that this disintegration may have already begun?

---

[53] Broadbent 1931. Broadbent describes this alternative Church through the history of the past 2000 years and shows its sufferings and triumphs.
[54] Chapman 1995:9.

Without a doubt, Islam is, and has been, the most formidable opponent of Christianity.[55] Three times in history, Muslims have sought to deal a death blow to Christianity. Yet it must be stated that there have been three serious assaults on the Muslim world by 'Christian' countries. These were:

1. **The Muslim assault on Western Europe** with the occupation of Spain in 714 and invasion of France in 732, which was defeated by Charles Martel at Tours and Poitiers.

2. **The Christian Crusades** from 1096 to 1291 which were aimed at regaining the Bible lands for Christianity lost to Islam in the seventh century. The cruelties, atrocities and carnality associated with the Crusaders are still a major stumbling block to Christian witness. It is significant that the Reconciliation March of Christians along the route of the Crusaders' armies in 1996-9 should take place at this time – 900 years after the launch of the First Crusade.

3. **The Turkish Ottoman invasion of Eastern Europe** 1396-1683. In the latter year the assault on Vienna was repulsed, followed by a long and slow Ottoman retreat from European countries until World War I in 1914. The 1,200-year Muslim rule over Christianized peoples of Europe have deeply and negatively affected Europeans to this day in their attitudes to Muslims and is one of the major factors in the bitterness shown in Bosnia today.

4. **European colonial Empires** gradually gained political control of nearly all the Muslim-majority countries of the world[56] beginning with the Dutch in Indonesia in the seventeenth century and culminating in the foundation of the Israeli state in 1948 as the ultimate affront.[57] The impact of colonialism, especially the existence of Israel which emerged from its shelter, has been one of the most painful realities for Muslims, and particularly Middle Eastern Muslims, and one of the major

---

[55] Colin Chapman's excellent book, *Cross and Crescent,* is superbly written to help Christians understand Muslims and Islam, and how to share their faith with them in a meaningful way. It is both comprehensive, up-to-date and has an excellent and full bibliography which I do not attempt to reproduce here.

[56] Jansen 1979:63-65.

[57] Chapman 1995:144.

motivations for Muslims to react in any way possible to end that ignominy.

5. **The Muslim response in the Yom Kippur War of 1973 and the first oil crisis.** Although the effort to crush Israel in 1973 failed, it was the beginning of the Muslim response to Israel and the West which continues to this day. It is a war being waged on every front – diplomacy, finance, elimination of Christian minorities in Muslim lands, ending any Christian mission work, military might and terrorism. It would be surprising if this did not lead to a war of apocalyptic proportions within the next few years in the Middle East.

6. **The invasion of Western culture into the Muslim World.** The pervasive influence of Western values and culture through the media is hated and rejected by many Muslims. Yet these influences are so powerful that they are seen as a further assault on Islamic society. Hollywood and Christianity are inextricably intertwined in Muslim thinking.

It is not a promising prospect for the Christian evangelization of the Muslim world, let alone its disintegration. Yet the promises of the Bible are true, the gospel is the only remedy for the sin of Muslims, and we are assured that every people, even those that are largely Muslim, will be represented before the throne, and that every stronghold and proud obstacle to the knowledge of God will be destroyed.[58] By faith we can expect this to happen, however we must be realistic about the challenge to our faith for this to be realized. It is not only the violent and confrontational interactions between Islam and Christianity throughout the history of Islam but also:

1. **The completely different world-views** between Christianity and Islam covering so many areas – politics and government, the place of women, food and drink, the meaning of love and so on. This maximizes prejudices and fears of both sides and makes deep friendships difficult to form.

2. **The Qu'ran, their holy book, and a theology** developed which openly denies the most important aspects of the Christian faith – the fatherhood of God, the deity of Jesus, his Sonship, his atoning death and resurrection and present reign. Only a deep

---

[58] 2 Corinthians 10:4-5.

work of the Holy Spirit and often years of exposure to the gospel can overcome these barriers.

3. **A social and legal system** so contrived as to make it almost impossible for a Muslim to become a Christian and where apostasy must be punished by death, often at the hands of relatives. On top of this, the long history of negative experiences makes indigenous Christians from other backgrounds extremely cautious of any converted from Islam. No wonder conversions have been so few, and why so many that have taken the step have given their lives for their new-found faith.

4. **A perceived threatening militancy** and the growth of "fundamentalist" terrorism and violence has gained prominence in the world's press. Islam is bent on world domination and has ample theological undergirding for the use of force to attain it, though this would only be advocated by a vociferous, but very influential minority.

What are the evidences in today's world for believing that there will be a decisive demonstration of the power of the gospel in the world of Islam before Jesus returns? I believe there are many! Some of these are shown in Part 3 of this book. There is such an increased volume of prayer, far more missionaries being called, more conversions than ever before, and in many countries churches are coming into being which consist almost entirely of those from a Muslim background.[59] Even fundamentalism itself is causing such stress[60] and disillusionment for Islam in the Muslim world that this in itself could be the means by which the disintegration of Islam before the gospel comes about.

Hinduism

It is hard to conceive of a more contrasting religion to Islam than Hinduism. Islam is fiercely monotheistic and rigidly exclusive while Hinduism is polytheistic and sponge-like in its

---

[59] Increasingly we are using the term **Muslim Background Believer** (MBB) churches. The commonly used term for believers from a Muslim background is "Muslim convert" – an unfortunately ambiguous and patronizing term which ought to be struck out from our vocabulary.

[60] Mohaddessin 1993; Zakaria 1988. These two books are expressions of dismay by Muslim authors at the manifestation of fundamentalism in Islam today as being a rejection of 'true' Islam.

inclusiveness.[61] Many Hindu temples have a portrayal of Jesus as one of the pantheon of gods they worship. Hinduism is as big a challenge to faith for Christians as Islam. It represents another religious ideology that has scarcely been dented by the gospel and relatively few won to Christianity from it. The great majority of Christians in India have been converted from the marginalized in society – the Dalits[62] and the tribal minorities scattered over India and regarded as outside the caste system. The number of Christians from the middle and higher castes, especially the priestly Brahmins, are very few in comparison.

There has been an increasing fascination globally with the Hindu religion and the civilization that gave it birth. Over 15 million migrants have left the sub-continent of India to reside and trade in every continent, most being Hindu, thereby exposing other cultures to their religion. Then there has been an increasing number of Hindu missionaries from 1893 onwards to the West. During this time Hindu practices and world-view have become part of the mainstream of non-Christian Western culture with yoga, transcendental meditation, reincarnation and the development of the whole New Age movement becoming intellectually acceptable. There is validity in saying that Hinduism has been far more successful as a missionary religion in the West than Christianity in the Hindu world.

The challenge of the spiritual need of the 800 million Hindus in the world is one of the greatest we face in seeking to complete the task of world evangelization.[63] In India itself a militant form of Hinduism is striving to do everything possible to legislate against conversion to Christianity making it difficult if not impossible and eliminate all forms of Christian witness. Also tribal and Dalit Christians are bribed or coerced to revert to Hinduism. The Church in India has an uphill battle, but there are encouraging signs. There has been a rising mobilization of prayer and massive increase in the

---

[61] Burnett 1992:18. David Burnett's lucid analysis of Hinduism is a 'must' for all who want to understand about Hinduism, and why it is so important for study as the Hindu world-view is becoming the mainstream of non-Christian Western culture.

[62] Dalit is the modern and politically correct term for those who have been called "outcaste" or "untouchable."

[63] *30 Days Hindu prayer Focus*, 1997. by The Reconciliation! Fellowship of Churches. Colorado Springs, CO 80936, USA: WorldChristian News & Books.

size of the missionary force from among India's Christians to approximately 15,000. Further, since 1990 there has been a great deal of research and analysis of the unfinished task that is leading to more effective deployment of that mission force to reach the mainstream Hindu castes and society. Much prayer will be needed to see the penetration of every level and segment of society.

Buddhism

Hinduism gave birth to Buddhism, but in Nepal and India, the lands of its birth, it has hardly any remaining following. Yet Buddhism in its various cultural adaptations has become the predominant religion of Sri Lanka, East and South East Asia.

There are nearly 700 million in the world who would probably consider themselves Buddhists. Buddhism is a religion that is the antithesis of everything we Christians regard as important or desirable. How can we understand a view of life where there is no God, where feelings and emotion are wrong, where salvation is earned by works and life is an endless cycle of reincarnations and where bliss is not heaven but to attain nothingness? How can we begin to communicate the gospel in a way that even makes it desirable to them?

Buddhism is highly syncretic and in every culture penetrated by it, it has absorbed the indigenous religions – in Tibet the demonic Bon religion, in Thailand the ubiquitous spiritism with every building protected by its spirit house, China with idolatrous Taoism and Japan with nationalistic Shintoism. Even the atheism of Buddhism is replaced by the deification of their founder, the Buddha.

In the Buddhist realms Christianity has only made significant inroads in Korea and where Communism loosened the grip of the old ways on the general population. The cultures named above remain mighty strongholds yet to be effectively impacted by the gospel.

Other Ideologies

More could be said about other political and religious ideologies – for example the Druze, Baha'i and Ahmaddiyah that came from Islam, Sikhism, Jainism, Parseeism, Animism, and the major deviants from mainstream Christianity. There is not the space.

In every philosophy or ideology devised by man or crafted by the enemy of souls we have the assurance that they will not stand before the Lord Jesus and the gospel he gave us. In Isaiah is the beautiful promise:

> ...you shall confute every tongue that rises against you in judgement. This is the heritage of the servants of the Lord and their vindication is from me, says the Lord.

It is such promises that give us confidence in our message in the face of all these persuasive ideologies. However it is a spiritual warfare. So it is to that level of conflict we briefly turn.

Chapter 25

The Spiritual Challenge

Isaiah leaves us in no doubt about the challenge of what we are about. We are involved in spiritual warfare:

> If anyone stirs up strife, it is not from me; whoever stirs up strife with you shall fall because of you.
> Behold I have created the smith who blows the fires of coals, and produces a weapon for its purpose.
> I have created the ravager to destroy; no weapon that is fashioned against you shall prosper... (Isaiah 54:15-17)

We see a world in which Satan has wrested control. He made the claim to the Lord Jesus Christ in the wilderness temptations that the kingdoms of this world had been delivered to him, and that he had the right to give them to whom he willed[64]. The Lord Jesus did not deny this. Jesus did not win them back by bowing to the devil, but by defeating him through death on the cross and the triumphant resurrection from the dead. The kingdoms of the world can now become the kingdom of Christ.[65] Jesus must reign until all his enemies are put under his feet.[66] All spiritual warfare is but an application of the finished work of the cross, not the loudness of our voice, the strength of our words, or even our close proximity to the scene of battle.

Jesus told his disciples "...how can one enter a strong man's house and plunder his goods, unless he first binds the strong man?" That authority is given to us to cast out demons, and over all the power of the enemy.[67] We should be under no illusion about the seriousness of the conflict or underestimate the power and cunning of the "strong man" whose goods we are bent on taking. His infernal majesty is no push-over. He certainly has no intention of releasing his captives, but now through our faith in the finished work of the cross, he has to yield. This is the spiritual warfare in which we are engaged. It is a reality, and we are involved whether we like it or not.

---

[64] Luke 4:5-8.
[65] Revelation 11:15.
[66] 1 Corinthians 15:25.
[67] Luke 9:1-2; 10:17-20.

The whole subject of spiritual warfare has come to the fore among Evangelicals in the past 15 years. Spiritual warfare is one of the "in" things today. We have whole libraries of books on the subject. Signs and Wonders conferences and Spiritual Warfare seminars are packed with eager Christians. We are trying to learn a new vocabulary – deliverance ministry, exorcism, power encounters, confronting the forces of darkness, tearing down strongholds, identificational repentance, spiritual mapping, territorial spirits. Tremendous claims are made for these new understandings and tools and their impact for world evangelization. Unfortunately this has brought polarization to the Body of Christ. There are two extremes I want to avoid:

1. **Under-emphasis of the spiritual nature of the conflict.** For too long Western Christianity has done just this and many missionaries have gone into situations ill-prepared for spiritual opposition.[68] This was certainly my experience in Africa. I was working among a people steeped in witchcraft and fear of spirits. I owe much to my godly African co-workers who educated me about the spiritual powers at work and their cultural and demonic setting. They also demonstrated how the Lord Jesus gives total freedom through a deep repentance with renunciation of the works of darkness and faith in Him and only in certain cases that exorcism is necessary. However those who hold this position can be too cautious, and even accuse the strong proponents of the more aggressive approach of being heretical, and even wrongly influenced by the very forces opposed to them.[69] This can be.

2. **Too great a preoccupation with the enemy.** There has been a rapid growth of awareness of, and fascination with, the occult. This, together with the infiltration of New Age Hinduism, has radically changed the world-view of many in the Western world. As a result people have become far more conscious of spiritual forces. We easily become too devil-conscious and lose

---

[68] Neil 1989:13. Arthur Neil is one of the most experienced pastors in Britain in this whole area of demonization and spiritual warfare. His book is one of the best I know for giving both a biblical balance and practical pastoral application – even if not too easy to read!

[69] Rommen 1995:9-87. In *Spiritual Powers and Missions* Priest, Campbell and Mullen even label this missiological syncretism in their section in this book.

sight of the reigning Lord Jesus. The more we know of God, his
Word and his power, the better we are able to deal with the
enemy. Dealing with the occult can become a morbid
fascination for Christians. It can be a dangerous side-track to
delve into every form of satanic stratagem and the techniques to
overcome them, for we can become ensnared in time-
consuming deliverance ministry or live in danger of
unconsciously making ourselves open to the dark powers. Jessie
Penn-Lewis's book *War on the Saints* which came out of the
1904 Welsh Revival warns of an over-preoccupation with the
things of Satan. Frank Peretti's popular novels on spiritual
warfare[70] were written to alert Christians to this unseen conflict.
These helped to fill the gap in Western theology with a
convincing interpretation of the real world, but despite Peretti's
pleas[71] not to build a theology based on these vivid portrayals of
demonic forces, we find many have. Our Christian bookstores
carry a plethora of titles on spiritual warfare – some
propounding exotic techniques and speculative solutions.

The result is that controversy has broken out among Evangelicals.[72]
We do not need civil warfare among believers about spiritual
warfare, but we do need balance and a biblical centrality in our
understanding and involvement in spiritual warfare. The book
Spiritual Powers and Missions edited by Edward Rommen gives
both views forcefully expressed in order to promote discussion. I
was asked to do a concluding section, but I declined to enter into
the polemics, preferring to look beyond the dispute to the real
weapon that God has given to win the warfare, namely intercessory
prayer. There are many books written that give far more coverage
than I can give here.[73] So I will not deal with important though
more controversial areas such as deliverance ministry,[74] spiritual

---

[70] Peretti 1986, 1989.

[71] Peretti 1989. This argument is also strongly stated by Mike Wakeley in
his article "A Critical Look at a new "Key" to Evangelization" in the
Evangelical Missions Quarterly 1995, 31(2):152-162.

[72] Rommen 1995.

[73] Wagner 1991, Silvoso, 1991, Otis, 1991.

[74] Many have moved so far into "deliverance ministry" and the emphasis on
the influence of the demonic that every wrong attitude or action is seen
to be demon-instigated. Some spend much of their ministry life casting
out demons of drunkenness, adultery, smoking, lying, etc. This leads to

mapping,[75] territorial spirits,[76] blessings and cursings.[77] The new terminology has a fascination of its own, but sometimes not only is the language para-biblical, but the teachings attached to them may be seen as stretching or distorting the truth. These matters are more in the area of terminology and techniques, but underlying all is the fundamental and biblical ministry of intercessory prayer. This is less controversial and, unfortunately, less practised by the average Christian.

Our prayers can and do change the world.[78] We do not have to understand everything about the forces arrayed against us, but we do need to understand the nature of the power and authority that is ours in Christ. Sometimes our technical knowledge hinders us. I have been impressed by the increasing concern among Christians for the evangelization of Muslims, yet often the best missionaries are the ones who have studied little more than the basics of Islamics but have a passion for sharing Christ. In their boldness for Jesus, they plunge in to witnessing to Muslims, where an Islamist would fear to go. By saying this I am not advocating that a

---

failure in taking personal responsibility for sin and effectually denies the biblical basics of repentance and faith.

[75] This is a term developed by George Otis Jr. in his book, *The Last of the Giants*. His thesis is that study of the cultural and spiritual history of an area or people will reveal the spiritual power points or strongholds on which intercessory prayer and spiritual warfare must be waged. Then once these have been confronted, the opening of the people or area to the gospel is then possible. There are many examples in his writings and in missions history to demonstrate this as a valid approach. However many fear that this can be extrapolated too far.

[76] Territorial spirits is a subject admitted by all sides to be controversial and based largely, but not exclusively, on the enigmatic passage in Daniel 10:13 [See Rommen, 1995]. I personally do not like the term, but the concept of satanic power points has much validity and value in our intercessory warfare against the enemy.

[77] Prince 1986, 1990. Derek Prince has been one of the leading proponents of the importance of investigating curses made on forbears in previous generations for living people to be freed from bondages. This again is controversial. I am sure there is some validity in these claims about the effects of ancient curses on subsequent generations, but such curses are nullified by a clear and definite repentance from sin which includes a renunciation of all works of darkness. For Christians to believe that the curses of the enemy's minions, whether demonic or human, can affect them is a bondage in itself (see 1 John 5:13).

[78] Piper 1993:41-70; Billheimer 1975:43-56.

knowledge of Islam is wrong, but we must not let that knowledge cripple our faith that the Holy Spirit can bring about the conversion of Muslims through our witness. The same is true as we confront the devil and his kingdom of darkness and forces of evil. We must not be ignorant of his devices[79] but nor do we have to know everything about demonism, the occult, the hierarchies of the spirit world, before we dare bind the strong man and spoil his goods.[80] Donald Jacobs, a Mennonite missionary in East Africa testifies powerfully to the godly balance of African Christians associated with the East African Revival and how their longing was to know more of Jesus and even turn their backs on the detailed information their traditional religionist compatriots sought about demons.[81]

We need the simplicity and faith of children in our warfare against the strongholds of Satan. My late wife, Jill, was long burdened to write a book to help children pray for the world.[82] Its title, *You Can Change the World*, came about in a beautiful way and illustrates this principle. When Jill began to write the book in 1990, she described Albania which was then a Communist hermit state proudly claiming to be the first truly atheist country in the world where all religious expression was illegal. At our mission headquarters in England there was a group of praying children who interceded for each country or people as Jill completed the chapter. These children took on their hearts the need of the children of Albania where the Gospel was banned and where there were no known believers. They prayed for religious freedom to come to that land. A few months later the Communist government fell, and freedom for worship and witness came. Jill had to re-write the chapter. When these children heard of the answer to their prayers they were delighted. One of them shouted out, "We've changed Albania!". That was true, their prayers were joined with others praying earnestly for the Gospel to have free entry to that needy land! Just four years later we now know there is scarcely a town in that land which does not have a group of witnessing believers. May God give us their faith and simplicity. May these words encourage the reader not to engage in controversy, but to confront the enemy in the combat of intercession!

---

[79] 2 Corinthians 2:11.
[80] Matthew 12:29.
[81] Wagner 1990:319.
[82] Johnstone, Jill 1993:8-9.

Earlier I described how God has used the intercession of groups of believers for the expansion of the Church such as the Moravians in the eighteenth century, intercessors for China in the nineteenth and global prayer for the fall of the Iron Curtain in the 1980s. There have also been remarkable men whom God has used in a notable way and have been known as intercessors – men such as Job, Elisha, Daniel in the Old Testament and others such as David Brainerd,[83] George Müller,[84] Rees Howells,[85] Praying Hyde,[86] and many others. May God give us in our generation like men and women who know their God and how to walk with him, making mighty requests of him in prayer.

Do we not see this happening? During preparation of the last edition of *Operation World*, I was awed by the number of prayer requests listed in the 1986 edition which were no longer points for prayer but rather for praise because the answer had come. For the first time in history we can meaningfully speak of seeing a church planting movement within every ethno-linguistic people and making the Gospel available for every person in our lifetime. This has become the driving vision of the AD2000 Movement. I can only attribute the advances now taking place and described in part 3 of this book as a direct answer to strategic prayer by millions around the world.

I have become aware over the past 20 years of a growing number of prayer initiatives and networks unprecedented in the history of the world. There is, in fact, a **prayer awakening** under way, the scope of which would astonish us were we to know the whole story. The availability of information and the globalization of the world missionary force have increased the emphasis on strategic praying for Gospel advances in unevangelized parts of the world. What are some of the characteristics of this prayer awakening? I point out some:

1. **The intensity** – of an early morning Korean prayer meeting in almost any Protestant church in the country or of the well attended Friday all-night prayer meetings in many congregations in Brazil.

---

[83] Tucker 1983:90.
[84] Pierson 1899.
[85] Grubb 1952.
[86] Carré, probably 1920.

2. **The militancy** – of praying Christians expecting Satan's forces to yield in power encounters, leading to significant movements to Christ in hitherto resistant peoples. I well remember a Dorothea Mission Week of Prayer we held in then Portuguese-ruled Mozambique in 1965. Up to that point little Protestant mission work had been permitted in much of the country. We definitely claimed that land for Christ and an opening for the Gospel. Within weeks missionaries had gained entry into that land.

3. **The variety of expression** – in simultaneous prayer at full volume, prayer walking, marches for Jesus, hands raised to heaven, lying prostrate before the Lord.

4. **The global networks of prayer.** Peter and Doris Wagner, co-ordinators for the AD2000 Movement Prayer Track have links with dozens of prayer networks around the world – with millions of Christians involved – **The Day to Change the World** (now becoming an annual event on a day in October involving millions to pray for the nations, Gateway cities, Key Unreached Peoples), the **March for Jesus** events (involving 16 million by 1995 with a major component of praying for world evangelization), **Intercessors International** (launched by Dennis Clark in 1969), **Concerts of Prayer International** (in which God has used David Bryant to revive the vision of the Scottish Cambuslang ministers and then the great Jonathan Edwards over two centuries ago), **The Lydia Fellowship** (mobilizing women for intercession), **The Esther Network** (mobilizing children as intercessors), The **YWAM** initiative to mobilize Christians to fast and pray for the Muslim World during Ramadan, and many more.

5. **The specific nature of the praying** – A decade ago we were wondering whether most of the unevangelized world would be closing to any form of Christian presence. Yet in answer to prayer country after country has opened up for witness, whether overt or covert. Such countries as Nepal, Cambodia, China, Russia, Uzbekistan, Kyrgyzstan, Bulgaria, Ethiopia, and many others are evidence of this. Many of the closing or closed doors have proved to be revolving doors in answer to prayer.

We are therefore in the early stages of a prayer-fuelled advance of the Kingdom of Christ – a fact that gives me great hope for the future despite the evident negatives in the world and failures in the Church. What could happen for the Kingdom were that prayer mobilization to further increase? The majority of evangelical churches have yet to catch this vision; the wider world is so big, complex and remote and their own outreach often discouraging. Their energies and resources are spent on local concerns and programs that benefit the gathered saints more than the millions of Satan's captives heading for a lost eternity.

I need to interject a word here about prayer walking. This has become a remarkable feature of intercessory prayer today. The number of Christians engaged in prayer walking or prayer journeys has escalated. A number of books have been written[87] on this subject. It is an exciting development. However it is important to realize that the physical presence of the intercessor does not increase the power of the prayers. The physical presence of the intercessor gives new insights, increases burden, more opportunity for prayer, and can give real encouragement for embattled little groups of indigenous believers. The commitment of a group of intercessors and agreement before the Lord in what they pray is powerful in effect. Prayer moves the hand that moves the universe, so it is being in his presence rather than in a physical location that pulls down strongholds. Further words of caution need to be given. The theology of prayer walking needs to be defined. There is a danger that if the premise of territorial spirits is accepted (a moot point), this can easily extend to the premise that physical presence of intercessors in the area controlled by the territorial spirit is essential for its binding. This is not true. The practise of prayer walking needs to be examined – I see negatives that need to guarded against; the huge expense of what could just be Christian tourism to the detriment of funding for workers on the front line, the motivations for going can be mixed, the drain on the time and energies of workers serving in glamorous places. It can even endanger ministries in sensitive areas.

Here is not the place to elaborate on the biblical basis for intercession, nor the passionate pleas of Jesus for his disciples' involvement in prayer or how we pray. Nor can I here go into the wonderful truths of Scripture about the authority we have in Jesus by right of redemption, and because of our being seated with him in

---

[87] Hawthorne 1993.

heavenly places. Jesus has given us the keys of the kingdom, he has promised us the greater works than he could do, but what are these other than intercession in the leading and power of the Holy Spirit?[88]

There is a solemnity about intercession because there is always a price to pay. Jesus had to pay with his life to become an intercessor for us. We follow Jesus bearing a cross. Intercession is cross-bearing. Paul saw this and pointed out to the Colossians that his sufferings were to complete what was lacking in the sufferings of Christ for the Church.[89] Grace was freely given to us in Christ, and is freely available to us day by day, but if we are to become ministers of that grace it will cost. It is only as we are willing for that cost that the task of world evangelization is achievable. Intercession is the ultimate weapon. No subterfuge, sin, bondage or stronghold of Satan can withstand it. Let us wield it.

Conclusion of Part 5

Much ground has been covered. The challenges before us are big, but God's promises even bigger. World evangelization must be accomplished, and this as soon as possible. May the twenty-first century also be the one in which the Bride of Christ is readied for the consummating Wedding Feast.[90]

If this is to happen we need to see breakthroughs for the gospel in:

1. Every geographical region, country, state, province and district of the world.

2. Every people discipled with a missiological breakthrough leading to the indigenization of the gospel message in their cultures.

3. Every city penetrated and uplifted by the power of the gospel in our urbanizing world.

4. Every social network and structure influenced by the absolute standards of the Bible.

---

[88] John 15:1-14; Luke 18:1-8; Ephesians 2:6; Matthew 16:19; John 14:12-14; Romans 8:26-27.

[89] Colossians 1:24.

[90] Revelation 21:1-2; 21:9-14.

5. Every ideology, whether human or demonic, openly disarmed and discredited in the light of the Lord Jesus Christ.

6. Every manifestation and stronghold of Satan himself despoiled by the power of the Risen Lord Jesus.

Part 6

Precious Promises for Harvesters

Isaiah 54:4-17

God is more interested in us as individual people than for the work he can squeeze out of us. We are not toothpaste tubes to be discarded when the contents are finished. He did not redeem us for service but for fellowship with himself for ever. He is less concerned about our structures and strategies that he is about our relationship with him. His loving handling of us may sometimes appear harsh, the way dark, the heavens like brass and the fruit so long in appearing. God works for the long term by dealing with our relationships and out of these comes our effectiveness. Moses was forty years in the wilderness before he could come to the point where he spoke to God face to face – how many baby boys did Pharaoh kill in Egypt in those years?

So far we have looked at the big picture – God's plan, world evangelization and the strategies and structures needed. Now in conclusion we look at the marvellous promises God gives to us as individuals. Each one of us is special to him. The barren widow of Isaiah 54:1 is us collectively and individually. He makes us collectively and individually his special bride on whom he lavishes all his love and concern. I was so blessed by the statement of a Chinese Bible School student some years ago. She made the remarkable statement, "I know God has not got any favourites, but I know I am one of them!" How true.

We are never closer to God than when we share his heart for the unevangelized. In the closing verse of Matthew, Jesus promised to be with us until the close of the age. Yet in a very real way, that promise is only applicable to the ones who go making disciples. In the verses in Isaiah 54:4-17 we find an equivalent to that Great Commission promise. May we find encouragement in the immortal words that Isaiah penned. Here, in closing, are God's promises to the ones involved in enlarging tents and spreading out across the face of the earth. These six precious promises are for us as we obey the Great Commission.

Chapter 26

The Six-fold Promises of God for Harvesters

1. Freedom from fear (54:4)

Fear of the unknown, of people, of failure, of poverty, of danger, of bugs, of spiders, of disease and a host of other phobias keep many from wholly following the Lord in obedience to whatever he calls us to do. The command "Fear not" comes with great frequency in Scripture. Isaiah said:

> Fear not; for you will not be ashamed; be not confounded; for you will not be put to shame; for you will forget the shame of your youth, and the reproach of your widowhood you will remember no more.

This is a double promise. Firstly there is no need to fear the future, and secondly that the things of the past need no longer tie us down with feelings of failure and inadequacy.

God guarantees our future integrity whatever our outward circumstances. The future of our world is grim. We have ample grounds for fear, for the threats are real, whether through violence, war, disease, economic stability or lack of security. This is even more true for those who become ambassadors for Christ in other cultures and lands. To be a missionary today does not command the respect it did. His sanity or theology can be questioned by Christians at home, and his career overseas maligned or soon terminated by government legislation, police intimidation, terrorism or hostage-taking. Even the very word "missionary" has gained a negative connotation. Yet there is no need to fear the consequences of going. The Lord Jesus Christ will be with us, the Holy Spirit will empower us, and the Father guarantees that we will not be put to shame by the enemy, by those who oppose us, or even by fellow Christians. Everything may fail whether finances, health, co-workers, cherished methods, but God will not let us down. We may suffer, get cancer, be tortured or martyred but our relationship with God, our eternal fruit, our future and our crown are secure. We believe Paul's words to Timothy; "I am sure that he who began a good work in you will bring it to completion at the day of Jesus Christ." We can then have an unshakeable assurance in the character of our God who undergirds these promises. He will perform what he promised whatever the physical evidence may be to the contrary. With such promises we can go out in his name to subdue kingdoms, liberate captives, build the Church and see Satan bruised under our feet and world evangelization achieved.[1]

The promise is also for the past. Isaiah makes mention of two tragic types of event; the shame of youth and the reproach of widowhood. Our past foolish mistakes, our sinful actions, our wrong life-style and also tragic events in our lives leave wounds and scars. God forgets them all. They no longer need cripple our future ministry, but can even become weapons in our armoury for that ministry. The blood of Jesus is sufficient to cleanse those who repent and give us a testimony of power to help others. The indwelling life of Jesus lifts us up to resurrection life where the pains and wounds of past events and the sins of others against us no longer restrict our freedom in serving the Lord.

Greg Livingstone, the Director and founder of Frontiers, a mission dedicated to church planting among Muslim peoples, once made the comment, "Missionaries today need more servicing." He was expressing the problem of so many Christians wanting to serve the Lord today. The breakdown of moral standards, family life and the rampant sinfulness of today's society have left scars. Many have been wounded. Many are held back from service because of past abuse they endured and for the inadequacy and sense of failure this brings. Counselling, when rightly ministered, can bring such ones into the freedom that is their heritage in Jesus, but it can also be a snare and a byway when based on humanistic presuppositions of modern psychology. It can legitimize anger felt against those who knowingly or unknowingly harmed the victim. It can also breed a dependence on people and not on God. A comment I heard is apposite, "It seems that to be a good Christian today you need to give your heart to Jesus – and have 50 years of counselling!" Wonderfully, the gospel we proclaim has the power to totally neutralize the negative impact of past experiences on future ministry.

---

[1] Matthew 24:1-13; 1 Corinthians 4:13; Romans 8:31-39; 2 Timothy 4:6-8; Philippians 1:6 are some of the New Testament verses which underlie this paragraph.

2. Union with Christ (54:5)

Salvation from sin is the negative; the positive is that the saved are brought into a union with the Lord. This thoroughly New Testament truth is foreshadowed in the words:

> For your Maker is your husband, the Lord of Hosts is his name; and the Holy One of Israel is your Redeemer, the God of the whole earth is he called.

That we be *married* to our Maker, *joined* to the Holy One of Israel is overwhelming. The love and care he lavishes on us, on me, his bride, are more than the most perfect earthly, doting husband could ever bestow! From the New Testament perspective, Jesus is my Lover, my Provider, my All! The great pre-reformer in Italy, Savanarola, said, "What must a man possess who possesses the Possessor of all things?" All is mine in Christ. I can face the world and all its scorn and opposition with confidence because greater is he that is within me than he that is in the world.[2]

The Apostles in Acts preached more on the Resurrection than on the Crucifixion. Paul said, "For if while we were enemies we were saved by the *death* of his Son, much more, now that we are reconciled, shall we be saved by *his life*." It takes us so long to discover this. It can almost be like a second conversion to find out that I no longer have to *try* to work *for* the Lord, but I have to trust in his indwelling life and Spirit to do his work *through* me. For too many servants of God, their ministry is one of striving rather than resting. There yet remains a Sabbath rest for the people of God, but few have found it. They have entered the first rest of Matthew 11:28 *from* a burden, but they have never entered into the rest of Matthew 11:30 *with* the burden of the yoke shared with Jesus. The mystery hidden for ages and generations is now made manifest to the saints...which is Christ in you, the hope of glory. Sadly, this is still a mystery to many.[3] Hudson Taylor had to learn that hard lesson on his first furlough. He was at the point of breakdown in 1868 when he met with God in a new way on the beach at Brighton in England[4]. In that meeting he discovered the true meaning of Galatians 2:20:

---

[2] 2 Corinthians 9:8; Ephesians 3:19; 1 John 4:4.
[3] Romans 5:11; Philippians 4:13; Hebrews 3:12-4:10; Matthew 11:28-30; Colossians 1:25-29.
[4] Taylor 1932. *Hudson Taylor's Spiritual Secret*

I have been crucified with Christ; it is no longer I who live,
but Christ who lives in me; and the life I now live in the flesh
I live by faith in the Son of God, who loved me and gave
himself for me. (RSV)

Hudson Taylor went on to found the China Inland Mission,
probably one of the most trend-setting and innovative missions in
the nineteenth century. He found the secret of abiding in Christ; of
trusting his indwelling presence for every task.

I had to learn these truths in Africa as a missionary. Why did I
struggle so long to see what should have been obvious – that is a
mystery too! However once the Lord revealed this to me – both
through the writings of Norman Grubb,[5] the witness of Jill, who
was to be my future wife, and the reading of the Scriptures, it
changed my ministry. From then onwards I knew that it was not me
doing the work, but I was quietly expectant that God would do all
he desired through me if I let him. Would that I always lived by
that precious truth. It is this truth that makes all things possible –
even to me. I can expect hard-hearted people to be converted,
prayers to prevail, ministry to have fruit. It is not me but him in
me – no cause there for pride. If it works, it is him, if it doesn't, it
was me interfering. That is why we have confidence that the
lordship of Jesus will be manifested in this age and before the
return of Jesus in Muslim Mecca, in Hindu Varanasi, in Tibetan
Buddhist Lhasa, in Communist Beijing and that peoples at present
with no disciples of the Lamb will soon provide them – such as the
Qashqai of Iran, the Maldivians of the Indian Ocean, the Mzab of
the Sahara and the Qatar Arabs of the Gulf.

3. Purpose and Guidance (54:6)

These words are hauntingly beautiful:

For the Lord has called you
like a wife forsaken and grieved in spirit,
like a wife of youth when she is cast off.

It is moving to see the pathos of this poor woman deserted and
thrown out by a husband who obviously did not deserve her. It is

---

[5] Grubb 1955, 1962. Norman Grubb, for many years the Director of WEC
International, had a deep influence on my early Christian life and
ministry through his writings about our union with Christ.

painfully up-to-date for so many today with such a high divorce rate. Yet in the midst of the grief, overwhelming self-pity and hopelessness, she is called, given a welcome to a perfect union, and offered a prospect of fruitfulness.

That forlorn woman is you and me! God calls us in our desperate hopelessness not only to a salvation from misery, but to a union with him, and to a life of purpose and usefulness. Maybe I am taking some exegetic licence in applying this call to the call to Christian service and the assurance of guidance in that service, but I think not! God has a plan for you. There is a YOU shaped hole in his kingdom that only YOU can fit!

God has an eternal purpose for us that we should live to his praise and glory here on earth and later in heaven. He also has an earthly purpose in the works ordained for us that we should walk in them. He reveals that purpose, for, indeed, it is our birthright, for all who are led of the Spirit of God are the sons of God.[6] So within his calling to himself is also embedded the guarantee that he will never leave us in the lurch without a knowledge that we are in the centre of his will.

We must know his general leading as revealed in the Scripture, but we must also know his specific leading in the personal and in the detail. The life of Peter and Paul in Acts demonstrates this again and again. It is just as valid for us today. Yet it is in this area I find so much confusion and uncertainty today. Many ask, "How can I know the will of God, how can I be absolutely sure?" Here are just a few words to you if this is your problem.

We are guided by the Holy Spirit – we *know*, but may not be able to explain why we know! If I ever hear anyone using the words "the Spirit (or God) guided me to...", I see amber lights flashing. It can be used in defence to protect oneself from a challenge to a dubious step. As we move ahead with what we already know is right, the peace of God in our hearts is a precious assurance from the Holy Spirit. We can get it wrong, and therefore there must always be a gracious humility to those who may question or challenge us.

---

[6] Ephesians 1:3-14; 2:10, Romans 8:14.

God's guidance is conditional. Romans 12:1-2 shows that the good and acceptable and perfect will of God can only be proved *after* three tough conditions:

1. Presenting your bodies a living sacrifice. All must be yielded to God. How can he guide you if you have a bias in your thinking, a sin in your life or an unwillingness to do anything he desires?

2. By not being conformed to this world. How can you know God's will if you want to please others or yourself, or if you are more concerned about what others think or say?

3. By being continually transformed by the renewal of your mind. Your mind must be bathed continually in the Word of God; your mind set on the godly, the good, the wholesome. Then you can hear the still, small voice of God in your spirit.

God's will is proved or confirmed through four safeguards:

1. Is it in accordance with the revealed will of God in the Bible? Personal guidance will never be in contradiction to what has been recorded in God's Word.

2. Is it with the prayerful agreement and approval of the leadership of your church or fellowship?

3. Is it in line with other confirming circumstances in your life?

4. Are there any unsought, but beautiful evidences of God working things out for you in a supernatural way? This could be a special ordering of events, a word of prophecy or knowledge from the Lord, a vision, a special word from God in your daily reading of Scripture.

Any one of these can help towards proving God's will, but ultimately, as with Paul and his team in Phrygia and Galatia in Acts 16:6-10, you must gather the pieces of evidence together to conclude what God is really saying about his will. It is a risk, but our Father has his ways of checking us even if, with all the best intentions of our heart, we make a mistake.

In Christian ministry there must be the deep assurance that God has personally led you. This is ultimately the one thing that will keep you true to that calling when the going gets rough. I always advise Christian workers never to leave God's will for a negative reason. Run away from one difficulty, and you will end in darkness and in situations far worse than those from which you fled. The safest place for you is in the centre of God's will – even with chains on your feet as a hostage, with your body racked with fever or trembling in a cellar with RPG rockets crashing into the house above.

4. Redemption from every failure (54:7-10)

Isaiah has a word for those who fail:

For a brief moment I forsook you, but with great compassion I will draw you. In overflowing wrath for a moment I hid my face from you, but with everlasting love I will have compassion on you, says the Lord, your Redeemer.

God sometimes seems far off, the heavens like brass, prayer a battle and service drudgery. We can even feel rejected by God. This can be the enemy attacking (resist him), our minds overburdened by work (get the balance right between work and relaxation), or spiritual failure (repent). It is the latter I want to address briefly.

None of us can look back in our lives and say we have never made a mess of things. We have all had times of failure. Such failures can sometimes be major – in the moral realm, in finances, in relationships or in the ministry itself. The terrible sense of failure and uselessness can crush and lead such a one into spiritual darkness.

Yet this wonderful promise assures us that we have never gone too far for the Lord not to pick us up again, forgive, restore, and even lead into a new ministry of a fruitfulness that would never have been possible without the failure. His grace cannot be explained, but is marvellous! God can be angry, and turn his face from us, but that is for a brief moment. What matters is that his everlasting love chases us down the years of wilderness experience and brings us back again. There may be consequent limitations with which we must live – divorce, harm done to others, or an illegitimate child, but the Lord takes us up where we are and has a new start for us. What love, what a Father, what a Redeemer! Let no failure rob you of the expectation of further usefulness for world evangelization. God is resourceful – he always has a Plan "A" for you and me, whatever our past.

5. Eternal Fruitfulness (54:11-13)

Now follow three verses that are both beautiful and poetic. Their meaning is not easy to discern, but these are fragrant promises for the servants of the Lord involved in world evangelization. Here I see our fruitfulness assured. Here are the words themselves:

> O afflicted one, storm-tossed, and not comforted,
> behold, I will set your stones in antimony,
> and lay your foundations with sapphires.
> I will make your pinnacles of agate, your gates of carbuncles,
> and all your walls of precious stones.
> All your sons shall be taught by the Lord,
> and great shall be the prosperity of your sons.

In spite of agonies and sufferings, the Bride will be complete, beautiful and glorious. The imagery is a preview of the New Jerusalem in Revelation 21, filled with the redeemed of the Lord. Yet the precious stones are, in other parts of Scripture, identified with God's people. The breastplate of the high priest had twelve precious stones[7] set in it. They represented the sons of Israel. Could it be that these stones here in Isaiah speak of the fruit of the preaching of the gospel that will adorn the heavenly Jerusalem? The concept is not wrong, though that interpretation may be!

We are promised fruit. The Church will be perfect and complete and we will have had a part in that completion by our commitment to world evangelization. Therefore the sufferings of this time, these slight momentary afflictions are preparing us for that eternal weight of glory! How small the sacrifices, how minimal the pain will seem when one day we gaze on the Lord Jesus and admire his wonderful work to bring us all to that glorious consummation! We know our labour in the Lord is not in vain.[8]

Then follows a promise for our spiritual and physical children. They will be taught of the Lord, and be prosperous. As we go out in obedience to disciple the nations, we can expect the Holy Spirit to work in them just as in us. Our primary task is not to inculcate a dependence on us as the disciplers, but on God, and in the direct leading of the Holy Spirit. We must expect this whatever the

---

[7] Exodus 28:15-21.
[8] 2 Corinthians 4:17; 1 Corinthians 15:58.

unlikely human material, the degradation of the surrounding culture, or the lack of literacy, literature and the Bible. We can trust him in them.[9]

Finally for those of us called to serve and sacrifice for the cause of Christ, our own physical children also will be taught by the Lord. Some are afraid to obey because of the effects of that obedience on their children. The thought is, 'How can I bring suffering to my children because I become a missionary?' Our loving Lord never forgets them! His call to the parents is just as valid for our children. My son Tim was six years old when the Lord led Jill and me to leave our ministry in Zimbabwe and serve for a year on the Operation Mobilization ship, M.V. Logos. Our children loved their life in Zimbabwe, and did not want to leave. Tim prayed a beautiful prayer! "Lord Jesus, thank you for calling us children to be on the ship. You've called Mummy and Daddy, and they've got us, so we know you have called us too!" He had his theology right. Years later my eldest son, Peter, was speaking with a friend, not realizing that his mother could hear him. He said, "I've had a marvellous childhood!" We thought of the stresses of living through the war in what was Rhodesia, the poverty under which we lived, and cross-cultural shocks to which we subjected the children. It was all worth while. By God's grace all of our three offspring are active in serving the Lord Jesus. God taught them as he promised. We do not deprive our children in obeying God's call, we enrich them with a heritage and blessings otherwise unobtainable.

6. Supernatural protection (54:15-17)

We are involved in the greatest and most bitterly fought war ever to be waged. The enemy will not surrender his final grip on his crumbling empire until the King of kings and Lord of lords comes in triumph at the end of time. Every stronghold, every bunker, every sinful heart will be a battle. Our wounds and casualties will be severe. Suffering and martyrdom are our expected lot. Yet we have the promise of supernatural protection in it all! Isaiah's words assure us of this:

---

[9] Allen 1912. Roland Allen spoke strongly about trusting the Holy Spirit in indigenous converts in a time when Western missionaries were noted for their patronizing paternalism. Sadly this fleshly paternalism is not so easy to shake off for missionaries even today!

If anyone stirs up strife, it is not from me; whoever stirs up
strife with you shall fall because of you...
no weapon that is fashioned against you shall prosper,
and you shall confute every tongue that rises against you in
judgement. This is the heritage of the servants of the Lord and
their vindication from me, says the Lord.

The words of Jesus give the same message. He warned us that in
the world we would have trouble, but assures us that he has
overcome the world. He told us that he has given us authority to
tread on serpents and scorpions, and over all the power of the
enemy. Paul assured us that in all trials and difficulties and all that
the world and the devil can throw at us we would be more than
conquerors.[10]

Conclusion

What promises and what assurance of victory in world
evangelization! We are privileged to be able to participate in the
most certain final triumph of the Crucified Lamb. We are even
more privileged to be alive today to see the consummation of all
things unfolding before our eyes. My prayer is that this book will,
in some small part, contribute to uplifting the hearts of God's
people by showing that this is so, and to better equip them to be
participants in the action that brings it about.

---

[10] John 16:33; Luke 10:19; Romans:8:35.

Bibliography

AARGAARD, Anna Marie. 1974. *Missio Dei in Katholischer Sicht,* Evangelische Theologie vol 34, pp420-433.

ADDISON, James Thayer. 1936. *The Medieval Missionary; A Study of the Conversion of Northern Europe A.D. 500-1300.* New York, USA: International Missionary Council.

ALLEN, Roland. 1956 (originally 1912). *Missionary Methods: St Paul's or Ours?* London, UK: World Dominion Press.

————— 1962. *The Spontaneous Expansion of the Church.* Grand Rapids, MI 49516, USA: Baker Books.

BAKKE, Ray. 1997. *A Theology as Big as the City.* Downers Grove, Ill 60515, USA: InterVarsity Press.

BANKS, Robert. 1995. *Paul's Idea of Community.* Peaboy, Mass. 01961, USA: Hendrickson Publishers.

BARLOW, Sanna Morrison. 1952. *Mountains Singing; The story of Gospel Recordings in the Philippines.* Chicago, Ill. USA: Moody Press.

BARNES, Lemuel Call. 1902. *Two Thousand Years of Missions Before Carey.* Chicago, IL, USA: The Christian Culture Press.

BARRETT, David B. Ed. 1982, *World Christian Encyclopedia; A comparative study of churches and religions in the modern world, AD 1900-2000.* Oxford, England: Oxford University Press.

————— 1984. The Five Statistical Eras of the Christian Church. *International Bulletin of of Missionary Research* April Vol 8 No. 4, New Haven, Conn. 06511, USA: Overseas Mission Study Center.

————— 1986. World-Class *Cities and World Evangelization.* Birmingham, Alabama, USA: New Hope.

————— 1987a. *Cosmos, Chaos and the Gospel.* Birmingham AL, USA: New Hope.

————— 1987b, *Evangelize! A historical survey of the concept.* Birmingham AL, USA: New Hope.

————— & REAPSOME, James W. 1988, *Seven Hundred Plans to evangelize the world: the rise of a Global Evangelization Movement.* Birmingham AL, USA: New Hope.

————— & JOHNSON, Todd M. 1990, *Our Globe and How to Reach It.* Birmingham AL, USA: New Hope.

————— JOHNSON, Todd M. & JAFFARIAN, Michael. 1998, *World Christian Encyclopedia.* Oxford, UK: Oxford University Press.

BEACH, Harlan P. & FAHS, Charles H. 1924. *World Mission Atlas*. London, England: Edinburgh House Press.

BEALS, Paul A. 1995. *A People for His Name*. Pasadena, CA 91114, USA: William Carey Library.

BILLHEIMER, Paul. 1975. *Destined for the Throne*. London, England: Christian Literature Crusade.

BORTHWICK, Paul. July 1985. *Evangelical Missions Quarterly;* Article: The Crucial Roles of the Church Missions Committee.

BOSCH, David J. 1991. *Transforming Mission: Paradigm shifts in Theology of Mission*. Maryknoll: Orbis Books.

BRIERLEY, Peter. and WRAIGHT, Heather 1996. *The UK Christian Handbook*. London, England: Christian Research Association.

BROW, Robert. 1968. *The Twenty Century Church*. Grand Rapids, MI, USA: Eerdmans.

BROADBENT, E.H. 1931. *The Pilgrim Church*. London, UK: Pickering and Inglis.

BRUCE, F.F. 1958. *The Spreading Flame*. London, UK: Paternoster Press.

BRYANT, David 1979. *What it means to be a World Christian*. Madison, Wisconsin, USA: Intervarsity Press.

————— 1984a. *In The Gap. What it means to be a world Christian*. Ventura, CA 93006, USA: Ventura Books.

————— 1984b. *With Concerts of Prayer: Christians joined for Spiritual Awakening and World Evangelization*. Ventura: Regal Books.

BURKE, Tidd & DeAnn. 1989. *Anointed for Burial*. Seattle, WA 98155, USA: Frontline Communications, YWAM.

BURNETT, David. 1986. *God's Mission: Healing the Nations*. Bromley, Kent BR2 9EX, England: MARC Europe, World Vision.

————— 1992. *The Spirit of Hinduism; A Christian Perspective on Hindu Thought*. Tunbridge Wells, Kent TN3 0NP, UK: Monarch Publications.

CALVIN, John. 1536 & 1957. *Institutes of the Christian Religion; Beveridge edition.*. London, UK: James Clarke & Co.

CAREY, S. Pearce, 1923. *William Carey*. London: Hodder & Stoughton.

CAREY, William 1792, *An Enquiry into the obligations of Christians to use means for the conversion of the heathens*. Leicester, UK: Anne Ireland. Also 1988, Dallas, TX: Criswell Publications.

CARRÉ, E.G. probably 1920s *Praying Hyde: A Challenge to Prayer*. London, England: Pickering and Inglis.

CHAO, Jonathan 1989, *The China Mission Handbook*. Shatin, N.T. Hong Kong: Chinese Research Center.

CHAPMAN, Colin. 1995. *Cross and Crescent.* Leicester LE1 7GP, UK: Inter-Varsity Press.

CONYBEARE, W.J. & HOWSON, J.S. 1957, *The Life and Epistles of St. Paul,* Grand Rapids, MI, USA: Eerdmans Publishing Co.

CONYERS, A.J. 1988. *God, Hope and History; Jürgen Moltmann and the Christian Concept of History.* Macon, GA 31207, USA: Mercer University Press.

DAVIES, Ronald E. April 1997. *Jonathan Edwards: Missionary Biographer, Theologian, Strategist, Administrator, Advocate – and Missionary.* Newhaven, Conn 06511, USA: International Bulletin of Missionary Research April 1997.

DAYTON, E. & WILSON, Sam, eds., et al. 1974–1984 *Unreached Peoples Annuals.* Monrovia CA, USA: MARC Publications.

DINNEN, Stewart 1995. *A Rescue Shop Within a Yard of Hell.* Fearn, Scotland: Christian Focus Publications.

————— 1997. *Faith on Fire; Norman Grubb and the Building of WEC.* Fearn, Ross-shire, IV20 1TW, UK: Christian Focus Publications.

DOUGLAS, J.D. ed. 1962. *The New Bible Dictionary.* London: Inter-Varsity Press.

————— ed. 1975. *Let the Earth Hear His Voice: International Congress on World Evangelization, Lausanne, Switzerland.* Minneapolis, Minnesota 55403, USA: World Wide Publications.

EDWARDS, Jonathan. 1748. *A Humble Attempt to Promote an Explicit Agreement and Visible Union of God's People through the World, in Extraordinary Prayer, for the Revival of Religion and the Advancement of Christ's Kingdom on Earth, Pursuant to Scripture Promises and Prophecies, Concerning the Last Time.* A Published Sermon.

ESHLEMAN, Paul. 1995. *The Touch of Jesus.* (The story of the Jesus Film). Orlando, FL 32809, USA: NewLife Publications.

FETTNER, Ann Giudici. 1990. *The Science of Viruses: What they are, why they make us sick, how they will change the future.* New York: Quill.

FISCHER, 1997. *Intercessor's Prayer Guide to the Jewish World.* Richmond, Virginia, USA: YWAM Jewish-World Office .

FOMUM, Zacharias Tanee 1988. *The Way of Victorious Praying.* New York: Vantage Press.

FORSTER, Roger & RICHARDS, John 1995. *Churches that Obey; taking the Great Commission seriously.* Carlisle, Cumbria CA3 0QS, UK: OM Publishing.

FULLER, Andrew, 1791. *The Pernicious Influence of Delay.* A published sermon. London: Matthews.

GARRETT, Laurie 1994. *The Coming Plague: Newly Emerging Diseases in a World Out of Balance.* New York: Farrar, Straus and Giroux.

GAUKROGER, Stephen. 1995. *Why Bother with Mission?* Leicester LE1 7GP: Inter-Varsity Press.

GEORGE, Timothy. 1991. *Faithful Witness.* Birmingham, AL 35202, USA: New Hope.

GREENWAY, Roger S., Ed. *Discipling the City.* Grand Rapids, MI, USA: Baker Book House.

GRIGG, Viv. 1984. *Companion to the Poor.* Monrovia, CA 91016 USA: MARC Publications.

———— 1992. *The Cry of the Urban Poor; Reaching the slums of today's Megacities.* Monrovia, CA 91016 USA: MARC Publications.

GRIMES, Barbara 1951 -1996. *The Ethnologue, Languages of the World.* Dallas, TX, USA: Summer Institute of Linguistics.

GRUBB, Kenneth 1948, 1952, 1957, 1962. *The World Christian Handbook.* London, England: World Dominion Press.

———— 1968. *The World Christian Handbook.* London, UK: England: Lutterworth Press.

GRUBB, Norman G. 1933. *C.T. Studd, Cricketer and Pioneer.*

———— 1952. *Rees Howells, Intercessor.* London, England: Lutterworth Press.

———— 1955. *The Liberating Secret.* London, England: Lutterworth Press.

———— 1962. *God Unlimited.* London, England: Lutterworth Press.

HALL, Douglas John. 1997. *The End of Christendom and the Future of Christianity.* Valley Forge, PA, USA: Trinity Press International.

HAMMOND, Peter. 1995. *Faith Under Fire in Sudan.* Newlands, South Africa: Frontline Fellowship (Box 74, Newlands 7725).

HANNA, John, ed., SMITH, Marti & JOHNSTONE, Patrick. 1997. *Praying Through the Window, Vol III.* P.O. Box 55787, Seattle, WA 98155, USA: YWAM Publishing.

HAWTHORNE, Steve & KENDRICK, Graham. 1993. *A Guide to Prayer Walking; Awaking our Cities for God.* Milton Keynes, UK: Nelson Word, Ltd.

HAY, A.R. 1947. *The New Testament Order for Church and Missionary.* Temperley FNGR, Argentina: New Testament Missionary Union.

HEFLEY, James and Marti. 1974. *Uncle Cam: The Story of William Cameron Townsend*. Waco, TX, USA: Word.

HENGSTENBERG, E.W. ca1850. *Christology of the Old Testament* in 2 vols. English translation 1854, reprinted ca. 1960. Florida 33608, USA: MacDonald Publishing Company.

HESSION. Roy. 1950. *The Calvary Road*. London, England: Christian Literature Crusade.

HUTTON, Samuel K. 1935. *By Patience and the Word, The story of Moravian Missions*. London, UK: Hodder & Stoughton.

JANSEN, G.H. 1979. *Militant Islam*. London, UK: Pan Books.

JOHNSON, Todd. M. 1988. *Countdown to 1900; World Evangelization at the end of the Nineteenth Century*. Birmingham, AL, USA: New Hope.

JOHNSTONE, Patrick J. St.G. 1993. *Operation World*. Carlisle, Cumbria, UK: OM Publishing and WEC International.

KANE, J. Herbert 1971. *A Global View of Christian Missions*. Grand Rapids, MI: Baker Book House.

KENNEDY, John 1965. *The Torch of the Testimony*. Bombay, India: Gospel Literature Service.

KEYES, Lawrence E. 1983. *The Last Age Of Missions*. Pasadena, CA, USA: William Carey Library.

KILBOURN, Phyllis. 1995 *Children in Crisis*. Monrovia, CA, USA: MARC-World Vision International.

————— 1996. *Healing the Children of War*. Monrovia, CA, USA: MARC-World Vision International.

————— 1997. *Street Children: A Guide to Effective Ministry*. Monrovia, CA, USA: MARC-World Vision International.

KOCH, Kurt. 1970. *The Revival in Indonesia*. Berghausen, Bd, Germany: Evangelization Publishers.

KUHL, Dietrich 1996. *Internationalization of an Interdenominational Faith Mission: How acceptable and effective are multi-cultural teams in WEC International?* Thesis submitted to Columbia International University, Columbia, SC, USA.

LANGTON, Edward. 1956. *History of the Moravian Church*. London, UK: George Allen and Unwin.

LATOURETTE, Kenneth Scott 1975. *A History of Christianity*. New York: Harper & Row.

LEWIS, David C. *The Unseen Face of Japan*. Tunbridge Wells, Kent TN3 0NP, UK: Monarch Publications.

LEWIS, Peter 1992. The Glory of Christ. London: Hodder & Stoughton.

LOWE, Chuck. 1998. *Territorial Spirits and World Evangelization?* A biblical, historical and missiological critique of Strategic-Level Spiritual Warfare. Fearn, Ross-shire,

IV20 1TW, Great Britain: Christian Focus Publications & Sevenoaks, Kent TN15 8BG, Great Britain: OMF International.

LYALL, Leslie. 1963. *Missionary Opportunity Today; a brief world survey.* London, UK: Inter-Varsity Fellowship.

McEVEDY, Colin & JONES, Richard. 1978. *Atlas of World Population History.* Harmondsworth, Middlesex, England: Penguin Books Ltd.

McGAVRAN, Donald A. 1955. *Bridges of God – A Study in the Strategy of Missions.* London, England: World Dominion Press.

————— 1966. *How Churches Grow – The New Frontiers of Mission.* New York, USA: Friendship Press.

————— 1970. *Understanding Church Growth.* Grand Rapids: William B. Eerdmans Publishing Co.

————— 1987. *Zaire, Midday in Missions.*Valley Forge, PA, USA: Judson Press.

McQUILKIN, Robertson. 1984. *The Great Omission: A Biblical Basis for World Evangelism.* Grand Rapids MI, USA: Baker.

MAYS, David 1996. *Building Global Vision.* Wheaton, Ill., 60189, USA: ACMC.

McGRATH, Alister. 1995. *Evangelicalism and the Future of Christianity.* Downers Grove, IL 60515, USA: Inter-varsity Press.

McLEISH, Alexander. 1952. *Christ's Hope of the Kingdom.* London, U.K.: World Dominion Press.

MOHADDESSIN, Mohammed. 1993. *Islamic Fundamentalism; The New Global Threat.* Washington DC, USA: Seven Locks Press.

MOLTMANN, Jürgen. 1977. *The Church in the Power of the Spirit: A Contribution to Messianic Ecclesiology.* London, UK: SCM Press.

MONTGOMERY, John W. Summer 1967. Wheaton, Ill. USA: *Evangelical Missions Quarterly* pp 193-202. An article on Luther and Missions.

MONTGOMERY, James & McGAVRAN, Donald A. 1980. *Discipling a Whole Nation.* Santa Clara, CA, USA: Global Church Growth Bulletin.

————— 1989. *DAWN 2000: 7 million churches to go.* Pasadena, CA: William Carey Library.

————— 1997. *Then the End Will Come.* Pasadena, CA: William Carey Library.

MURRAY, Andrew 1900 reprinted 1979. *The Key to the Missionary Problem.* Fort Washington: Christian Literature Crusade.

MURRAY, Iain H. 1971. *The Puritan Hope.* London, England: The Banner of Truth Trust.

NEELY, Lois 1980. *Come Up to This Mountain: The Miracle of Clarence W. Jones and HCJB*. Wheaton: Tyndale.

NEILL, Stephen 1964. *A History of Christian Missions*. Harmondsworth, Middx.: Penguin Books Ltd.

NEIL, Arthur 1989. *Aid Us in Our Strife*. Vol 1. England: Heath Christian Trust.

NELSON, Marlin L.1976. *The How and Why of Third World Missions*. Pasadena, CA, USA: William Carey Library.

OLSON, C. Gordon. *What in the World is God Doing?; The Essentials of Global Missions*. Cedar Knolls, NJ 07927, USA: Global Gospel Publishers.

ORR, J. Edwin.1973. *The Flaming Tongue*. Chicago, IL: Moody Press.

————— 1975 *The eager feet: Evangelical Awakenings, 1790-1830*. Chicago : Moody Press.

OTIS, George, Jr. 1991. *The Last of the Giants*. Tarrytown, New York, USA: Chosen Books.

————— 1995. *Strongholds of the 10/40 Window*. Seattle WA 98155, USA: YWAM Publishing.

PATE, Lawrence. 1989. *From Every People, a handbook of Two-Thirds World Missions*. Monrovia, CA, USA: MARC.

PENN-LEWIS, Jessie. 1912 *War on the Saints*. England: Overcomer Literature Trust.

PERETTI, Frank. 1986. *This Present Darkness*. Westchester, IL, USA: Good News Publishers.

————— 1989. *Piercing the Darkness*. Westchester, IL, USA: Crossway Books.

PETERS, George W. 1972. *A Biblical Theology of Missions*. Chicago: Moody Press.

————— 1981. *A Theology of Church Growth*. Grand Rapids, Michigan 49506, USA: Zondervan Publishing House.

PIERSON, Arthur T. 1899. *George Müller of Bristol*. Westwood, NJ, USA: Fleming H. Revell Co.

PIPER, John. 1993. *Let the Nations Be Glad; The Supremacy of God in Missions*. Grand Rapids, MI 49516, USA: Baker Books.

PIROLO, Neal. 1991. *Serving as Senders*. Waynesboro, GA 30830, USA. Operation Mobilization Literature Ministry.

ROMMEN, Edward, Ed. 1995. *Spiritual Powers and Missions; Raising the issues*. Pasadena, CA, USA: William Carey Library.

ROOY, Sydney H. 1965. *The Theology of Missions in the Puritan Tradition*. Grand Rapids, MI, USA: William B. Eerdmans Publishing Co.

SANGSTER, Thelma. 1984. *The Torn Veil, The Story of Sister Gulshan Esther*. Basingstoke, Hants RG23 7LP, UK: Marshalls.

SAUER, Erich. 1914 & 1978. *From Eternity to Eternity*. England: Paternoster Press.

SCHERER, James A. 1996. My pilgrimage in Mission. *International Bulletin of of Missionary Research*, April 1996, New Haven, Conn 06511, USA: Overseas Mission Study Center.

SHENK, Wilbert R. ed. 1984. *Anabaptism and Mission*. Scottdale PA, USA: Herald Press.

SILVOSO, Edgardo. 1991. *Prayer Power in Argentina*. In *Engaging the Enemy: How to Fight and Defeat Territorial Spirits* (Ed. P. Wagner, see below).

——————— 1994. *That None Should Perish: How to reach entire cities for Christ through prayer evangelism*. Ventura, CA, USA: Regal Books.

SKEVINGTON WOOD, A. 1960. *The Inextinguishable Blaze: Spiritual Renewal and Advance in the 18ᵗʰ Century*. UK: Paternoster Press.

STEARNS, Bill & Amy. 1991. *Catch the Vision 2000*. Minneapolis, Minnesota 55438, USA: Bethany House Publishers.

STOTT, John. 1975. *Christian Mission in the Modern World*. London: Falcon Press.

STUDD, Charles T. 1900-1932. Assorted quotes from letters and sermons. Some published in *Fool and Fanatic* (Ed. Jean Walker, WEC International).

TATFORD, Frederick A. 1982. *That the World May Know, Vols 1 - 10*. Bath, England: Echoes of Service.

TAYLOR, Dr. and Mrs. H. 1932. *Hudson Taylor's Spiritual Secret*. Chicago, IL: Moody Press.

TAYLOR, William 1991. *Internationalizing Missionary Training*. Exeter, UK: Paternoster Press.

TIPPETT, Alan R. 1977. *The Deep Sea Canoe*. Pasadena, CA, USA: William Carey Library.

THOMPSON, Phyllis 1978. *Count It All Joy: The Story of Joy Ridderhof & Gospel Recordings*. Wheaton: Shaw.

TUCKER, Ruth A. 1983. *From Jerusalem to Irian Jaya, A Biographical History of Christian Missions*. Grand Rapids, MI, USA: Zondervan.

VAN DEN BERG, Johannes 1956. *Constrained by Jesus' Love; an enquiry into the motives of the missionary awakening in Great Britain in the period between 1698 and 1815*. Kampen, Netherlands: J.H. Kok.

WAGNER, C. Peter. 1991. *Engaging the Enemy: How to fight and defeat Territorial Spirits*. Venture, CA: Regal Books.

——————— Ed. 1993. *Breaking Strongholds in your City: How to Use Spiritual Mapping to Make Your Prayers More Strategic, Effective and Targeted*. Ventura, CA: Regal Books.

WINTER, Ralph D. 1971 Churches need missions because modalities
need sodalities. Article in *Evangelical Missions
Quarterly*, Summer 1971.

———— *Mission Frontiers Magazine*; numerous references, U.S.
Center for World Mission, Pasadena CA.

———— & HAWTHORNE, Steven C., 1981 & 1992. *Perspectives on
the World Christian Movement*. Pasadena CA: William
Carey Library.

WOODFORD, David B. 1997. *One Church, Many Churches: A Five
Model Approach to Church Planting and Evaluation*.
Ann Arbor, MI, USA: UMI.

YOUNG, Edward J. 1972. *The Book of Isaiah Vol III*. New International
Commentary. Grand Rapids, MI: William B. Eerdmans
Publishing Co.

ZAKARIA, Rafiq. 1988. *The Struggle Within Islam: the Conflict between
religion and politics*. Harmondsworth, Middx.: Penguin
Books Ltd.

Index

Also published by Christian Focus

Territorial Spirits and World Evangelisation

A biblical, historical and missiological critique of
Strategic-Level Spiritual Warfare

CHUCK LOWE

'This is a methodologically-clear, admirably lucid, and mission-hearted challenge; a challenge not merely to our theories about strategic-level spiritual warfare, but to our evangelical technocratic quest for success-ful 'method'. Lowe argues that the floodtide of confidence in this 'method' has swept away exegetical, historical and empirical caution, and that it has unwittingly produced a synthesis uncomfortably closer to *The Testament of Solomon* (an intertestamental magical writing) and to animism than to any *biblical* understanding of demonology and spiritual warfare. In place of this questionable construction, with its quick-and-easy answers, Lowe points to the grittier, more robust ex-ample provided by James O Fraser, a CIM missionary to the Lisu in China. A great read!'

Max Turner
Vice Principal and Senior Lecturer in New Testament,
London Bible College

'So easily do many accept the new and the novel! To all who care deeply about world mission, Chuck Lowe's evaluation of strategic-level spiritual warfare is a needed clarion call; a call to reject what is built on a foundation of anecdote, speculation and animism, and to walk in the established paths of biblical truth and practice.

'Lowe has set himself up as a target for those who follow the SLSW theology. It will be interesting to see how they respond to this book.'

George Martin
Southern Baptist Theological Seminary
Louisville, Kentucky

'I am pleased to commend this careful examination of a controversial subject. The new interest in demons and the demonic, lately fanned by Peretti's novels, obliges Christians to reflect carefully on the biblical basis of all contemporary thought and practice. Not every reader will agree with the conclusions, which are sharply critical of Peter Wagner and others. But you do not have to go along with their theology to take seriously the devil and his minions.'

Nigel M. de S. Cameron
Distinguished Professor of Theology and Culture,
Trinity Evangelical Divinity School, Deerfield, Illinois

'The evangelical community at large owes Chuck Lowe a huge debt of gratitude. With his incisive, biblical analysis of strategic-level spiritual warfare, he shows clarity and sanity. He thoughtfully analyses the biblical, historical and theological tenets of our times with regard to spiritual warfare, showing them to be the re-emergence of the inter-testamental period and the medieval age. He makes a complex subject readable and concise, while remaining charitably irenic toward other Christians with whom he takes issue.

'The greatest strength of this book is the author's dogged insistence that, whatever one's approach to SLSW, one must not build doctrine on vague texts, assumptions, analogies or inferences, but on clear, solid, biblical evidence alone. I fully endorse the contents of this exceptional work.'

Richard Mayhue
Senior Vice President and Dean,
The Master's Seminary, Sun Valley, California

'The Bible makes it very clear that the forces of evil are strong, and that the followers of Jesus are engaged in an unrelenting battle against them. But little attention is given to this struggle in a good deal of modern writing, so Dr. Lowe's study of spiritual warfare is important.

He is concerned with modern approaches that do not do justice to what the Bible teaches about the forces of evil. Specifically he deals with those who advocate strategic-level spiritual warfare. His book clarifies many issues, and encourages readers in their task of opposing evil.'

Leon Morris
Ridley College,
Australia

Chuck Lowe studied at Oral Roberts University (B.A.); Westminster Theological Seminary (M.A.R.); and the Australian College of Theology (Th.D. under Leon Morris). He has served with OMF at Singapore Bible College since 1984, where he teaches New Testament interpretation, theology and preaching. He is also theological researcher with OMF since 1995. His research interests are in Chinese folk religion and sociology of religion. Chuck is married to Irene Wong, a Malaysian Chinese, and they have two children.

Published by Christian Focus

60 Great Founders
Geoffrey Hanks

ISBN 1 85792 1402   *large format 496 pages*

This book details the Christian origins of 60 organizations, most of which are still committed to the God-given, world-changing vision with which they began. Among them are several mission organizations.

70 Great Christians
Geoffrey Hanks

ISBN 1 871 676 800   *large format 352 pages*

The author surveys the growth of Christianity throughout the world through the lives of prominent individuals who were dedicated to spreading the faith. Two sections of his book are concerned with mission; one section looks at the nineteenth century missionary movement, and the other details mission growth throughout the twentieth century.

Mission of Discovery

ISBN 1 85792 2581   *large format 448 pages*

The fascinating journal of Robert Murray McCheyne's and Andrew Bonar's journeys throughout Palestine and Europe in the 1840s to investigate if the Church of Scotland should set up a mission to evangelise the Jewish people. From their investigation, much modern Jewish evangelism has developed.

Also published by Christian Focus and WEC

You Can Learn to Lead
Stewart Dinnen

ISBN 1 85792 2824   *B format 176 pages*

A practical manual for missionaries, church leaders, or anyone in a position of leadership. The author was International Secretary of WEC and therefore had plenty of hands-on experience.

Patrick Johnstone says of this book: 'It was my privilege to serve under Stewart's incisive and courageous leadership. I commend this book as a means for equipping others with like vision.'

And Brother Andrew comments: 'Stewart, your book is a gem! Diamonds! I wish I had written it.'

Rescue Shop Within a Yard of Hell
Stewart Dinnen

ISBN 1 85792 1224   *pocket paperback 272 pages*

The remarkable story of evangelism by Betel among the drug addicts and AIDs sufferers in Spain. In addition to the strategies of the workers being explained, there are testimonies from converted addicts, some of whom became leaders in the church.

Faith on Fire
Norman Grubb and the building of WEC
Stewart Dinnen

ISBN 185792 3219   *large format 240 pages*

Norman Grubb 'inherited' the leadership of WEC from his father-in-law, C. T. Studd. Leslie Brierley said of Grubb, 'To experience his dynamic leadership ... was my unforgettable experience.'

In 1969 **William Carey Library Publishers** was founded for the exclusive purpose of publishing the best in current thinking on missions at a reasonable cost—the only company of its kind then in existence.

It is our aim to aid the work of the mission executive, the missionary on the field and his/her home church and the student of world mission. In addition to its own publishing program, WCL distributes mission related books from 90 other publishers—all at discount prices.

Publications include:

Communicating Christ in Animistic Contexts, Gailyn Van Rheenen
The Holy Spirit and Mission Dynamics, C. Douglas McConnell, editor
Kids for the World: A Guidebook for Children's Mission Resources (2nd edition), Gerry Dueck
Missionary Care, Kelly O'Donnell
On Being A Missionary, Thomas Hale
Scripture and Strategy, David J. Hesselgrave
Then the End Will Come, Jim Montgomery
Unfamiliar Paths: The Challenge of Recognizing the World of Christ in Strange Clothing, David E. Bjork
Too Valuable to Lose: Exploring the Causes and Cures of Missionary Attrition, William D. Taylor, Editor

Since 1976, WCL has been associated with the **U.S. Center for World Mission.** The USCWM is a frontier mission mobilization organization and has produced the following items which are of special interest to World Christians who read this book:

Vision for the Nations — a 13 week Sunday School-style video curriculum

Perspectives on the World Christian Movement — a college level course offered by extension in 60 locations in the U.S.

World Christian Foundations — a 32 semester hour distance based, mentored MA or BA degree completions curriculum with U.S. regionally accredited institutions.

For more information on both WCL and the USCWM visit web at:
www.uscwm.org

To order, contact: William Carey Library
P.O. Box 40129, Pasadena, CA 91104
Phone: 1-800-MISSION (1-800-647-7466)
Fax: 1-626-794-0477
Email: orders@wclbooks.com